Hold Fast
A Hollywood Pirate's Tale

MARK RYAN

with John Matthews

Copyright © 2015 by Mark Ryan & John Matthews
All rights reserved. Except as permitted under the U.S. Copyright Act of 1976.

No part of this publication may be reproduced, distributed, or transmitted in any form or by any means, or stored in a database or retrieval system, without the prior written permission of the publisher.

This paperback edition published with permission in the U.S. by LMB Entertainment, November 2015.
Originally published by Mythwood Books.
This U.S. edition published by LMB Entertainment with permission from Mythwood Books.

ISBN: 978-1-5188127-7-4

U.S. Cover Design and Formatting by Dayna Linton

Cover photos of Mark Ryan by Tom Korbee

DEDICATION

To my children, Daniel, Daniel and Katherine, so they might understand
M.R.
To Emrys—for the wisdom
J.M.

"In everything that can be called art, there is a quality of redemption. It may be pure tragedy, if it is high tragedy, and it may be pity and irony, and it may be the raucous laughter of the strong man. But down these mean streets a man must go who is not himself mean, who is neither tarnished nor afraid. The detective... must be a complete man and a common man and yet an unusual man. He must be... a man of honour. He must be the best man in his world and a good enough man for any world. The story is this man's adventure in search of a hidden truth, and it would be no adventure if it did not happen to a man fit for adventure. He has a range of awareness that startles you, but it belongs to him by right, because it belongs to the world he lives in. If there were enough like him, the world would be a very safe place to live in, without becoming too dull to be worth living in."

~ Raymond Chandler - *The Simple Art of Murder*, 1945

Contents

Foreword — *vii*
Preface — *ix*
Introduction — *xi*

1. BEGINNING NOW — 1
2. THE SHOW GOES ON — 13
3. A WORLD OF SECRETS — 30
PHOTO PAGES 1 — 43
4. LIVING MAGICALLY — 45
5. BLURRING THE EDGES — 61
6. PLAYING WITH SWORDS — 75
7. ADVENTURES WITH JULES VERNE — 91
8. SWORDS, SONGS, AND SPARKLY DRESSES — 108
9. PRIVATE INVESTIGATIONS — 123
10. ON THE WALL WITH KING ARTHUR — 148
11. A LONG DRIVE INTO THE DESERT — 169
12. THREE WISE, IF VERY ODD, MEN — 187
PHOTO PAGES 2 — 215
13. BECOMING SEVERAL GIANT ALIEN ROBOTS — 220
14. TRIBAL STATES—THE RESERVATIONS — 239
15. HOLD FAST: SAILING UNDER NEW COLORS — 254

Acknowledgements — *273*
Further Reading — *274*
Filmography — *276*

Foreword

I FIRST MET MARK on the set of *Robin of Sherwood* around 1982. We were based in Bristol, though the first two episodes were shot in Northumberland. I didn't think much of him on first impression, and I don't suppose he thought much of me—the big mouth from London. He was this black leather, shoulders back, chest out, northern geezer from Doncaster, who professed to know how to skin a rabbit… so fucking what… and shoot a bow… big fucking deal!

To be honest I thought he was full of shit: stories about undercover this, SAS that. He dressed, as I thought then, like a proper northerner… Black leather trousers (it's that black leather again!) and a white shirt with, if I remember rightly, a faint grey-blue pattern in it—faint because it had been washed so many times. It was undone to the waste. Mark was like a young Doncaster version of Tom Jones… And I have to tell you—boy, could he sing!

I guess seven boys living and working so closely for a long period of time brings you together, gives you the chance to get to know the real person behind your personal judgment. So, 30 years later we're all still very close, and I consider all the cast as my very greatest friends.

You've always been there when I needed you. Nothing is forgotten Mark Ryan, my friend.

Ray Winstone, 2015.

Preface

IT WOULD BE VIRTUALLY impossible to invent Mark Ryan. In his life he has been a singer, soldier, a TV star, a Hollywood actor, a private investigator and an advisor to a variety of intelligence and law enforcement organizations. He has written two books about the Tarot and a best-selling comic, taught soldiers how to uncover secrets and actors how to fight, while he has worked with some of the biggest names in Hollywood. All this time he has followed a code of living, and a philosophy, which have enabled him to survive many different kinds of danger.

When Mark first approached me to help him write this book—"a kind of long rambling story," as he called it—we had been friends for over twenty years, and had worked together on blockbuster epics like *King Arthur* (2003), but I knew very little of the "other" Mark Ryan, or of the secret life behind that of the screen and TV actor. To me he was a friend with whom I could be sure of a great conversation, more than a few beers and a lot of laughs. I also knew he had a more profound side and that he lived his life according to an unusual set of beliefs.

The story told here, for the most part in Mark's own voice, begins with his journey from Doncaster, Yorkshire, to his work in musical theatre in the London production of *Evita*, branching out into TV in the global hit series, *Robin of Sherwood*. It takes us through adventures wilder than most of us can imagine to the often bizarre world of Hollywood, the ending of a disastrous marriage and beyond, as Mark found himself drawn back into a world he thought he had left behind when he resigned from a unique position as a highly vetted operator in the British Army's Intelligence Corps and Special Operations community in 1997.

Invited to help an old friend and veteran SWAT team police officer, now running a private investigation company and dealing with a complex international extortion case, Mark soon found himself risking life and limb in the hunt for South American money launderers, threatened by lethal corporate blackmailers, searching for murdered Israelis in the vast deserts of Nevada, consulting with various U.S. agencies engaged in "state-of-the-art" counter-terror operations in the wake of 9/11, and helping some of the best-known names in Hollywood deal with a variety of celebrity "issues."

At the same time Mark continued to pursue a career as an actor, singer and swordmaster, working on such blockbuster movies as *The Prestige*, *First Knight* and *King Arthur*. Few knew of his secret other life and the dangers and thrills it brought in its wake. Yet the two strands continued to overlap, enabling him to bring his acting skills to the art of detection, and his military training to teach actors to fight better on screen. Recently he became a familiar name as the voice of Bumblebee—the best-loved robot in the *Transformers* movie franchise, and found himself travelling the world, signing toy replicas of the famous yellow car. In the past year, he has been filming in South Africa as a leading character in executive producer Michael Bay's TV series *Black Sails* from Starz. As I write this, Mark is voicing the latest addition to the Transformers stable as "Lockdown," the most popular villain in the fourth film of the series.

Writing this book with him, listening to many hours of taped conversations and gradually editing Mark's wonderful anecdotal words into written prose has taught me a lot about him that I might never have known. It's an amazing story by any measure, full of danger, tragedy, laughter and heart. It was a privilege to work on and it remains a privilege for me to know the man who has been called, rightly in my view, "an angel in the dark," and who I am proud to call my friend.

John Matthews
Oxford - Los Angeles, 2015

Introduction

AS I SIT HERE TYPING this in late 2014, I sometimes shake myself and wonder how I got here. I have often told people that if I hadn't stumbled into the music industry and thereby theatre, film and TV, I would probably have been a career criminal. It's been an amazing roller coaster ride so far, and I guess I've lived five of my allotted nine lives up to this point. So I still have four in hand to roll the dice with!

Having completed five grueling months on eight groundbreaking hours of the Starz TV blockbuster pirate series *Black Sails* in Cape Town, South Africa, I bounced across the U.S. on *Transformers: Age of Extinction*. In between Chicago and Detroit, I'd been to San Diego, New York and Miami to promote *Black Sails* at the San Diego Comic Con, New York Comic Con and at corporate events for Starz.

Legendary filmmaker Michael Bay, under his highly successful filmmaking division, Platinum Dunes, is the executive producer of *Black Sails*. The show was a huge undertaking and the production values were everything you would expect from a Michael Bay project. Having also worked on all four *Transformers* productions for Michael, I knew the days would be complex, challenging and rewarding as we always had a laugh, and I was sincerely honored to be a small part of this now-legendary production team.

As a boy in Doncaster, I looked out from my bedroom window, wondering what was beyond the red brick boundary that comprised rows of stoical terraced houses and the small backyards and alleys that made up our universe. This massive Hollywood machine was without doubt the most extraordinary experience and one I could never have dreamed possible as that unruly and rebellious tyke.

From a young age I escaped the boundaries of my Yorkshire life by imagining and writing adventure stories for a rogue's gallery of colorful characters, exotic locations, fast cars and derring-do. The settings for these were New York, the African continent, London, Zurich, South America, Eastern Europe and Washington, D.C., all places I could only imagine and had no real expectation of being able to experience in real life.

These young, escapist explorations usually included international travel, rare artworks, lethal and complex weaponry, well-appointed Manhattan apartments and sophisticated and stylish protagonists entwined in complex, duplicitous and dangerous plotlines. I never wrote about being an actor, a writer or a singer. Somehow that was inherent in my personality and I just accepted it was something that could be within my grasp if I decided to throw my hat into the showbiz ring.

As I began to detail some of the darker and morally uncompromising experiences for John in the original series of interviews that became this book, I realized just how those early stories had colored and foreshadowed my imagination and my eclectic view of the world. Maybe it was always my nature to accept and absorb changing circumstances and improvise, adapt and overcome, albeit sometimes with physical and psychological damage and occasionally leaving emotional wreckage in my wake.

But whatever the source of this drive, the sense of going beyond my own skills, wits and knowledge has propelled me to go way beyond fear of failure and manifest a life I couldn't even imagine as that hardy if socially awkward Yorkshire lad.

Recently, when sitting around a dinner table with a collection of showbiz reprobates that included fellow Merry Man and now icon of the British film industry Ray Winstone, I expressed the feeling that we'd been lucky to survive the lives we had lived. Ray looked at me with his usual conspiratorial grin and said, "We've been lucky? We made our own luck, mate."

I countered that, as working-class chaps, the odds against us ending up where we were, let alone negotiating the unseen barriers we had overcome to get here, must include an element of good fortune at least. Ray said, "There are plenty of barriers out there, but we just didn't realize that. So for us they didn't exist and we went straight through 'em!"

This profound nugget of insight from "Raymondo" gave me pause for thought and I pondered this simple concept for days. I had never even thought about seeing barriers or feeling inadequate to the task. It had never occurred to me that I couldn't do something if I put my mind to it, and if I couldn't, I'd take my father's advice and apply whatever I had learned from the experience to the next challenge or ambition. In this way there would never be any loss or waste of effort. Any negative feelings, emotions or influences, however painful, would be turned into positive and practical drives that would be useful, applicable and valued somewhere along life's rocky and invariably unpredictable road.

As an example of this odd journey's eclectic reflections, a couple of years ago I was walking alone through Dublin's famous Temple Bar on a warm, wet April evening after working on the editing for *Blood Type*, a vampire/time travel concept, shot in the home of Robin Gibb, and written by John Matthews and his production partner Wil Kinghan.

As the aroma of stale beer and the dull throb of "sensory depravation torture," thinly disguised as rap music, floated from the bars and through my senses like nails through kneecaps, I felt the weight of tremendous melancholy and sadness as I strolled past the teeming hordes of hen parties and Eastern European revelers, stumbling merrily and unsteadily through the cobbled streets of this ancient and robust city. An unexpected welling of emotion stopped me in my stride for a few moments and a terrible realization stumped my breath and halted the usually successful attempts to redirect my thoughts.

I had been talking to the hotel barman for several nights. His name will remain, as he would wish, confidential, but his stories, inside knowledge and stark images of world conflict and strategic international politics appeared authentic. His Blackwater "Challenge Coin" had provoked an unexpected emotional reaction in me that's difficult to express, even now. I still travel carrying a challenge coin from the Los Angeles TEWG (Terrorism Early Warning Group). This U.S. military tradition allowed anyone with a service history to challenge someone else to produce their unit "coin" or buy drinks for the rest of the night for everyone who does.

I chose not to expose the L.A.-TEWG coin to this interesting chap, as many federal agencies and intelligence units had been involved in the extensive field training exercises I'd organized and co-directed at LAX for the Chameleon Group; but from our conversations it soon became clear that we might once have fought on different sides. We might even have even been in the same conflicts! We might have been bitter and vicious hunters of our own comrades, friends and families. Who knows? But here we were, just two old geezers in a hotel bar. He later emailed me a scan of a faded black and white photograph of a very young man proudly holding a Sterling submachine gun, somewhere with brick terraced houses and cobbled alleys. Whose side had he been on then, I wondered?

As I wandered back to my hotel, I had never felt so alone in my life. I had been alone in many strange and exotic places, many times, but I had grown to love Dublin, its energy and its people. Being no longer emotionally or romantically plugged into the city was a strangely numbing experience. The first time I came back I actually dreaded it, and wondered if I actually should stay away for my own peace of mind. A pint of Dublin Guinness and a dozen oysters soon sorted that out.

The woman I had loved was here. The home that I thought we would create together was here. And my spiritual and cultural roots, however conflicted and convoluted, seemed deeply entwined with the ancient morphic pulse and rebellious ghosts that wander freely through the complex and labyrinthine societal confluences that are still flowing just under the opaque skin of 21st-century Ireland.

From being in the clique of the Jerry Bruckheimer movie *King Arthur*, to having a stranger from the North put a finger, assassin style, to my head after a day of (none too subtle) surveillance and an amateurish "cold contact" approach in a public toilet, to running up and down the polluted canal pathway on frosty winter evenings, trying to stay fit, to the glory of the Bray Studios and the joys of the Ardenode Hotel in Ballymore Eustace, Ireland had got under my skin. More to the point, *she* had got under my skin and, just as in some Victorian melodrama, it was "the love that could never be."

As I walked down the busy streets I realized just how far I had gone from the terraced house I was born in, across the Irish Sea in Yorkshire, and just how far away from there and alone I truly was.

It struck me how much the world had changed since my childhood. I remembered watching sleek Vulcan "V" bombers armed with nuclear weapons, roaring aggressively into the Cold War air from RAF Finningley to patrol in a holding pattern over the North Sea, maybe one day to receive the fatal encrypted order that would send them eastward to the Soviet Union, bringing plutonium-fuelled Armageddon to their designated Russian targets. Now, RAF Finningley was the Doncaster/Sheffield "Robin Hood" Airport where I would land in a few days on my journey back home to visit my family.

Here in Dublin, just as in the Doncaster marketplace of my childhood, all manner of language, dialect and accents mingled and floated in the damp air—Russian, Serbian, Nigerian, Romanian, Korean, Polish and Turkish. How far we have come. Now, in this city, where I had lived and hoped to make some kind of home, that sense of separation was a stark reminder of the life I had lived and the price I had paid for that life.

I was a stranger again.

As I walked back to my hotel, my mind wandered through memories of standing on the stage of Carnegie Hall to armed confrontations in the Southern California desert reservation of a Native American Tribe, secret interrogation training facilities in Cornwall and Scotland and the back streets of Budapest and Montreal, Hollywood's very rich and very famous and the very sad, lost and fatally messed-up.

AK-74s and broadswords. Carbon-fiber *Sgian Dubhs*. A diminutive Seacamp .32 semi-automatic, tucked into a tight sports ankle support so that the little gun wouldn't "print" in public places. Glock 9-mms, spring-loaded Kershaw knives and Sabre pepper spray.

Hidden cameras and dead witnesses. Israeli mothers of murdered sons. Federal agencies, human intelligence, .40 Hydra-Shok rounds and humanitarian disasters. Talented and enthusiastic "wannabees" and fatally flawed and sometimes fatally overdosed A and D-listers.

9mm Walther PPK/Ss and watering holes. Misdirection and malfeasance. Monty Python and bridgewire nuclear triggering mechanisms. Organized crime and disorganized film sets. Multi-million-dollar New York art scams. Suicides, lies, brutality, honor and loyalty. Lovers present, past and passed-on. Shallow graves, hidden motives and Neuro-Linguistic Programming, CCWs and false imprisonment, roving Chinese ambassadors and royal family confidence tricksters. The stuff of my childhood imagination was now a living if ironic tableau, and the makings of a dozen or more novels.

All of this had been a normal and daily part of my life for so long. Maybe that time was drawing inexorably and naturally to a close. Maybe it was time to tell the story? In doing so, my intent is not to offend or otherwise cause personal distress or pain to anyone who has been in my life as a friend, lover, collaborator or comrade. For the most part, I have the deepest respect, regard and affection for the people I've served with, worked for or otherwise have trodden the boards with. Some are still roaming the Sand Box, or some grey concrete corner of "Legoland on Thames," [aka. MI6 Headquarters] and some are not so quietly retired and wish to retain their pension. Some wish their secrets to remain lost to the shadows of history (I honor their request) and many have passed quietly, or sometimes rather noisily, into the Otherworld.

The notable showbiz likes of Martin Grace, Bob Dick, Jay Larkin, Diane Cilento, Robin Gibb, Danton Burroughs, Lewis Collins, Terry Walsh, Billy Dainty, Ingrid Pitt, Terry Forrestal, Bob Anderson, Roy Castle, Jimmy Doohan, Peter Matz, Terry Nation, Francesco Quinn, Meg Webster, Richard "Kip" Carpenter, Ronnie Cass, Robin Williams (to name but a few) and those that shall remain anonymous for now, I shall never see the likes of again in this lifetime. Bring on the next, I say. I honor their lives, their friendship and their legacies.

Some elements of this story, for real reasons of security classification or U.S. legal statute, have also been left for those who were actually involved in the situations described, to either claim or deny their parts, if they wish to do so. Where possible, documents, correspondence and photographs have been reproduced with permission.

I've erred on the side of caution (for the most part) and abided with the old saying that, if you can't say anything nice about the dead, better say nothing at all. For other reasons that many of those named in this book will fully understand, some details of actual identities, incidents and cases have been changed or masked for the protection of either those still alive, serving or serving time.

Most of the actual events recounted here take place after my move to Los Angeles and the granting of my California Private Investigator (PI) License in 2002. My MoD vetting was still active and I was involved in other work. So much remains left to sleep "unquiet slumbers in that quiet earth." Better that way.

Much of the *Robin of Sherwood* era has been covered in great detail in other works, for which reason we decided not to dwell on that period, albeit one of the most enjoyable and productive decades in my career. (We may choose to revisit it in a later edition).

Rather, John and I agreed to tell the tale as a sojourn, not as a simple showbiz kiss and tell or a Boy's Own yarn, but rather to acknowledge those anonymous close friends who survived life's rich tapestry of challenge, and also to recount what was learned from a lifetime of stepping onto the Rainbow Bridge or into the dark labyrinth of the clandestine life.

Hopefully, some of the lessons and experiences will be useful to folks who decide to beat their own unique if thorny path through life in future and dare to ask the question: What's over that next wall…?

WHY *HOLD FAST*, YOU MAY ASK. Crew members of the old sailing ships used to tattoo these words on the knuckles of their hands. They did it to remind themselves that if they did not, indeed, hold fast to the ropes that formed the rigging of these mighty vessels they would almost certainly end up in the sea. My own life has been a little like that. As I navigated the sometimes-uncertain seas of Spookdom and the acting profession, I have held fast to my beliefs, my trust in an ability to elicit a response from the universe and move forward.

When I took on the role of Gates in the Starz series *Black Sails*, I would be playing a pirate quartermaster and I realized I had been in this role for a great deal of my life. I chose to have Hold Fast applied to my hands by the makeup department. It seemed right then, and it seems just as right now that we use it as the title of this story.

As I began to write, the tensions in my bones and sinews began to ease, slowly. When you're young, you do not think of yourself as complex, merely invincible. As you grow older, you realize you are simply uncomfortable in too much light. Maybe that's why we write.

Now it was Cape Town, Edwards Air Force Base, the Magic Castle, Cape Canaveral, the Union Jack Club, spies, vampires, tarot cards and being the iconic voice of an alien SR71 Blackbird spy plane, as well as an honorable if cunning pirate quartermaster! Then there is Lockdown, the laconic and merciless alien bounty hunter whose view of the universe is detached, unyielding and amoral. Funny old world…

Surreal and solitary most of it has been.
But it is my life.
Welcome…

Los Angeles, October, 2014

Hold Fast
A Hollywood Pirate's Tale

1.
BEGINNING NOW

"Whatever you do or dream you can, do it. Boldness has genius, power and magic in it. Begin it now."
~ W.H. Murray—*The Scottish Himalaya Expedition, 1951*

I HAVE BEEN SHOT AT SEVERAL TIMES IN MY LIFE. Not only on screen, but sometimes by live rounds from real weapons. For most of my professional career I've lived a double life, moving in and out of two worlds, crossing from the twilight world of military intelligence to the tinsel world of film and TV. I've done TV shows including *Robin of Sherwood* and *Frasier*, movies including *The Prestige* and *Transformers 1* through *4*, plays including *The Mystery of Edwin Drood* and musicals such as *Evita* and *1776*, and most recently played a pirate in the Starz TV show *Black Sails*. For much of that time, I was part of the international intelligence and Special Operations otherworld. Whether as a member of the British Army's Intelligence Corps or a California licensed private investigator and security consultant in the U.S., I journeyed through this labyrinth with a profound fascination and focused sense of moral duty.

Sometimes people I was working with (in both areas) knew about this; sometimes they had no idea at all. Over the years, this double life has taken me to some strange places and brought me into contact with some fascinating and seriously dangerous people. That's how my life has been: living with two valid passports, each with a different name, and carrying some very serious ordinance about my person when I needed to.

The one thing that has kept me sane, through bad times and good, through a disastrous marriage and some dangerous places and situations, is a belief that if you face the universe head on and ask the question, "Whom Does the Grail Serve?,"[1] you'll always get an answer. It might throw you a few curveballs, but it also gets you onto the right road at the right time.

I have three grown children. My relationships with them have been good and bad, torn and battered. This has led me to think that some kind of explanation of the life their strange father has lived would be a good thing. This book is dedicated to them, in the hope that they might understand some of the history told here. There are a lot of misunderstandings and misconceptions, not just about my life, but the lives of others who live in the strange shadowy world I've known over the past thirty years.

My family knows very little about any of this. We don't talk about it, or at least very little—certainly not over the last fifteen years, while I have lived and worked in California. They know virtually nothing about the dark labyrinth that often paralleled the bright lights of show business.

The other reason for writing this book is because, having reached a kind of watershed in my life, I felt a need to take stock. These watersheds, where smaller rivers flow together into one great big one, have made a huge impression on me over the years. It seems as though, on numerous occasions, my steps have been led, guided you might say, to be in the right place at the right time. So whether you believe in coincidence or a higher power operating in the universe, it seems to me that my life would have taken a very different turn had I not repeatedly and unexpectedly run across people and situations that have sent me off on roads very much less travelled.

But we need to go back a few years if this is to make any sense.

I'm not sure whether words or music came first. I always wanted to be a singer, but I was forever writing stories as well. The best Christmas gift I could get was a blank book to write in. I would sit in my room in my parent's house in Doncaster and write long rambling adventure stories in which—I now realize—I was always the central character. Looking out of

---

[1] From the epic stories of King Arthur where the knights, going in search of the Grail, ask this question as a way of opening the path before them.

my bedroom window at the red brick wall across the alleyway between my house and the next I would think: *There's got to be something beyond this for me.*

I remember writing a story when I was still at school about the theft of a rare stamp that featured a character living in New York and London. It was a real adventure story of the kind I loved. I remember listening to the music from On Her Majesty's Secret Service by John Barry—perhaps the best instrumental James Bond soundtrack ever! I think it was really that which got me interested in music and drama in the first place, because that soundtrack played in my head for years after. Like most lads of that age I was entertained by plenty of TV gung-ho adventure stuff, like *The Saint, Danger Man* or *The Man From U.N.C.L.E.*, but had no interest in living that kind of life myself. It was an escape! I really wanted to be in show business!

As I was sitting in my old bedroom in Doncaster recently, looking out at that alleyway and the blank wall on which I had played out so many childhood scenarios, it seemed surreal that I now live in L.A. and work in film and TV, as well as being a licensed PI. My mother had recently passed away and I was reflecting on both her extremely moving passing and the stable and safe home environment in which we had grown up that enabled my siblings and me to take so many life risks and achieve the things we had.

Would I have made the same decisions if I had known then, as a boy aged twelve or thirteen, what was ahead? Even then I was making swords and knives in metalwork class at school. Once I even took the teacher's keys, put them in a sand press, and made my own master set for all the classrooms!

This was all about exploring boundaries—I didn't smoke or do drugs, wasn't out fighting on a Friday night. I wasn't a football fan either; I didn't do any of that. I could not find where I fitted in, and I think I was always asking what the boundaries were—what are these rules that society asks us to live by? But of course I had no idea that I could actually make things happen. I didn't really know what goal I was reaching for.

I kept asking questions: Why? How? Why not? I was constantly inviting the universe to challenge me. I couldn't articulate it then, but it was a process I knew instinctively would work for me. I don't know how I knew that either, but I was convinced that if I kept asking questions and pushing at the walls, the universe would shift and reveal a different pattern and a route to a more challenging and fulfillling future.

Variety is the Spice of Life

Like many another performer before me, I started out on the club circuit. Before I had turned 17, I had established myself in the Yorkshire Working Men's Clubs—some of the big ones like Batley Variety Club—and I was trying to find a route into an agency in London. I had a singing teacher called Judy Bowman in Doncaster (still alive, full of energy and boisterously teaching music and singing) who was enormously influential in getting my career started.

Things began to change when I entered the Adwick-le-Street Working Men's Club Talent Competition. Judy told me she had entered all her pupils—and that all of them had won. Clearly, she expected me to do the same. I was still working at "March—The Tailors," part of a Yorkshire chain. When I walked into that competition, there were a lot of people there who had been performing for a long time and knew the business.

In those days, the Northern club circuit was a very tough environment indeed. This was really the beginning of me thinking I could do anything if I just went for it—aimed for it—just kept going. Even if it didn't work out, and I didn't hit that target—as my dad used to say—I would at least be higher up the ladder than before. This is something I still believe, and practice every day. (I also learned another useful lesson from a Grimethorpe miners club MC—be nice to people on the way up as you'll be sure to meet exactly the same people on the way down!).

Judy knew that I wanted to try my luck down in London. At that time, my then-girlfriend Judy Turner was also a club singer, and we talked about going to London and wanting to take it head on. She used to say, "You know, there are a lot of good singers in London—probably the best in the business—so be prepared for failure." To which my response was, "I guess I'll find out." (Terry Nation, Original *Doctor Who* writer and inventor of the Daleks, put it more succinctly to me some years later: "Always prepare for success. Failure takes care of itself.")

I talked to Judy Bowman and she said, "I tell you what we'll do..." She opened up a copy of *The Stage*, where the London agencies were listed, and said, "Close your eyes. Here's a pin—stick it in." That's what I did. It stuck in an agency called Forester George, on Park Lane. I remember thinking: *Park Lane—I don't think that's a good idea.* But Judy said, "So what? Write to them, send some photographs—go for it."

I did some research and found out they looked after big names of the time, stars like Mike Yarwood and Ken Dodd, so I really did think I'd made a bad choice. I decided to give it a go anyway, so I sent a handwritten letter with some pictures and basically said, "You don't know me now, but you will, and you'll regret it if you don't give me an interview."

The letter landed on the desk of Frank Woodruff, who sadly died from cancer about eight years ago. He was a wonderful, warm, funny, intelligent man. He called me back because he couldn't believe the audacity of the letter, and said that normally they would have just tossed it in the round file, but there was something that intrigued him and he just had to find out more about me. So we talked on the phone and he said to come into the office when I was next in London.

I did exactly that. I met him and his boss, Nancy George, and told them what I had been doing and what I wanted to do and they got me a couple of gigs: one in Blackpool and one in Bournemouth at the Roundhouse Hotel, just singing. I was still only eighteen.

Then there was a gig at the Savoy Hotel in London—in cabaret. I had no idea what I was doing or what I was walking into at that time. It was in London, in an important venue, and I knew I could compete. When it was all said and done, the agency didn't actually take me on, but used me as a filler act for more established performers, but I didn't mind. I was working and learning. They even got me a chorus part in *Cinderella* in Manchester in 1974, and I ended up understudying the legendary variety artist Billy Dainty, who was playing Buttons. That was the first time that I had worked in a real theatre other than the Royal Festival Hall.

The director of *Cinderella*, Dougie Squires, was also choreographing *The Young Generation*, a top dance group of the time. He gave me a lot of solid advice. I also quickly realized how talented Billy Dainty was. When you talk about variety, these guys could really do it all—sing, tap-dance, juggle, play instruments. Dainty was a true comic genius whose trademark was the Max Wall funny walk—he was a consummate professional, as was the late, great Roy Castle, with whom I worked later on. In fact,

Roy got me out of trouble during the taping of a *Good Old Days* episode some years later while I was still in *Evita*. I simply could not remember the lyrics to the song I'd been given and Roy filled in the airtime with more of his amazing act. They mercifully cut my less than stellar performance from the show and I learned another very valuable lesson about never committing to doing something in public you don't feel 100% connected to, confident about, and are prepared for.

During the run of *Cinderella*, Dougie advised me to get into drama school to get a real understanding of stage performance and technique. It just happened that he was a patron of the famous Italia Conti Stage School, so he told me to go down there, introduce myself, tell them that he had sent me, and that I might get some lessons as a result.

I drove down to London, slept in the car for a couple of nights, and basically walked in and introduced myself and told them what Dougie Squires had said. They were quite taken aback at me just walking in off the street, but I guess because of Dougie they said, "Okay—do some classes—we'll work something out."

You have to understand this was a stage-school that charged high tuition fees, but after that first time, I just used to wander in and out, joining in the classes I needed. The family that owned the school were very benevolent about it. One day I walked into the singing class, taught at the time by Roy Gregory. Like me, he was a Northerner and one of the best singing teachers in the business. He was also known as a very tough guy. He looked at me and asked who I was and what I was doing in his class. I explained that I was taking some lessons and that I was a singer. He said, "Oh, you're a singer are you—do you have any music with you?" I said I had. So he picked out something and played it. I can't remember what we started with, but he said, "Let me hear you sing." This was in front of the whole class, and I sang for most of the lesson—about an hour—while Roy played through all my music on the piano. At the end, he gave me back the music and said to the rest of the class, "This kid is a singer."

That's how my career really started.

At this time, Conti's were planning a stage show version of the popular film *The Young Ones*, written by Ronnie Cass and Peter Myers, with additional material by Cliff Richard and the Shadows. Someone said that Ronnie Cass was coming in to do some auditions and I happened to be in on that day. Somebody else (maybe Roy Gregory) said I should go and sing for him. I had no idea who Ronnie was at that time, though he was actually an extremely well known and respected writer and musician. He asked me for my music and we went through three or four songs. At the end he said, "Come and talk to me before you leave today. There may be a part for you in this show." I really thought the show was not for me, so I didn't go back to see him. Then I got a note the next day saying, "Ronnie Cass wants you to call him—here's his number—you'd better call!" When I did, he said, "Come to my house and meet my family. I want to talk to you."

So, I went along to his fantastic house in West Hampstead, met his wife and family, and we chatted. He played the piano and went through some more songs. Then he said he was interested in managing me. At the time, I had no idea what that meant. He later produced a management contract—in fact, a three-year contract—in which he guaranteed to find me X amount of work. I was still being partly looked after by Forester George at that time, but now my career went into the Ronnie Cass phase.

Ronnie was incredibly generous to me and we spent many hours running songs and building an act we could take on the road. Ronnie had been very involved writing a show called *This Is Tom Jones*, and many other film scores and revues. His family basically adopted me into their fold and saw to it that I was fed and watered when things were tough. I owe Ronnie and his family a huge debt of gratitude and probably the career I have now.

Because of Ronnie, I did the famous TV show called *Opportunity Knocks*—a kind of Seventies version of *The X Factor*—and a few other gigs, one of which, believe it or not, was in Zambia. One of Ronnie's contacts wanted someone to work with a six-piece band in this string of hotels in Zambia and he thought it would be good for me to experience a different environment. I didn't know it then, but this gig was going to have a very far-reaching and totally unexpected effect on my life.

With Ronnie playing the piano, I landed a part in my first West End show called *Dean*, about the life of James Dean, the movie star who died tragically young. I played all the bad guys in James Dean's life, including the singer Vic Damone.

This was in the mid-Seventies and, at the time, I used to hang out at the Bar Italia on Frith St., Soho. I got to know the owner, Mr. Nino, quite well. Everyone in the show went there between performances because it was close to the stage door. While talking to Nino, he told me he was looking for a singing teacher for his son Anthony, who was running the restaurant, and that he would really like the bloke from "that place that was on the telly the other night"—the Italia Conti Stage School (there had been a documentary about the school a few days earlier). So I told him I still went in from time to time and Nino asked me if I could get Roy Gregory to coach Anthony. I said I could ask. Roy did end up coaching Anthony and Nino never forgot it. He's still a friend to this day.

Dean was not a great box office success and I was ready for a change, so off I went to Africa for Ronnie and that is essentially where the other side of my life began—though I didn't realize it right away.

I flew out of Heathrow on Zambia Airways in an aging Boeing 707 and, after last-minute repairs we ascended into the grey London skies with one engine ablaze and flew all the way to Central Africa on three engines! Both passengers and crew were staring out of the windows the whole way, wondering if the wing would fall off. It took a very, very long time and we later found out the flames were from escaped fuel leaked during the repairs to the engine starter motors, that began burning off during take-off.

I arrived in Zambia in early March 1977, just as President Nikolai Podgorny of the U.S.S.R. arrived to visit President Kenneth Kaunda in Lusaka. What neither I nor anyone else among the British general public knew at the time was that Zambia was at the heart of a very secret, vicious and clandestine war involving the CIA, MI6, KGB, BOSS (South African Intelligence Service), Cuban forces and the Chinese—all over mineral resources and embroiling various African Marxist liberation movements in a bloody and protracted struggle.

Added to this was the presence of a shady secret alliance of various intelligence organizations and arms dealing interests known as the Safari Club, operating out of Cairo with a loose charter for military intervention and secret diplomacy, aimed at countering and opposing Soviet Cold War efforts in Africa. Reputed to be involved in this alliance were the SDECE (French intelligence), the Mukhabarat (Saudi intelligence), billionaire Saudi arms dealer Adnan Khashoggi and members of SAVAK, the infamous Iranian intelligence service.

Relatively peaceful, Zambia at the time was one of the biggest copper producing countries in the world; it had one of the largest man-made holes in the ground, called "the Nchanga Open Pit." Together with the Chingola mine, it made Zambia the second largest copper source in the world and, therefore, strategically very, very important indeed.

Zambia was also geopolitically central to the wars of liberation against Namibia, South Africa and Rhodesia, backed by Cuba and the U.S.S.R., and resisted by the clandestine actions of the various intelligence services. The Soviet president had pledged material support for these liberation causes during his visit, and had met with Joshua Nkomo, amongst others, in Lusaka. The Russians were supplying arms to Nkomo (ZAPU) based on Zambia's southern border with Rhodesia and Robert Mugabe (ZANU) based in Mozambique and backed by the Chinese.

East Germany (proxy for the U.S.S.R.) was recruiting and training ANC operatives and supporters, sometimes flying them to East Berlin from Mozambique or Zaire (the Congo) for special operations training in subversion and sabotage, as well as indoctrination by Soviet intelligence. I actually spoke recently to one such individual who was an ex-prisoner and now a guide at the Robben Island Prison Museum, the location of Nelson Mandela's eighteen-year incarceration during the apartheid era. He recalled that terrible time clearly, giving me a very different view of that period in African history, through which he had survived and I had sojourned in a state of naiveté.

Zambia, which was part of the Commonwealth until 1972, was the hub of this vicious and deadly undercover activity. Britain was trying to engineer a peaceful solution to the conflict and had stood against the Smith government's declaration of independence. Kaunda had also fallen out with the Soviets because of their involvement in the Angolan civil war, and bridges needed to be rebuilt between the various conflicting groups to keep Zambia itself stable and safe from war.

So I stayed for three months in the middle of this political hotbed with a social ticket to just about every strata of Zambian society. Being young and adventurous and foolish, and not really understanding what was going on or who I was talking to, I spent a lot of time travelling backwards and forwards from Livingstone Falls, Lusaka and Kitwe, which was on the northern side of Zambia and bordered by Zaire.

I swam in the Zambezi River, went on a photo safari, dined with ex-pat mining families at community Braais (BBQs), dated the transiting British Caledonian air hostesses, drove my VW Beetle around local villages and drank the local beer known as "Mosi" after *Mosi-Oa-Tunya*, the Kololo name for the Livingston Falls. It means "The Smoke Which Thunders," and holding the beer to the light to see if there were any foreign bodies floating in it became a prudent habit!

There was a lot of political activity in Kitwe. At the time, there was a vicious civil war in Ethiopia, and many of that country's government ministers, officials, teachers and civil servants, some of whom I met, had fled to Zambia to escape torture and assassination by rival "Red Terror" Derg Marxists. Adding to this disaster, Somalia's invasion of Ethiopia was brewing, and torture, executions and mass murder were rampant in the region.

Everywhere I went in these African towns, I ended up in some hotel bar where I would talk to anybody, unaware at the time of who they were and their significance. I did realize that there was a tricky political situation going on, but that was about as far as it went. Sometimes of course you couldn't ignore it. Everyone was taking about human rights violations in what was once part of the British Commonwealth, and how we were supplying arms and using these people to our advantage. Dr. Kenneth Kaunda was known to be under the British wing, but he was still playing people off against each other. The Brits supplied financial aid, mining expertise, Sterling SMGs and WWII vintage Webley revolvers, while turning a blind eye to tribal rivalries and limited local bloodshed.

The bar at the Intercontinental Hotel in Lusaka had become the hub of a whole network of spies, adventurers, diplomatic refugees, mercenaries, arms dealers, casino sharks, journalists, hookers and various spooks of every political persuasion.

The KGB were easy to spot, sweating in cheap, ill-fitting, boxy suits, downing tumblers of neat vodka in one go and with Makarovs bulging under damp armpits. The Americans weren't much better, wearing loose-fitting and colorful Hawaiian shirts to hide 2.5 inch .357 Model 19 SWs and drinking ice-cold Saki, a habit, I was later informed, picked up from time spent in Saigon during the Vietnam War and R&R in Tokyo.

It was an odd atmosphere when tired and emotional Russian "trade delegates" sang hearty folk songs and bemoaned the days when we were all friends and beat Hitler together as allies!

Eventually I left Africa a changed man—little knowing I would be back there in 2013. As I now realize, you can leave Africa, but somehow Africa never quite leaves you. Its colors, primal energy and attitude to life and death linger in the subconscious and sometimes your secret life, as I was to discover.

After my departure from Lusaka, Joshua Nkomo's forces had committed one of the worst atrocities of the conflict, shooting down a civilian jet and killing 56 passengers. Ten of the survivors, including women and children, were subsequently murdered on the ground. Some months later, Nkomo's forces shot down yet another civilian aircraft, killing 59 passengers.

In revenge, the Rhodesian SAS drove over the border and blew up Nkomo's house in a mission apparently called Operation Bastille. To this day, rumors persist that the British warned Nkomo and later Mugabe of various assassination attempts, as it was judged both men would be indispensable in any peace negotiations involving Rhodesia and South Africa, for which the U.K. was instrumental in trying to broker a settlement.

On my return home I auditioned for and got a part in the show *Evita*. There was already an album of the music featuring Tony Christie and Julie Covington and "Don't Cry For Me Argentina" had been a huge hit. I was a big fan of Tony Christie and used to follow him around and steal his act. I mean that as a joke, but Tony Christie was one of the best live club acts I have seen anywhere. He was a great performer, and I liked his style and his music and his songs. People used to say that I did a great Tony Christie impersonation and kept insisting I go for the part of Magaldi in *Evita* because I could sing it just like him. Ronnie told me to audition, even though I personally thought it was a very long shot.

Ronnie told me the main thing was to get me in front of Hal Prince. I remember saying to Ronnie, "Who's Hal Prince?" not knowing he was one of the most famous musical theatre producers and directors in the world. Ronnie went with me, we met the producer, Bob Swartz, and did the audition with Ronnie playing piano. We did a version of Old Man River that Ronnie had arranged, and Hal Prince stood up in the stalls at the end and said, "What a great arrangement—and what a great voice." He walked up to the front of the stage and said, "You're my Magaldi!" We chatted for a while and I walked away not really understanding what had just happened. Ronnie was absolutely delighted, of course. Bob Swartz met us backstage and confirmed that we would get a contract in the next week or so. It was still going over my head—I had no idea that it would change my life again.

Almost a year later, we went into rehearsals and the first few weeks were hell. Hal Prince knew it was not going to be easy for me—being still a bit raw to the business—and he made me work extra hard. I learned later that at one point they had even talked about replacing me. I had no idea that I had an "enemy" in the production, musical director Anthony Bowls (I never found out why), and that I was being undermined almost continually and didn't realize it.

After the very successful opening night, Anthony left the production following "artistic differences" with Hal. I had seen this coming, but stayed well away from it all. On the opening night, I was one of the "crowd-pleasing elements of the show," as the London *Evening Standard* proclaimed!

So there I was—a leading man in a West End musical. Not bad for a tyke from Yorkshire! But right around the corner, a whole new part of my life was waiting to get underway.

2.
THE SHOW GOES ON

"We travel not for trafficking alone:
By hotter winds our fiery hearts are fanned:
For lust of knowing what should not be known
We make the Golden Journey to Samarkand.
- James Elroy Flecker

WORKING ON *EVITA* MEANT that I spent a lot of time in Soho, where the theatre was situated. In all I was there for about four years, during which time I got to know a lot of colorful characters, particularly the Italians and Maltese who ran restaurants, clubs and the porn industry.

I also came across people working in the arms business, and others who were serving police officers: some Special Branch, some in the Diplomatic Protection Group and others in the security services. I had a couple of unintentional brushes with terrorist organizations and major organized criminal figures that broadened my understanding of this dark and secret underbelly of London's "polite" society.

I even came under suspicion once myself, and became the focus of a major criminal investigation in Yorkshire because I drove up and down regularly to visit my family, usually late at night after the show. It seems that I bore a superficial resemblance to the identikit image of a suspect in the case. Once it was realized that when the horrific crimes were being committed I had about sixteen hundred and fifty eyewitnesses watching me running around the stage at the Prince Edward Theatre in London, and that it was thus physically impossible for me to have been involved in any crime, the police accepted that I was totally unconnected to the case. One of the officers later explained the misunderstanding to me in my dressing room. I expressed my opinion that, considering the transient and random nature of the crimes and the physical description, I totally understood and was not offended in any way by their investigation, because I was totally innocent.

I also came to understand that after my African adventures I was on somebody's official radar in the security world. On my return from Zambia I received a brief and business-like phone call requesting a sit-down, and was later visited by "Mr. Brown" and "Mr. Green," representing a benign-sounding bureaucratic enclave of the Home Office. I was grilled in depth, for some hours, about my personal contact with various characters while in Lusaka, and what I had actually been doing there. These gentlemen were polite, subtle and skilled debriefers, but they did not look like paper-pushing civil servants, and their official credentials suggested they had a large and effective machine behind them. They also impressed on me, very firmly, the requirement that I *never* disclose the nature of their enquiries, or that they had approached me at all!

It might seem odd that a perfectly innocent person returning from a harmless foreign trip would be approached by British security personnel in this way, but as I learned for myself later on when I took part in many training scenarios, the practice of "cold contact" approaches for information gathering or "along-side" recruitment are a regular, inexpensive and sometimes highly effective tool in the intelligence business. On many occasions I was the training target of officers honing these skills, and I made them meet me in places like the British Museum to ask me a seemingly random and innocent question regarding the exhibit I was studiously looking at.

Having the trainee ask me if "Horus was blind in one eye?" while standing in front of a statue of the Egyptian god was always a good start to a cold contact, as was "Mirror, mirror on the wall" while looking at a highly decorated Iron Age mirror in the Celtic art collection. These details were sure to confuse, distract or challenge the conversational and social skills of even a hardened officer, who expected complete compliance and docility from his assigned target and suddenly found himself discussing Celtic art and burial traditions! Considering the variety and historical importance of some of the exhibits in the British Museum, it meant I could mix business with pleasure and put the officer in a situation that would test his adaptability and fortitude.

I enjoyed these regular London training exercises immensely and it helped my colleges at JSIO (Joint Services Intelligence Organisation) get the most out of their courses by varying the nature of their scenarios. However, that came much later; for now the purposes of the visit from Messrs. Brown and Green (in various guises) would remain something of an anomaly for several years to come.

While I was still at the Italia Conti Stage School in the 70s, one of the young actors I met was Jamie Foreman, to whom my then-girlfriend Susan had been engaged for a while. Jamie and I had only spoken a couple of times, but I knew he was the son of Freddie Foreman who, if you haven't read the book *Respect*, was one of the most feared figures in London gangland at the time. Freddie had been heavily involved with gangland interactions during the 60s and 70s, sometimes finessing various rival gang feuds and, when required, enforcing peace. I met Freddie, or "Brown Bread Fred" as he was known, and found that he was actually both a very likeable person and a gentleman. That can't be said for some of the other figures that roamed around Soho at this time.

It was after I started going out with Susan that I came into contact with what you might call the "grey area" of society: the shadowy place where the world of criminals, terrorists, arms dealers and intelligence groups collide and intermingle. It's the same whether you're in London, New York or Los Angeles.

At the time there was a club in London called The Candy Box, just off Oxford Street. I went there with a friend, John Turner, who was also in *Evita* playing Peron while I was playing Ché, the part I graduated to after playing Magaldi for over a year and a half. It was the only club that opened at 2 am and closed at 8 am. I remember John knocking on the door, which was made of shotgun-riddled metal, and a little slit opened so the doorman could see us and let us in (eventually I became a member). It was like a scene from *Casablanca*. I remember John saying, "That's the Richardsons over there, and that's the Kray firm and that's the Finchley mob over there. All the girls in the middle are hookers, but they're off duty now: this is where they come when they're not working. That guy's a drug dealer, that one's an MP and yes, he is wearing a dress..." There were police officers from West End Central, the Sweeny, gangsters, all sorts of groups, all drinking together. It was a kind of weird neutral zone and I found it fascinating. I got to know some of the individuals after a while and saw how they fitted in and moved around each other.

People got to know me as well, and began to trust me. While I was still in *Evita*, a Royalty Protection officer who was responsible for looking after the British Royal Family, and whom I knew, went off with one of the showgirls one night and left his S&W .38 Model 10 revolver in my dressing room. I remember thinking, *What the hell I am going to do with this?* If I got caught with the weapon I could get 15 years. But I took it home with me anyway, and called him and told him I had just driven home with it in my car. He came round later to collect it, but it would have been difficult to explain away if I had been stopped. He would have lost his job and I would have been arrested. This kind of thing meant people knew I had a cool head on my shoulders and that folks on both sides of the fence could trust my discretion.

Knowing some of these faces had a useful side effect. One day my brother came to visit me at the theatre. He left his car, which was a Wood & Pickett-style Mini Cooper, done out like a Rolls Royce inside with a wooden dashboard and leather seats, parked outside. After he left me to go home he found it had been broken into; somebody had smashed in the back window and stolen his briefcase off the back seat. He was all for reporting it to the police, but I dissuaded him because I believed we could get better results by talking to some of my new Soho friends.

We went round to see as many people as we could and told them what had happened and asked if they could point us towards anyone who might know the whereabouts of my brother's stuff. No one said much but everyone agreed it was bad for business to have theatre folks' cars being robbed and damaged because we spent so much money in the restaurants and Soho pubs! Over the next few days just about everything, including my brother's passport, his building society account book and so on, was handed in at the stage door—mostly in plain brown envelopes. The only thing he did not get back was the actual briefcase.

I went back to thank some of the people I had spoken to and told them we had everything back except for the briefcase. They said that it would have been thrown away: only the valuable stuff would have been kept and was able to be returned. I learned from this that there was indeed honor among thieves—at least towards their friends.

Gradually, I began to be aware of a whole "other" world out there, which played by a different set of rules. All kinds of doors suddenly opened to me—many of which I had no desire to open at all, but they were there anyway. "Messrs. Brown and Green" made odd, unannounced and discreet appearances, but were only interested in African, Eastern-Bloc or terrorism-related issues. Criminals were of no concern to them, leaving Soho villains to the local "plod" as they called them. That was never an issue for me and not a conflict of interest as I was not into robbing post offices!

Later in the mid-80s I was part owner of a paintball company. My business partners were John Newman and Sam Madge. Both were involved with the military, and John was ex-Para Regiment and had earned a BEM (British Empire Medal) for his service around the globe. Sam had been the Stage Manager during my run on *Evita*, but was also involved with the Royal Corps of Signals and was working for the DSF (Director of Special Forces). We ran into a problem almost straight away when we were told that the CO_2 guns we used in the paintballing would not pass the rigorous Home Office forensic tests. So we had to have them "retuned" by a lovely guy called Martin, who used to call himself my soft-core weapons supplier. Because I was purchasing various bits of military equipment for the paintball game, I found myself in the company of some pretty curious characters who were shifting military equipment all over the world. Once again there was a crossover between the everyday corporate world and the sinister.

Later, we became the only paintball company ever to get a contract with the Home Office, helping with stress evaluation for their personnel. We never knew who they were exactly, but the Home Office would regularly bring down two teams of ten or twelve people, and we'd have them running about in the woods shooting at each other. We designed special games for them, and they would rotate captains and put a psychologist in with each team to evaluate how they reacted under stress.

The one thing you can say about the paintball experience is that it does put people under stress, because although the paintball doesn't hurt that much, it really does sting! You don't want to get hit. It's also a game of strategy that brings out the leadership abilities in people.

Another colorful character who worked with us on the paintball game was my old friend Brian Hamilton, an interesting and complex man who has done a lot of work for British security elements and the military. Brian had been in the Royal Marines and did several tours in Northern Ireland. He used to get in touch with me when he needed help with odd jobs—some of them very odd indeed. We are still friends today.

Once, Brian sent me two supposed ex-special forces guys who wanted help finding a way to get equipment into South Africa and to get past the embargo that was then in place because of apartheid. They had found out that a well-connected Australian arms dealer with close contacts to the Australian government was living in London. He had access to just about any equipment you could think of: aircraft, tanks, artillery, helicopters, ground to air missiles and even torpedoes. These guys were interested in some Vietnam war-era C-130 Hercules cargo planes and a large shipment of spare parts for the aircraft, and the dealer was the man to get them. I went to meet this guy to ensure he was for real. After several conversations it became obvious that he was very well connected and could deliver from the catalogues of equipment he had in his possession. However, there was still the problem of the embargo, so they asked me to come up with a way to get around this. They needed a reason to purchase the planes so that they could get an End-User Certificate of ownership. They could then use them for transport and smuggle them to Africa.

Once again Messrs. Brown and Green made an impromptu and discreet appearance and suggested that I went along with the plot. I thought it over and came up with the believable and practical idea of buying a defunct American cargo company in Florida, filing flight plans as if they were actually going to carry regular cargo there, then buying the planes and flying them openly to Florida so that the authorities would know they had arrived. Once there, they could set up a fictitious series of deliveries and fly them to South America. These would appear as legitimate cargo shipments, and the planes would then be on their way to South Africa via Swaziland before anyone had worked out what was really going on.

I think there were three planes in all—worth about $12 million at the time—and I believe that they were intended for the South African army. However, no one was allowed to supply military equipment or anything else to South Africa because of apartheid. I was very aware of this and was obviously not going to break the law, but it seemed that somebody was setting up a sting operation and I had no intention of being on the receiving end of it. My job was simply to come up with a viable plan for the proposed operation.

It was never revealed to me whether this was a plot to ferret out the identities of those involved in this kind of deal, or whether it was an "unofficially" sanctioned operation. When it was all done and dusted the whole thing came to nothing. After several meetings with the mysterious buyers, it was quietly dropped. The two characters that had approached us disappeared, and that was the end of my involvement. However, I always wondered if Messrs. Brown and Green had seen to it that no C-130 ever made it to South Africa, and that a quiet and convenient "accident" had claimed the aircraft and their shipment of spare parts and engines somewhere over the Atlantic Ocean.

Hard Men

Another interesting character I met at this time, through Brian, was Benny Cellini, a very smart, very bright guy who had arrived in London from New York. Then in his mid-thirties, he was in London, supposedly to have a hip replacement operation. This is a common practice in organized crime: if you think you are looking at a life sentence you go somewhere for a supposedly serious medical procedure that will make you immobile for months.

The Cellini brothers, Eddie and Dino, were responsible for inventing modern gaming, as we know it still in Las Vegas, including the way the gaming floor is laid out, the games that are played and the lighting. They had done the same in the Bahamas. The family were well known in organized crime but I was told that they did not have a son known as Benny, so he might have been using that name as an alias.

One day he came to me and said, "You know about the film business. I want to buy the rights to a book called *Higher Than Hope* by Fatima Meer. How do I do it?" I asked what the book was about and he said it was a biography of Nelson Mandela. Somehow, this writer had got access to him and the book was written while Mandela was still in prison. His friends in South Africa wanted to buy the rights so that one-day they could make a film of it. It was arranged for "Benny" to meet with Fatima Meer's agent in London, and I went along with him.

We met in a restaurant before the meeting and he told me that he was going to offer them half a million dollars in cash, but that he was prepared to go up to one million. I said, "That's a lot of money for this kind of deal!" "Benny" hinted that the money was laundered, and told me he had a bankers draft, which he flashed at me. I saw that it was colored blue, which meant that it was almost certainly Barclays, so I said, "Oh, a Barclays draft out of Cyprus is it?" "Benny" looked amazed and asked me how I knew that. I said because that was where all the "bent" money came from. At the time Britain had a large listening post on Cyprus (and probably still does), and a lot of money for secret operations, both black and white, went through Nicosia.

We went on to the meeting and discussed how we could make sure Nelson Mandela actually received his slice of the money while he was still in prison. It was explained that the money would be paid into an account in Zurich, and that Winnie Mandela would distribute funds to the ANC from there, while holding some money back for Nelson when he came out of prison. The middleman told us this was how it would be. The lawyer who was also present said he would discuss it with the writer, Fatima Meer, based on an offer of one million dollars.

I knew that in these situations many people try to place themselves in the middle of a deal, even if they have no authorization or actual agreement to do so. Middlemen try to use that influence or deal brokering to make a commission or finders fee should the project go ahead. Usually they don't. This happens all the time in Hollywood with movie projects, so the situation did not surprise me. Because I wasn't personally involved in the deal or seeking a fee, and was only accompanying "Benny" as a favor to Brian, it did not really concern me. The only thing I baulked at was the thought of having one million dollars disappear into a numbered Swiss bank account managed by Winnie Mandela, possibly never to be seen again.

Once again the deal fell through because I believe Nelson Mandela's people or the ANC found out who was actually trying to buy the rights to the book, and the deal evaporated. This prompted me to make some of my own inquiries as to who "Benny" really was. The answers were not good.

Around this time, I got to know a man named Bob Dick. Bob was widely known as the best gold smuggler in the business and one of the only Scotsmen to be associated with Angelo Bruno and Philadelphia organized crime; things that he described in his semi-fictional autobiography *The Bagman*. Bob was known to a contact of Ray Winstone's at the time, an accountant who we nicknamed BR—a lovely bloke who seemed totally harmless.

Ray, Clive Mantle (another old friend from *Robin of Sherwood*) and I were looking for sources of financing for several film projects we were developing for our own film company, Odds On Films, and BR said that Bob knew his way around the film game and might be able to help. Bob was a gentleman and a very shrewd operator. He was dapper, smooth, thoughtful, and very wily. I learned a tremendous amount from him about how to think outside the box and how to operate in a very different environment. Bob used to park his Rolls Royce in the grounds of Brompton Oratory, which was right across from his and his wife June's apartment in Empire House, Knightsbridge. He apparently made bounteous and regular donations to the church!

I asked him about "Benny." His response was simple. If he were a "made" wise-guy [i.e. under the protection of the Mafia] on the run from American justice and "wildcatting" with mob funds, sooner or later it would end badly. If he was a fraudster using the name and claiming association with families in N.Y., it would also end badly. Either way we didn't want to be in the line of fire when the shooting started.

I took the warning seriously. Bob was totally honest and open with me about his former associations with various groups, businesses and organizations, although he was now retired and enjoying a quiet life tinkering with a variety of showbiz projects. Some mutual friends expressed real concern about our friendship, since Bob had a fearsome reputation and was a very highly sought-after smuggler at one time, with friends in some pretty scary places. I had to admit this all seemed pretty redundant because he had been nothing but honest and open with me, and appeared at ease with his life and infamy. He and June introduced me to friends in

New York, Las Vegas and Los Angeles, and I was genuinely fascinated by the way his mind worked and by what I could learn from him. He often asked me questions about how I would approach an issue or problem, and we had fun exchanging ideas and coming up with outlandish and yet workable scenarios. He gave me his book to study and told me many of the real backstories to the tales he included, which he had to polish and recount in a non-incriminating way.

Maybe that's why he took to me under his wing, so to speak. We thought alike but from different points of view. He was the poacher and I was the gamekeeper.

I learned a lot about poaching from Bob Dick.

Bob also became interested in my writing, partly, I suspect, because of my own colorful contacts gathered along the way. I had written a script called *Pendragon*, which was about King Arthur, and Bob was impressed with it and wanted to help me. He also had his own script that he wanted me to help him with. I read it and did not think much of it. The subject was very non-politically correct (PC) and I just didn't get it. In fact he had sent both scripts to a professional reader in Hollywood and the feedback on *Pendragon* was very good and on his was awful. The premise and structure of the script were wrong and I told him why. I think he respected me after that and trusted my judgment, and through those discussions Bob and I struck up a loose collaboration on a couple of TV and movie projects.

He was a very classy and subtle guy, and had reputedly worked for the CIA among others. Not long after we first met he told me he had been approached to come up with an idea for a TV soap set in the famous Palace Hotel, a glamorous tourist spot in St. Moritz, Switzerland. I did some research on the place and came up with an idea for something like *Dallas*, but giving the hotel another name. It was all about the comings and goings of the guests and I wrote the basic framework and character descriptions for it. Bob really liked the idea and decided to take it to a big film festival in Milan, where he had friends. We would show it around and try to drum up some interest. He asked me to go along. I learned later that Bob probably had another purpose for going, but at the time I knew nothing of this.

We met in Milan and drove up through Italy, around Lake Como and into Switzerland, then on to St. Moritz, where we stayed near the famous hotel. The city fathers of St. Moritz had heard about the project and wanted to take us out to dinner. They greeted us enthusiastically. We sat around talking about our ideas for the show, as well as the burning question of the Euro and how the European Union and Germany's banks were going to be running Europe. This did not sit well with me and we had some spirited and good-natured banter about "those bloody Brits" and their lead-lined, handbag-wielding Prime Minister.

We went round trying to sell the idea to a couple of TV companies from London, but there was no real interest because they all thought it would be too expensive to shoot. We also met with a charming American TV executive called Bill Cameron, who was working in the international TV sales market in London. He asked rather warily if Bob was still a member of the mafia. Bob, without batting an eye, explained patiently that he could never be a member of the Mafia because he was Scottish. He told Bill, in a very calm and matter of fact manner that he was an "associate" of organized crime and had retired from that life with the good graces and best wishes of Angelo Bruno. I wondered if Bill was really comforted by this honest and direct answer.

I later had further meetings with Bill about various projects, and he told me he had left the U.S. after being shot during a random gang initiation. The bullet had nicked his liver and exited through his left lung but his assailant hadn't stolen anything, despite the fact that Bill had the trunk of his car open, his wallet in his pocket and an expensive watch on his wrist. He had been left bleeding on the parking lot floor. This seemed odd at the time, but if that was his story he was sticking to it and I thought I'd better let it pass.

Bill was also in possession of what appeared to be a first generation copy of the infamous MJ-12 documents, a reputed government/alien conspiracy agreement. He told me he was trying to develop the concept as a TV show and asked me if I had any knowledge of this bizarre conspiracy theory. At that time I did not, so I couldn't help him with it.

As Bob, June and I drove back across Europe to the U.K. from Switzerland, I wondered if the wells of at least one of the cars we used might be full of Tola gold bars, being smuggled into Britain. Bob had once driven all over Europe doing this, but I didn't ask because I didn't need to know.

As far as I was concerned all we were doing was going to discuss a TV show; but there was a slim chance we had enough bullion on-board the car to pay for a TV series several times over!

Treading Strange Waters

All this gadding about and the odd relationships that came out of it began to get me an unsought and whispered reputation—most of it based on hearsay. A director friend of mine named Tom Clegg asked me outright about this over dinner when I was in Montreal years later, working on a show called *The Secret Adventures of Jules Verne*. He said, "You know you've got a reputation as being an ex-mercenary and maybe even a hired assassin?"

I liked and respected Tom and wasn't offended by the question. I told him that while we were working on a film called *Who Dares Wins* I used to go shooting at the London Wall Pistol Range with Lew Collins. Lew asked about my weapons skills and how I had become so familiar and competent with so many foreign firearms. I jokingly told Lew that I'd been a mercenary in Africa. Of course I was pulling his leg and wasn't going to tell him about my quiet visits to the Pattern Room at Enfield Small-Arms, then one of the greatest and most unique firearms collections in the world, which had started in the early 80s. I believe Lew told others and I'm sure that some people thought I really was an ex-mercenary, so the story might have stuck for a while.

Once, Brian even asked me if I was working for the CIA, because when you flit about all over the world, and hang about with some odd people, it might look to some as if that's what you've been doing. The reality was I had become a kind of freelance "fixer," although I preferred the term "consultant" because it is a more generic term.

I was gaining an education that would come in handy later on.

Instinctively, I have always felt a strong moral obligation to do the right thing. I know what is right and what is wrong. I do not break the law and have never taken drugs or dealt in them. Those in power know that I'm loyal to the democratic process, whatever that really means now! I do have secrets and I'll take them to my grave out of respect for those still serving and who wish to stay in the shadows of a quiet life. A Walter Mitty-type character lives in a fantasy world of their own making; but real life is much more challenging than any fiction I could have imagined or written about as a boy in Doncaster. In the end, that ability to see a moral line in the sand and walk down it, one foot in the light and one foot in the shadow, might have saved my life and opened other doors on more than one occasion.

Major Mitch Barking, my Intelligence Corps boss at one time, stated this as a matter of fact, quite pragmatically and with hand on heart, on my swearing the Oath of Allegiance in his office in Handel Street, "No pensions. No medals. No glory." Later, another Messrs. Green and Brown incarnation would say, "If you get caught, you're totally fucked and on your own." That seemed quite fair to me and it didn't require further explanation. Not only that but, in the early 90s, I welcomed it.

If I were asked to describe this period in my life, 1987—1992, I would say it was all very much a grey area, because I had one foot in both camps. On the one hand I was freelancing in a way that was not illegal or detrimental to the British Government or democracy, but at the same time I was aware of the relationships between the official line and some of these "unofficial" elements. I was doing my own thing within the law, and that was a narrow and limited path. I craved more of a rush and a sense of life purpose.

My friendship with Bob Dick—who was not your average "gangster" in my opinion—underlined the strange no man's land I found myself in. Bob never asked me to do anything illegal, but he gave me an education in criminality, which I have since used in other areas of investigation in the U.S. to help solve serious crimes. Whenever I have been asked to look into something, whether a homicide, a complex art fraud investigation or a criminal casino enterprise, I tried to look at the issue the way Bob would have done. Even if this has been challenging to the people I was possibly trying to protect, it always comes down to a question of truth, morality and personal judgment. I've always been fascinated by the underbelly of these other worlds and the duality of the human condition.

My friendship with Brian Hamilton was also like this. A true social wildcard, Brian could be charming, funny and truly chilling all at the same time. With those cold grey Irish eyes he could discuss South American plant extract poisons (which he grew in his greenhouse) or embarrass any female with a joke about sex that involved holding their hand... Brian is, and will always remain, an original.

Brian and I did many odd jobs together, and I often wondered to whom he was reporting; but I trusted him and sometimes that went all the way to putting my life in his hands. Together we have walked into strange situations without boundaries or fear, and I often marveled at his ability to charm his way out of harrowing situations with a smile and a wink. I was also amazed to find him, on several occasions, in the back of various restaurants during dinner, with his sleeves rolled up showing the chef how to cook various dishes and having the entire staff rolling about in laughter at this charismatic, unpredictable joker who had taken over their kitchen!

To put it in the language and symbolism of the Tarot, with which I have become familiar in recent times, it seems the universe takes care of The Fool and places the bridge beneath his feet as he steps into the void and refuses to carry the guilt, fear and doubt as baggage into the future.

One of the many interesting figures Brian and I met and worked with at this time was the beautiful and talented model L'Wren Scott, who passed away tragically in March 2014. L'Wren had come to us with a personal recommendation from mutual friends and required help to be extracted from a relationship situation that had turned sour and put her in fear for her safety.

She was concerned, sad yet stoical. She simply wished to leave England cleanly and completely, and without any further complications. She sat calmly in our office and was weary, realistic and genuine. This tall, eloquent and very likable woman had the knack of making you feel at ease and confortable in the presence of her stunning beauty.

Over the next few days we plotted, planned and arranged her removal from London to a safe and secure location in Paris. One of L'Wren's most treasured possessions was a Keith Haring painting that the prominent New York artist and activist had given her when they met there and became friends during the 80s. Haring was also a favorite of Madonna, who donated ticket sales to AIDS charities in his name, dedicated a tour to his memory and used his artwork on her album covers.

Haring died of AIDS in February 1990, and the painting had a special place in L'Wren's heart. She wanted to make sure it went with her to Paris. Brian and I both agreed that she was a genuine and rare person. After some initial background checks proved her claims, we took the view that we could trust the painting was really hers and that the situation was as she described.

Later, after L'Wren had been spirited away to France and housed within the "A Class" model fraternity, she was helped by many friends, including Jean Paul Gautier, to re-establish her life and career. Brian continued to keep in touch with L'Wren, who was now well protected by armed guards. One of her main desires was to contact her real parents, from whom she had been separated at birth, and this was achieved a few months later. I personally received very angry and coldly threatening calls from her jettisoned London "baggage." I explained I had been threatened before and would probably be threatened again, and that the caller did not scare me in the least. In any case the job was done and L'Wren was safe and sound and well out of his reach.

One of the many other enigmas with which we became involved, was finding some kind of resolution to was the assassination of Olof Palme, the Swedish Prime Minister who was shot dead in February 1986. This had come through a very mysterious group who actually had a piece of the pavement where he had died and thought it might be possible to get some information from it through psychic or telekinetic means. There was a reward of about five million dollars for information on those responsible for Palme's death, but nobody claimed it. After doing some research it was obvious that this was a murky case. Although the probable weapon used was an S&W .357 magnum revolver (they knew this because of the ballistic striations on the recovered bullets) there were many strange and twisted political angles to the case and it was obviously not as straightforward as it seemed.

Every conspiratorial angle, from secret Bofors arms deals (with a weird U.K. twist), to Chilean fascists, an Iraqi revenge assassination squad and South African agents, supported by right-wing Swedish police elements opposed to Sweden's financing of the ANC, were all in the convoluted mix. Nevertheless, the motive for the killing has never been resolved completely, and there are serious and enduring flaws in the case that was brought against one apparent assassin who allegedly never confessed to it but was eventually convicted. To date, several dozen would-be assassins have apparently confessed to the killing, but none have seemed viable or have been charged or convicted.

In the murky world of assassination, how you kill the target serves as a signal to various agencies so that they know who did what. Normally, permissions are needed, as in the assassination of Dr. Gerald Bull, a super-gun expert who was selling weapons to Iraq. Despite working on the sale through the British Secret Intelligence Service (SIS), rumour has it that he was assassinated by the Israelis and that Mossad had to get the British to agree first, hence the overseas location of the murder. So when you read how a person was found hanging from a bridge in the City of London, killed in a single car accident in the middle of nowhere or committed suicide by shooting themselves in the head three times, it's normally a warning from one country to another that an example has been made.

After digging into the back-story of the murder and even planning a short trip to Sweden to walk the ground myself—an absolutely vital process to understand the actual distances, escape routes and vantage points—Brian announced we were dropping the whole thing. I protested, jokingly reminding him that there was a five million dollar reward on the table! Brian explained that nobody would ever live to claim the reward and we should just walk away while we could. He had been told that it was a trap and whoever came up with a viable explanation or the probable truth would not survive to claim the reward.

I still have the piece of pavement that was claimed to be from the spot where Palme fell, although I have no proof it actually is. Who can say what secrets it might hold and, as far as I know, the now seven-point-four-million-dollar reward has never been claimed—despite a strange twist in the story that emerged in 2012. Eva Rausing, billionaire wife of Hans Christian Rausing, had apparently contacted Swedish investigators claiming that her husband knew who the killer was and where the murder weapon was hidden. Her decomposing body was later discovered in their London home. According to Harvey Morris of the New York Times, she had told journalist Gunner Wall that she "was afraid, and to investigate if she should die suddenly."

Such public crimes seem to nag at the collective conscience and demand some kind of closure. When I walked the ground in Dealey Plaza, Dallas, where President John F. Kennedy was shot, I was struck by how small and close all the distances were. There is no doubt in my mind that Lee Harvey Oswald could have made a shot from the Texas Book Depository, if in fact he fired the rifle at all that day. I could have made at least one shot. Any trained marksman could, in my opinion. I was totally convinced that, if there was a second shooter that day, the best spot was on the grassy knoll, offering a clear and close-range shot at the motorcade with unrestricted escape routes. Lee Bowers in the railway-switching tower would have had an unrestricted view of the whole parking lot and of any people standing there. But he died in an unexplained single car motor accident.

Something I saw in Africa made me always view these tragic events through different eyes. There was a bridge that crossed the border between Zambia and the then Rhodesia, countries that were of course at war. The train used to go backwards and forwards over the bridge, while the guys underneath on the ground were killing each other. I was fascinated by the fact that trade continued on the borders of a vicious war, while down below people were shooting at each other and de Havilland Vampire Fighter/Bombers were dropping explosive ordinances on training camps.

This fascinated, horrified and saddened me. It still does. On one hand there's the ordinary world we live in, and on the other, just underneath it all, is a melee of spies, spooks, conmen, gangsters, security services, policemen, lawyers, banks, terrorists, money launderers and those with military corporate interests, which most people don't know or even care about. I was interested right from the start with the way it all functioned and how it had all got so terribly messed up.

I almost became a split personality through such encounters. Because I was an actor, and had the confidence to be able to sit down with any of these people and then get up and walk away, I had no fear of them because I had nothing to lose. I think that's what my military bosses once meant when they wrote in an official report, "We can send this man anywhere— he can talk his way in and talk his way out. We can send him into anything and he'll come back." I had to countersign the report. It was the nearest thing to a pat on the back I ever received.

All of this had put me on the radar, but nobody ever came to talk to me or tell me directly that I should not be hanging around with certain people, or ask me to come down to the nearest police station to talk to them. But it did lead me, in*evita*bly, towards a deeper involvement with the intelligence world.

3.
A WORLD OF SECRETS

Manui Dat Cognitio Vires (Knowledge Gives Strength to the Arm)
(Motto of the Intelligence Corps)

BACK IN 1981, I worked on the film *Who Dares Wins*, based on the best selling book *The Tiptoe Boys* by James Follett. The book was inspired by the world famous Iranian Embassy Siege at Princess Gate, London, known as "Operation Nimrod." The initial plot synopsis for the book was written by George Markstein, who had been involved with iconic 60s British TV shows *The Prisoner* and *Callan*.

I had lunch with George to talk about the background to the film, and we discussed his book *The Cooler* and Inverlair Lodge, which was the model for the Village in *The Prisoner*. We chatted about "The Mad Major" and his highly polished and well-worn Mauser C-96 Broomhandle pistol that I had seen in the Enfield Small Arms Pattern Room. I also had briefly talked to Trevor Lock, the police officer taken hostage during the siege, at a private gathering, and he had explained his reasons for not shooting "Oan", the leader of the terrorists, during the final SAS assault. George was a very intelligent man; an excellent and experienced writer and his insights were highly educational.

The script was written by Reginald Rose, and told the story of a captain in the Special Air Service (SAS), whose motto formed the title of the film, who infiltrates a radical political group planning a terrorist operation against American dignitaries. Lewis Collins was playing the hero, and I was playing a professional assassin called Mac, filming during the day and performing as Ché in *Evita* at night for the last six weeks of my contract on the show.

Before shooting began I had bumped into my old pal Lew while hiking in the Brecon Beacons, the endurance training area in Wales used by several armed forces groups. Lew had played Bodie in the hugely successful TV series *The Professionals*, and it was he who introduced me to the director Ian Sharp, who was shooting test footage for the forthcoming production. Ian came to see me play Ché in the West End and asked me to join the cast of *Who Dares Wins*. I'd known Lew since working on *The Cuckoo Waltz* at Granada TV and Albert Fennel, the producer of the show, had promised me a role in *The Professionals*, but I was fully engaged with *Evita* while they were filming the series and it never worked out time-wise.

Lew had passed selection for 10 Para (another reserve unit) and was planning on going on selection for 21 SAS, the Territorial Army (TA) element of the SAS. I later learned that he had passed selection but was RTU'd (returned to unit) as being too high profile for their specific role at the time. I was actually grilled about my friendship with Lew in some detail years later during a vetting interview at Stirling-Lines, the regimental headquarter of the SAS, and also about my role in *Who Dares Wins*. They must have been satisfied with my answers because I was cleared and given the famous sand-colored beret to wear while on attachment with the regiment.

I forged friendships with some of the anonymous guys who worked as extras on the film. One character I met during filming, who was a legend with "The Regiment" (as 22 SAS is known) was Peter Scholey. Pete was a colorful and engaging character who happily handed me his regimental tie at a gathering and challenged me to go on selection for 21 SAS, the Territorial Army element of the unit.

There is actually very little difference in the standing of the Territorial boys, who serve alongside the full-time soldiers. 21 had its own role in Germany at that time, and troopers from the TA could be deployed for limited periods of time in conflict areas—just like National Guard soldiers in the United States serving at various times in Iraq/Afghanistan.

Everything was the same for the TA boys as the regular army, except that they did not get a pension at that time—although that might have changed now. The selection process was spread over several weekends, and some regulars felt it was easier because the accumulated effect of injury and exhaustion could be overcome more easily when the recovery time was spread out over a longer period; but for the most part the physical endurance marches were the same. The British Army could not fulfilll its commitment to various theatres without the addition of the TA soldiers, and I only rarely encountered any "STAB" (Stupid TA Bastard) mentality from the mature, regular soldiers, and only occasionally from the younger squaddies. Generally, they just failed to understand what our actual role was; they wanted to know who these blokes were with the funny green berets, Sterling sub-machine guns and non-standard "belt kits" - and why they marched so bloody badly!

Shortly after committing to selection with 21 at their old barracks on the Kings Road and training like a mad thing around Tooting Bec Common and the Black Mountains for months, I got a call from Ian Sharp about a part in *Robin of Sherwood*, and that was the end of my military aspirations for the time being!

It was simply a choice between a major TV acting gig, or going on selection. I made the right choice and spent the next three years of my life running around Bristol (thinly disguised as Sherwood Forest) with the Merry Men, being another kind of warrior, fighting on a different kind of battlefield.

The enduring friendships and myriad of amazing experiences during the making of the show are now the stuff of TV legend. The show influenced a whole generation of filmmakers (as I discovered when working on *Black Sails*, where the director Neil Marshall confessed to being one of them) and continues to entertain, enchant and educate millions of new viewers every year. It's a fitting legacy for my dear friend and wise, esoteric mentor, Richard "Kip" Carpenter, and remains one of the most memorable, productive and joyful periods of my entire life.

New Ways Forward

It was after the bitter and ugly break-up with my then-partner Susan in 1990 that I officially returned to the military. The 90s recession was in full swing, and I had been wiped out financially due to a three year battle for visitation rights to my children. I eventually won the case in the High Court as an unmarried father under the Children's Act of 1989, with full parental rights and a visitation schedule; but that was not the end of the struggle and Susan was determined to close me out of my children's lives.

At one point I ended up delivering Indian food for a local South London restaurant just to keep some money coming in and pay the rent. The TV and film business was totally decimated and even the odd jobs with Brian were drying up. I decided to go back on selection for 21 SAS because it was better than delivering tandoori chicken and meat samosas around Tooting in my Honda Prelude.

My experiences of this time were as varied as they were strange. One day during a physical exercise on the Kings Road parade ground we were dragging a "wounded" comrade and ourselves along the ground, which was freezing cold and rock hard, and I sliced off the skin and a lump of flesh from both knees (I still have the scars). This happened just before my first full weekend selection course and, although I took whatever painkillers were available, I could not run fast enough to meet the time set for us because the wounds on both knees were bleeding and very sore. I completed the run but one of the DS (Directing Staff) supervisors came over to look at what had happened and pulled me off the course after seeing the injuries—not the same as me jacking it in, which would have gone against me. He knew that they could use my skills somewhere else, so over that weekend I went on a CTR (close target recce) exercise—one group getting past the guards of another group's base and so on, which went well.

The following week I got called back, and in effect they said that although I was 35—a bit older than the other squaddies—they did not want to lose me, and recommended that I go on selection for the Intelligence Corps. I was advised that an interview could be arranged for me if I was willing to try. I was warned, however, that it was a long course—physically as well as mentally—the equivalent of taking a degree course while "tabbing up the Fan" (or to put that in regular English, Tactical Advance to Battle up Pen-y-Fan in the Brecon Beacons).

I had to face the reality that I would have a hard time at my age completing selection with the injuries I had, but since I had originally considered volunteering for the Intelligence Corp back in 1986, soon after my stint on *Robin of Sherwood*, I still had the paperwork. At the time I was working sporadically and didn't know if I could commit enough time to it.

I called the contact that I had been given to me by the DS at 21 and went to see the Int. Corps staff. They explained the clearance process, and I started it right away. It involved different levels of security vetting and training to be completed over a year. I then began the official Intelligence Corps training. The actual A3 course was a very, very thorough breakdown of Military Intelligence in all its glory, with the main focus, at this time, being on the Russian Order of Battle (ORBAT)—not because they were the main enemy anymore, but because their equipment and systems were still being used all over the world. One of the things I excelled at on this course was FER (foreign equipment recognition and its capabilities) because I had been interested in this for a long time and had been studying it as part of my various interactions with the arms business—so that module was easy for me.

The hardest, driest module was the classwork in security—reams upon reams of paper dealing with rules and guidelines on every level of army security from the bottom upwards, which I found very boring—but all to do with securing a military base, equipment and operations. We also covered the mysteries of the Manifoil Mk IV combination lock and how to break it and reset it, and other interesting and quite useful subjects like that.

In addition to the weekly classwork, we went on weekend assessments. They sent psychologists to observe everyone—and had us doing some really odd things. Once I was told to go and talk to a fence post—to have a conversation with it. After about twenty minutes of me talking to my new concrete pal, the psychologist came over to me and said in a mildly surprised tone, "You have no problem talking to this post, do you?" To which I replied, "Not at all. Do you have a problem with it talking back to me?"

I had just completed work on my first tarot deck, *The Greenwood Tarot* around that time, so was able to talk Jungian Archetypes and collective human subconscious with the psychologist and not appear totally bonkers!

There were all sorts of people on the course—satellite experts, ex-members of the French Foreign Legion, computer engineers, language specialists, armored Mercedes dealers and retired Israeli Army personnel—people from all walks of life. One day, as part of a test, we ended up facing a deep pond that was deemed an "obstacle. We had to get a heavy ammunition container across this pond using just the basic equipment supplied—planks of wood and a couple of ropes etc.

I stood watching while the group tried out different ideas, none of them successful, observed by the sergeant in charge. Having had previous practice with this kind of lateral thinking test, I told them my own idea and was about to choose the most suitable person to walk out into the pond, when the Sergeant shouted at me, "You do it!" So I dragged and pushed an oil drum into the center of the pond and sank it as a central pontoon. Then I walked backwards onto the planks and dragged the container with me—getting to the other side within the test time.

That was when I knew that I could complete the course.

Most of the early part of the course consisted of the kind of things I had done for the paintball/war games company. We had virtually invented some of these game scenarios for corporate entities. I remember how one of the sergeants came over and talked to me about it. I told him how the Home Office had been to look at what we were doing with the paintball exercises and how they eventually became a client. He was obviously impressed with this concept. From then on it was just a case of keeping up my dedication to the study. I became so focused and absorbed by the physical and mental challenge of achieving this goal that I blocked out everything else: it probably saved me from depression and drifting into melancholy regarding the situation with my children.

I eventually passed the A3 course and was presented with my Cyprus-green beret and green lanyard (the intelligence equivalent of wings). We did a further two-week assessment at Strensall Camp near York, and there was a family day at the end of it. My sister Sandra, her family and my mum all came out. The assessment weeks were physically hard—men and women were injured. We ended up with one lad on a life-support machine with heatstroke and exhaustion, and several who were retired off the course as either injured or "unsuitable".

For those who might think Int. Corps training is "soft," let's be clear on this—an Int. Corp operator has to be a soldier first. All the basic skills of an infantry soldier have to be mastered; the drill sergeants made sure of that. Operating in any environment, whether a sub-zero German plain, sweltering North African heat or the heaving deck of a Royal Navel LPD (landing platform dock) warship in the Atlantic Ocean, was expected of the "Green Slime" operator. I was very proud to be a member of an elite squad amongst an even smaller elite.

I got through it without injury, and was pretty proficient at the rest of the stuff: navigation, field-craft, strategies, HUMINT (human intelligence) and FER (foreign equipment recognition). However, when you wear that green beret you are expected to be an expert amongst experts, so the studying did not stop.

The part I really enjoyed was being out in the field, working on mapping and strategy. The idea of "seeing over the horizon," something that has stood me in good stead a few times since then, really became clear at that time. I remember an instructor telling me that one of the things you have to be able to do when engaging the enemy is look at a big battle and know what's going on: you get signals from people all around, and you mark the map with what is happening in the main line, the flanks and the forward reconnaissance parties. You get so that you can tell where everyone is and where the enemy is going, just by what equipment they are using and where it is. But it's easy to get bogged down in this detailed map marking: it was all a bit "old school" at the time.

A Parachute Regimental Sergeant Major came along and wanted me to brief him about what was happening during an exercise. I started to talk about what was where, and he said, "No. Not what's *where*. I want to know what's *happening*—what's going on?" I started to explain in more detail and he said, "Okay, stop. Stand back from the map and look at where they are all going." I stood for a while and could see that they were going towards a port and said exactly that. He replied, "That's good intelligence. Now, *why* are they going to the port?" I said, "Because they're going to be landing equipment and supplies there and they need to secure the landing zone."

The Sergeant Major agreed, and I realized that this was what was called "a usable and timely intelligence briefing." By standing back from the map, not getting wrapped up in the details and seeing the pattern instead, I was able to understand the *how* and the *why*. I soon realized that the same principle is a big lesson that can be applied to life—not just armored divisions and battlefield scenarios.

I can honestly say this was one of the most interesting periods of my life. Soon after, I requested to go on exercise with a section that worked as a Joint Forward Intelligence Team. We were sent up to the middle of nowhere in Yorkshire and they wanted volunteers to set up what was called a J-FIT. I didn't know what this involved—I thought it was putting up 9 × 9 tents and living in the field and being comfortable in that environment! I was thinking that maybe they would need a hand doing this because I can tell you one of the funniest things I have ever seen was a squad of Intelligence Corps soldiers trying to put up a 9 × 9 tent!

I agreed to go along anyway but the "volunteers" were ambushed along the road, dragged out of the Land Rover, "bagged up" and taken away to a disused animal disease research station in the middle of nowhere. They questioned us for a day to gather as much information as possible. The funny thing was that I actually had things like a button compass, a wire saw and a small container of potassium permanganate concealed in the seams of my old DPM (disruptive pattern material) combat smock, so during the exercise I was pretty confident I could E&E (escape and evade) if they kept me there for more than a day or two.

This later led to my working more regularly with JSIO (Joint Services Intelligence Organisation) and supporting some of their longer and more intensive HUMINT [human intelligence] training courses. I did the Personnel Handling and Tactical Questioning Course myself, where you learn how to physically handle and question a POW (prisoner of war). The Geneva Convention was something I had an interest in from both ends of the equation, and being "Prone to Capture" was a concept that I was keenly interested in *not* becoming too familiar with during my service. The demands and techniques of R2I (Resistance to Interrogation) were also subjects I decided to study in some detail, but hoped never to have to rely on.

I had a good relationship with the Special Forces guys based at Ashford in Kent. They had their own little compound, which was part of the CACW (Conduct After Capture Wing), and I was invited to work with them a couple of times. I was then invited to teach acting and various "Tactical Questioning" and HUMINT techniques to the regulars being deployed overseas. These were guys going out to support intelligence operations on the ground wherever the British Army was deployed. A unit called SIW (Special Intelligence Wing) was responsible for this type of training, and it was quite an honor to be invited to go and play with them.

The work with SIW was highly sensitive, and the barracks we were billeted in at one point was a very secret location in Cornwall. Nobody really knew what the SIW's role was. Mostly it was work with agents, informants and clandestine communications. I was very at ease in this arena and enjoyed the work tremendously.

Clandestine Operations

Once they know you are not a liability to "The Group", operators who are inside but also working on the outside feel free to approach you with work when required, so I was not surprised when "Taff" from the Drugs Intelligence Unit came looking for me. I was asked to work with Customs and Excise and come up with a smuggling scenario to help train their officers. I came up with a legend (cover story) based on the real-life mercenary recruiter John Banks of the infamous Angolan mercenary fiasco.

John Banks was an ex-parachute regiment soldier and mercenary recruiter who claimed many secret government operations and connections and reputedly had a close working relationship with David Stirling, the founder of the SAS Regiment. Banks owned a company called Security Advisory Service and was deeply involved with supplying soldiers of fortune to several warzones around the globe, apparently with tacit if deniable support of both the U.K. and U.S. intelligence services. In 75/76 he recruited approximately one hundred men to fight against the Cuban backed forces of the PMLA (People's Movement for the Liberation of Angola) during the Angolan war of independence. The operation ended in a debacle and most of the men were killed, captured or murdered by Costas Georgiou (Colonel Callan), also an ex-parachute regiment mercenary who was given control of the FNLA (National Front for the Liberation of Angola) forces. The paranoid and sociopathic Georgiou was later executed in Luanda for murdering 14 of his own men, and Banks slipped out of Africa leaving his best friend and bodyguard "Sutch" Fortuin to serve a 24-year prison sentence in Angola.

I was to be "Banks" for a week, supposedly in the U.K. to swap a batch of .50 caliber Barrett sniper rifles for a shipment of cocaine. The rifles were headed to Africa and the drugs were headed to Europe. For a week, officers of Customs and Excise followed me around and eventually made a cold contact to try and debrief me and get some intelligence on the deal. The exercises were highly regarded and very successful training for the would-be customs spooks.

On another memorable occasion a captain in the Defence Debriefing Team (DDT) whom I had met during training with 24 Company called me in for a chat. 24 Coy had a dedicated JSIO support role, and the DDT team was gathering HUMINT and other evidence that would hopefully bring Bosnian war criminals Milosevic, Mladic, Karadzic and others to justice. Reservists who took a special contract to work for the MoD mostly staffed DDT, and they had some very notable success in the role.

I was not that concerned if they put the war criminals in the ground or in prison after hearing some of the many horrific and inhuman stories coming out of Bosnia. A lot of the guys that I was working with had been recruited to work on the Bosnia situation, and one of the reasons why mostly TA personnel were used for DDT work was that they were not quite so military-minded. They still had a common human touch with civilians and could step back into the civilian role easily, something that was an advantage if you were trying to get useful information from a traumatized and distraught victim. That was the kind of work that the DDT team did: gathering intelligence and providing evidence against war criminals for trials in The Hague. It was a harrowing, disturbing and yet vital job.

I got to hear some of the worst stuff you can imagine. I don't think they could ever make a film about the horrors that went on there. It was reported that Serbian military commanders ordered repeated acts of inhuman and depraved savagery. Zeljko Raznatovic, also known as "Arkan" (later assassinated in Belgrade) was one such commander. His reputed assassin was in Cape Town awaiting extradition while I was there filming *Black Sails*. It was well known that Arkan had executed male and female victims at will in front of press cameramen. Arkan and his Tigers were responsible for some of the worst atrocities in Croatia, including in Vukovar.

Colonel Bob Stewart, who was the commander of the Cheshire Regiment serving with the UN peacekeeping force, was inspecting the conditions near the village of Ahmici, and was told by Muslim fighters about an ethnic cleansing massacre of women and children. There's footage of his patrol coming out of a house where the Croats had piled entire families into the cellar and burned them alive. Colonel Stewart was visibly angry, horrified and ashen. Dario Kordic, who was the Croatian political leader in Central Bosnia, was given a 25-year sentence for crimes against humanity for this slaughter. This kind of war required a different approach, and eventually the Blue UN Berets were removed and the NATO berets took over.

I learned of the Omarska concentration camp, where torture, murder and rape were carried out in utterly barbaric conditions. I learned of the use of rape as a tactic of war, and some of the bestial acts of torture and terror reportedly carried out by Serbian forces were so incredibly heinous that Psi-Ops personnel came to us and asked if we had any insight into some of the more inhuman and medieval acts carried out on female victims. There appeared to be no definable historical or religious precedent for these acts, which defied all humane laws, logic or military purpose, except for the spreading of total terror through sociopathic depravity.

I met with a still serving member of the group just before Christmas in 2013 for a drink and we discussed some of those atrocities. We still could not believe the horror and depravity of that conflict, right in the heart of Europe at the end of the twentieth century. Who could have imagined such madness would overtake a modern society?

My eldest son, the product of a brief relationship when I was 17 and of whom I'm extremely proud, was also serving in Bosnia at this point as a member of the Royal Regiment of Fusiliers (RRF) but under the command of the UN. The blue berets were unable to return fire in most situations but once NATO took over and the blue berets came off it was a very different story for 1RRF. He later completed several intelligence and surveillance courses before leaving the army in 1998. The apple never falls far from the tree it seems.

Towards the end of this period, a Captain serving with DDT came to me and asked me what I was planning to do next because he might have a job for me. He asked me what I knew about some British guys who had been captured and held hostage in Bosnia by the Serbs. All I knew at the time was what I had read in the papers. So he said, "Here's the brief.

In about an hour from now I want you to *be* one of the guys who were captured. There will be a visiting officer group who want to assess what happened. They're going to interview you about your whole experience. I want you to make up everything you think might have happened. Can you do it?"

I said I could and so we went off into a classroom about an hour later with maybe twelve senior officers. For the next hour or so I played the part of a soldier captured in Bosnia, answering their questions, having a cup of tea and chatting. At the end they said, "Thank you. You're a very brave man," and I left. The captain told me later that when he went back in and told the officers I had never been to Bosnia (officially) or done anything that I had said, and that it was a set-up, some of them were really pissed off. They had absolutely believed me. The Captain was really pleased because it showed the value of the training that we were doing: if I could fool them, they needed to hone their HUMINT debriefing skills.

All this time I maintained a special relationship with various groups, and often brought in exotic weapons for the troops to assess. Every weapon from FN-P90s to AK74s and MP5s were displayed so that the men could familiarize themselves with them. In return we shared experience and training with other groups, and handled demolition materials like Semtex and C4 plastic explosive so that we could identify them if we came across them.

This training really cemented that phase of my life. It led to working with other Special Forces groups—including the SBS (Special Boat Service). I was deployed to *HMS Fearless* to work with the SBS and 3 Commando Brigade, and after that I got the invitation to join 243 Section of 24 Company. This again was a great honor, and meant that my vetting would be upped to a PV-TS, or D.V. (Positively Vetted-Top Secret, now known as Developed Vetting).

From the start I think they saw that I could apply my acting skills to the work they wanted me to do. Though no one ever actually said it, it was inferred. My CO said something like, "You'll have no problem standing up, briefing people and being able to talk publicly to groups of people." I had not considered at the time that not everybody was able to do this, but it had always been easy for me. So as well as being able to teach other people how to create a legend or cover story, I could *become* other people as well. I suppose you could say the theatre is the best training for the work of a spook!

That's when it all started to happen in terms of being "other people." There was always a sort of parallel, and for a while the two sides of my life merged—because there really was this other person who they were meeting at the British Museum, or on an exercise where they had to locate and recruit me; I was also comfortable being somebody else for an extended time.

But underneath it all I was still Mark Ryan the actor.

HOLD FAST

7.

8.

9.

10.

11.

CAPTIONS

1. Roger Rees (John Adams) and myself (John Dickinson) forcefully debate the merits of The Declaration of Independence during the L.A. production of 1776 Sep 2001. Pic: Marcia Selegson, Reprise Productions

2. The original concept Chevy Bumblebee Camaro from the first Transformers movie (with Ironhide GMC TopKick bringing up the rear). Pic: Abbie Bernstein

3. Charlie's Angels with Roberta Brown and Andy Armstrong

4. A quick visit to Doncaster during Dean at The Casino Theater, London Pic: Doncaster Free Press

5. Playing Magaldi in Evita

6. Directing "Blood Type" at the Prebendal, Oxfordshire Pic: Anthony Straeger

7. Mads Mikkelsen and the custom Yang-Ling styled 'flame blade' specially built for Mads during King Arthur by skilled armorer, Tommy Dunne.

8. Two SBS LRICs (Long Range Insertion Craft) cruise behind HMS Fearless as members of C Squadron wet-jump into the very cold Atlantic during an exercise with 3 Commando Brigade, Royal Marines. Pi8. c: MR

9. Clive Mantle and I bookend the legendary Jimmy Doohan in Toronto. What a proper geezer! Beam me up Scotty!

10. The Honorary Knight of The Round Table during King Arthur with L-R: Sean Gilder, Pat Kinevane, Ray Winstone, Ioan Gruffudd, Joel Edgerton, Clive Owen, Mads Mikkelsen, Hugh Dancy, Ivano Marescotti and Ray Stevenson

11. At The London Wall shooting range during filming of Who Dares Wins with Lewis Collins, Ingrid Pitt and a trio of early H&K MP5A3s courtesy of Baptys & Co. Pic: The Daily Mail

4.
LIVING MAGICALLY

*"I believe that imagination is stronger than knowledge,
myth is more potent than history, dreams
are more powerful than facts,
hope always triumphs over experience,
laughter is the cure for grief,
love is stronger than death."*
~ Robert Fulghum: *All I Really Need To Know I Learned
in Kindergarten (1986)*

It's Magic

THERE ARE CERTAIN IDEAS and beliefs by which I have lived most of my life. I call these beliefs magic, and though some of you who read this might be skeptical, I'd like to say something about them here.

I believe magic can make an intangible idea, an elusive creative impulse, manifest in our reality, and I've found that living this way, trying to see how I, as a solitary individual, can interact with the rest of the universe, has made it possible for me to survive a range of odd, fantastic and ugly situations throughout my life. I've said it before but I'll restate it here: thought creates action. I believe that you have to step forward and initiate an action, and that when you do, the universe will respond. There's no point in just waiting for it to come to you. It might do so, but I believe

I'd rather initiate something specifically, ask questions, and challenge the universe to respond directly than wait for it to arrive by chance.

Attitude defines outcome.

How is this magic? Let me explain.

Real magic consists of taking an idea, a concept that comes out of the back of your head, and changing it into a material and living thing. To borrow an example from science—the Heisenberg Uncertainty Principle says that the way you view particles in matter changes them, making them no longer fixed and irrevocable. I try, on a daily basis, to practice changing the particles around me by pushing them the way I want them to go, rather than letting them channel me down a predicable path. I don't believe in fate, but I do accept the principles of the possible and the probable, the practical and the appropriate. I also put energy into the intuitive, the innovative and the honorable.

For me, every time something new comes to light in the scientific world, whether it's in subatomic physics, like the Higgs-Boson Particle, the observations of the Hubble space telescope or the theory of Morphic Resonance proposed by Rupert Sheldrake, it opens up a new area for spiritual discussion.

In April 2014, Massachusetts Institute of Technology (MIT) physicist Max Tegmark presented a paper dealing with the concept of a conscious state of matter and coined the phrase "perceptronium." He also referred to what is called the IIT (Integrated Information Theory), which postulates that parts of the human brain functions only as "feed forward" neural network processors, an idea that was also suggested by neuroscientist Christof Koch's research into the workings of the cerebellum. If this is correct, where does human consciousness actually reside? Within the brain matter, or connected on the subatomic particle level to an external framework of information and energy that our brains order and filter, which we then perceive to be our reality?

I believe that we can, consciously and subconsciously, communicate with the universe. We don't need a person or a belief structure to enable that communication, whether we see the organizing principle behind everything as an old guy in the sky with a beard, or a green goddess. We can do it for ourselves. Somehow we have an intrinsic and instinctive connection to reality on the same level as subatomic particles. We can affect our reality by the way we think, observe and interact. This belief comes from my early study of the ancient mystery religions and some of the curious and amazing experiences I have had since then.

Let me turn back the pages for a moment.

I WAS BORN ON THE FLOOR of a small terraced house on Beechfield Road, Doncaster, Yorkshire, which had no bathroom and an outside toilet. My mum's parents and my father's parents also lived on Beechfield Road. Other relatives lived there as well. We were a very close-knit family. My mum's side was Church of England and my father's Catholic - and thereby hangs another story, because as a result we grew up with a rather conflicted religious background, never knowing who was talking to whom on a regular basis. My father's large Catholic family were always falling out with each other as well as with my mother's side because of their beliefs.

Consequently, we ended up going to a Baptist Church as a compromise, which further confused the situation. But my father always told us that we could take whatever religious path we liked—nobody forced us into anything. I was therefore free to think about spiritual issues without any pressure to go one way or the other, which is probably why I have ended up with my own way of seeing things.

My uncle Eric, my mum's brother, lived at home with his mother, my Grandma, until she died. Then he lived alone for quite some time. During World War II, he was one of many thousands of British troops dropped into Burma and subsequently captured by the Japanese forces. He had a horrendous time, finally coming back from the war a shadow of his former self, having contracted TB and lost most of one lung. I remember him as a very gentle, intelligent and well educated man, and probably the smartest in the family.

Eric, talented and successful, had been a pupil at the very formal, scholastically respected Doncaster Grammar School. He worked for Doncaster County Council after the war and was my favorite uncle, and I was his favorite nephew. When I was very young I could not say the word uncle and I called him "Panky," some kind of strange mixture of the words "uncle" and "Eric!" For some reason, I became known as "Little Panky," while he was "Big Panky." He bought me Matchbox cars (some of which I still have) and took me for walks around the town and into his offices when mum was ill or busy running the household.

In the mid-1970s, Eric contracted cancer in his one remaining lung. He ended up coming to live with us for a while so my mum could look after him while he was going through this sad and painful decline.

While my mum was nursing him, I was in London doing my stint in *Evita* as Magaldi, but ultimately I came home and sat with him for several nights before he died. On one occasion, he hemorrhaged through his mouth and nose, which caused huge distress throughout the house. I cleaned him up and sat with him through the night, talking about his life. He always said he did not want to be a burden to my mum. At the same time, my father was also very ill with lung cancer, so my mum had both her brother and her husband terminally ill in the house. It was a truly brutal period.

After Eric died, my mother gave me his signet ring, which she and her sister Joan had bought for him on his 21st birthday. I began wearing it, and I still have it today.

After *Evita*, I went to the Brecon Beacon mountain range whenever I could, to train and keep in shape. At the time, this was one of the places where a lot of military training was done. For me, it was not only a physical training ground but also a spiritual retreat. I would go off for three or four days at a time, basically to clear my head and get back in tune with nature.

When the big hurricane hit the U.K. in 1987, I was actually in Torpantau Wood, bashered-up (a military term for being in a make-shift shelter made from a poncho, also called a basher) in a grove of trees. Later that night I got up, feeling very restless, although I couldn't say exactly why. I hiked out in the dark, got into my car and moved to a different spot. I was out in the hurricane overnight, and it was pretty wild too. When I went back to the spot where I had originally been trying to sleep, there were several trees lying across the area where I'd camped. If I'd stayed there, I would probably have been injured, maybe even killed.

I believe nature has a way of telling you when something is wrong. I've always had the belief that trees, woods and forests are my friends, and always feel very comfortable in and around them. Later this would lead to creating *The Greenwood Tarot* and, in a revised form, *The Wildwood Tarot*, both based on a primitive shamanic culture that was at one time native to Britain.

At the time, I was exploring the area of the Horseshoe and Pen-y-Fan and sleeping in the woods for a couple of days, even though the weather was awful. One day, while I was packing up and loading my stuff back into the boot of the car, I noticed that Uncle Eric's ring was missing from my finger. I pulled out my Bergan rucksack and sleeping bag and went through everything in the car, but it wasn't there. So I just stood and thought, *Oh shit, the ring is out there somewhere.* I remember looking back along the Roman Road leading to Pen-y-Fan, thinking, *I can't go back to my mum and tell her I've lost Eric's ring.* So I decided I would go and look for it. I didn't really believe I had any chance of finding it, but I just had to try.

Because of the time of day—it was around noon—I didn't have time to walk all the way back, so I drove as close as I could to the places where I had stayed the night before and retraced my tracks. It was a completely hopeless task, and most of the time I just looked out at the wilderness, knowing the ring could be anywhere.

Eventually I got back to the first couple of places I'd stayed, one of which was by a little waterfall. I found nothing on the muddy track, so I went to the next place—and again found nothing. By that time the weather was closing in again and I was ready to give in.

The final place was where I had spent the previous night, and I parked as near as I could and set off on foot for the spot, a small copse of trees by a little river on the side of a valley. I found where I thought I had camped the night before, and as I walked into the dark and shadowy area, I found myself looking at a carpet of golden-brown pine needles under the trees. I looked at this sea of bronze in the fading light and thought I was never going to find the ring, but as I was there, I decided I might as well look around.

I couldn't see anything, so I went to one of the trees I had been sleeping under the night before and put my forehead against the trunk and said, "Listen, I know this is not very important to you, but it's really important to me, and if you could help me with this, I would be very grateful. I've lost my uncle Eric's ring somewhere out here, maybe even in this wood.

I'd be very grateful if you could return it to me, please..."

I literally prayed to the trees. Then I turned my back and looked across the gloomy, darkening wood, and almost in despair, slid down the trunk to sit at the base. I felt in my heart of hearts that this was an impossible quest, and that I had gone as far as I could. It was time to let it go. But as I put my right Danner boot down into the thick carpet of gold-brown kernels, I heard a *clink* and looked down.

There, at the heel of my right boot, was Eric's ring.

I picked it up, stammered out my thanks to whoever or whatever was listening and put it back on my finger.

The philosophical and spiritual lesson I learnt from this is that, however hopeless, dark or even foolish the situation might seem, you can't give up. If I hadn't walked down that path, if I hadn't gone to the end of the journey, if I hadn't sat down by that tree and asked the question, I would not have found the ring. My guiding light has always been that however impossible or foolish the quest, if you ask the universe, if you take the step, if you initiate walking down the path, you will get an answer. Sometimes it's not the answer you expect, and sometimes you may not find what you're looking for, but sometimes the impossible solution arrives.

You could say finding the ring was just good luck or coincidence, a random, billion to one happenstance. But I believe on that occasion the universe provided the miracle for me, and it affected my whole philosophy thereafter. I still look at the challenge or the quest and set off down the road with conviction and hope.

Psychic Questing and Other Adventures

I still have my army dog tags. They have "Atheist" on them because I was advised not to have "Pagan." If I had been caught in a strange place, it would have been quite disastrous if my captors thought I was some kind of daemon-worshipping, blood-drinking heathen. I did try to explain quantum physics, human psychology and the concept of talking to mountain streams or the ocean to the Intelligence Corp unit clerk that dealt with these things, but soldiers don't tend to have those conversations with squaddies, even Int. Corps squaddies, so I let them put "Atheist" on the tags. The rationale is that an atheist, while not much better than a pagan in the eyes of much of the world, might still have a revelation while someone was pulling off his toenails or jumping up and down on his kneecaps—and that just might buy some time!

In actual fact, I would describe myself, philosophically and spiritually, as an eclectic pagan. This form of belief has helped me come to terms with a lot of the mistakes and losses that I've had, especially the defeats in life. There have been moments when I have sat somewhere thinking, *It's over, this is it, I've come to the end, I can't do any more, I've fucked this up so badly it is never going to be okay and maybe it's better if I find something else to do with my life.* But every time this happens, I get a response, something that could be summed up as, *You have to go to the end of that path – you have got to go and sit under the tree and ask the universe to give you back what it was you lost.* Whenever I have been in a dark place, those lessons have helped me survive.

I've grown to be philosophical about this life process and have accepted that, for me at least, I always have to go that little bit further down the road or take the extra effort to see the best results. I see it as the universe challenging me to take the journey for the journey's sake and to be aware and absorb the experiences and interactions along the way, to take the path less travelled and stop to enjoy the view. So many nuggets of wisdom and moments of joy have been presented to me through this process that it's become second nature and a part of my daily routine. Because of this, I endeavor to live by a simple axiom: be comfortable not knowing.

I've dealt with many dark things in my life, and some of them still keep me awake at night. But because I don't believe in the concepts of heaven and hell, and because I don't believe in fate, whenever I've had to deal with real evil, violence or depravity, I don't blame God. I look at people and think: this person got like this somehow; what was it in their life or psyche that caused this? It's not a question of judging them morally, because I don't believe the universe judges people morally in human terms at all.

I also don't believe the universe understands the concept of money or wealth or credit cards. I would suggest it understands abundance, generosity, and fecundity. Just as it reacts to creative/positive energy, it appears to respond to negative/destructive drives in its own primal fashion. To borrow from the writer Norman Mailer, "Either God is all powerful and not all good, or all good and not all powerful." I have enough proof of that for my own peace of mind.

Over the years, I've done quite a bit of personal research into various esoteric and mythic practices. I've experienced enough unexplained happenings to convince me that human consciousness can interact with and affect what is often called the "Otherworld." Exploring the esoteric world and its ideas and finding comfort in the mysteries of creation have been both healing and empowering for me, and much that has happened to me is best explained in these terms.

One example of this process was my involvement with writer and mythical researcher Andrew Collins and his psychic questing group. Andy and his associates would set out in search of strange and curious objects hidden somewhere in the land, using their innate psychic abilities to direct them to the right place. I was never a part of the actual group, but occasionally went along as an outside observer, offering detached and objective opinions. It was difficult not to get involved with the personal trials and tribulations of the various psychics but for the most part, I just listened and watched.

During my adventures with the group, several odd and yet important gifts were literally thrown at me to remind me how strange the universe is. Some of these experiences are documented in Andy's book *The Seventh Sword*, but some events occurred that I didn't tell Andy about. I wanted a kind of control line to see whether anything that happened during my interaction with the group was mirrored within their own investigations. Andy did the same to make sure that imaginations did not run amok or be influenced by subconscious suggestion.

In *The Pilgrim*, a graphic novel I began writing in the 1990s, I talked a lot about Col. Kim Seymour, who is one of the main pivotal characters in the story. Seymour was a real person, a veteran intelligence officer and one of the unsung heroes of the magical warfare stratagems used against the Nazis during WWII. Seymour was also deeply involved in ritual esoteric work. The first time I heard his name was from one of Andy's psychic friends, who told me I should look into Seymour's story.

I knew there had been a secret history of psychic battles going on during the Second World War, with magicians working for the Allies fighting those working for Hitler, but somewhere in the conversation a particularly magical place was mentioned that I had not heard of before. Apparently there was a rare white-leafed oak there, and a well dedicated to the old British goddess Ellen of the Ways. There was something about the description of the place that struck a chord in me. I couldn't say why, but it seemed important that I go there and take a look.

White Leaf Oak was apparently a nexus point for various ley lines and Earth energy vortices. These are believed to run through the Earth itself and to influence the energy of certain spots. The secret location to which I was headed included a water source that bubbled from the ground, held by a stone well with an ornate steel covering. I had only a very sketchy description of the actual location and wasn't even sure where it was, only that it was somewhere in or near the Chiltern Hills.

One sunny Sunday morning, I suddenly got the urge to seek this spot out and drove to a village that had a similar-sounding name. After driving for a couple of hours, I arrived there and looked around. The place looked exactly as it had been described to me, with a gentle hill rising up behind a graveyard to where stands of trees clung to the earth. I decided to explore.

A small pathway led away from the graveyard and further up the side of the hill, skirting the forest. A quarter of a mile or so up the path, the fence bordering the path was broken where it had obviously been climbed over. On the other side, a small track led deeper into the forest. I climbed over the fence and followed it into the trees.

Then, off to my left, I spotted what appeared to be a low stone structure nestling in the heart of a clearing. As I got closer, I saw an ornate well covering with hinges. I lifted it to find a clear well of bubbling stream water, percolating from the ground and covered by a steel grille above the floor of the well.

I sat quietly on a small rise of earth to one side, taking in the beautiful setting and watching the spring water trickle through a small runnel and back into the soil. I found myself wondering what the point of all this was, and what my connection with the well—if any—might be.

Once again, I trusted the universe and asked the well, rather impatiently, what the point of all this was and what lesson, if any, was to be learned from this pleasant sojourn in the country. I sat there in the dappled sunlight for a while and decided to push the question a bit harder. *Okay!* I thought. *If there's any point to this whole thing, give me a sign. Show me there's something practically useful to be learned from this.*

I aimed the thought directly at the well, and in response heard a fairly loud *plop* somewhere to my right. I immediately turned my head to see what it was, and my eye was drawn to sunlight glinting on something that was rolling down the bank toward me. As I sat there, watching what appeared to be a glass sphere tumbling down a small gully in the soil toward my boot, I looked up to see the source from which the sphere could have dropped. I saw nothing! No cheeky magpie circling overhead or sitting on a branch, not even the remains of a nest. As I looked back down to the ground, a small quartz sphere came to rest by my boot. What appeared to be a small, clear marble of the kind used by children for decades—a chipped but perfectly circular piece of glass or quartz—had literally dropped out of the sky, in the middle of a wood, landed near me and rolled to my foot.

I looked up again into the trees to see if there was anything that could have dropped it, but I couldn't see a squirrel or a bird or any movement of any kind. I was totally alone in the forest and nothing stirred above or even near me.

I couldn't explain it then, and I can't now, but sometimes, when I don't have the answer to a question, I hold that marble, which I keep by my bedside, and think, *Maybe you don't always need to understand everything straight away. Maybe you just need to keep looking, until at some point in the proceedings you find its true meaning.*

Universal Questions

The nineteenth century American philosopher Henry David Thoreau wrote something that sums up the way I understand the universe in his book *Walden: Or, Life in the Woods:*

> *... if one advances confidently in the direction of his dreams, and endeavours to live the life which he has imagined, he will meet with a success unexpected in common hours.*

That's the way the universe works, as I understand it. You don't always see everything right away, or understand all the answers you get, but you do get answers. Sometimes there's a lesson to be learned from just taking the knowledge you've been given and hanging on to it, waiting for it to find its own place in its own time. It's like the lesson I learned years before in my military training—how to see the whole picture by standing back from it until the patterns make sense.

The belief I have in the responsiveness of the universe has grown out of experiences like this. There are bits of quantum physics, Jungian psychology and a bit of Rupert Sheldrake's idea of morphic resonance mixed in with it. From these, I have come to believe that some part of the universe is conscious, aware and responsive. It doesn't necessarily understand human concepts, the material needs and requirements we deal with in our daily reality, but it does understand simple, profound and primal emotions and drives.

By asking questions, you are creating a void that nature does not like and which will get filled—which is why you've got to be careful what you wish for, because you *will* get a response. However we choose to dress this up, in cultural or religious terms, this energy, this force, this consciousness permeates everything. Jesus, the Buddha, the Goddess are all manifestations of the same energy, the same force, the same consciousness. I believe we access it through whatever is most philosophically, culturally or spiritually accessible for us. Another way to put it would be to say that we are opening our own channel to the divine.

I found my own channel by chance. It's not a particularly religious system, but I know that if I approach nature, whether in the form of a waterfall, a river, the sea, a mountain or a forest, and if I talk to whatever you perceive deity to be through those, you get a response. I believe my conduit to this field is through nature.

This doesn't mean I don't believe in a sentient and responsive universal consciousness or that karmic forces don't exist, but rather that these things function along the lines of a morphic field. This field has no human concept of good or evil, rich or poor, but is pure energy and is accessible to all of us to draw upon empathically.

My belief is that, as human beings, we're responsible for the actions we take, and we are not fated to do one thing or another. We all make choices and sometimes they're wrong, sometimes bad or foolish, but I don't believe there is any "devil" whispering in our ears telling us to do something evil. What I try to do when I have to deal with the dark side of life—and believe me, some of the cases I have worked on in the past ten years as a PI have been pretty dark—is to come at it from this simple point of view: there's enough evil in the world produced by the human mind and soul; we don't need to invent the Devil to have bad things happen.

This takes a lot of the fear out of dangerous situations. I don't mean that to sound like I don't worry, or feel fear, but I do believe, as Ian Fleming put it in *On Her Majesty's Secret Service*, "Worry is a premium paid to disaster before it is due."

Thinking that the person you are facing or hunting is not mad, bad or dangerous, but that he, or she, is just another flawed and malfunctioning human being and the product of some pitiful and destructive human fear and weakness puts things into perspective.

As I mentioned previously, between 1992 and 1997 I worked with the Defence Debriefing Team, which dealt with Bosnian war crimes investigations. Some of the atrocities I heard about were so medieval and horrific that you had to think, human beings did this, but it's so far from normal, so horrific and violent, that it really isn't human at all.

You ask yourself what part of human nature could allow someone to do these things? Sometimes you might think they must have been driven by something else—something inhuman, even alien—a part of human nature that is so detached from the loving, caring, supportive aspect of life that it becomes totally savage.

But if you can understand what motivates a human being to do cruel and bestial things, you take out the supernatural element and the concept that there is something big, bad or evil out there. Once you understand that, it becomes a more human-sized question. It's not about God or the Devil. It's just the sick aspects of human nature, and how I deal with that is in accordance with my own conscience and moral compass.

There's an idea I've come across a few times in certain types of esoteric philosophy, which talks about different rays of energy—a Green Ray, a Red Ray and a Blue Ray. These can be seen as influences, old streams of consciousness from a very distant time that continue to resonate in our minds to this day. My take on this is that the Green Ray represents ordinary human nature, and the Red Ray an alternative reality that is alien to us and outside ordinary human experience. Maybe even an alien intelligence. The Blue Ray is something else entirely and I'm not sure I understand it!

My friend Chesca Potter, co-originator of *The Greenwood Tarot*, believed that the Red Ray originated from an ancient race of alien or dinosaur/reptilian origin that could have emanated from ancient Mars, long before recorded human history began. Chesca described how a race that settled on Earth from a failing Mars became the origin of the Atlantis mythos, and that their science was esoterically based. She believed this was at the core of the occultist Dion Fortune's magical work, as expressed in writings such as *The Sea Priestess,* a fantastic magical novel full of strange and wonderful ideas.

I tried to explore something similar in the graphic novel, *The Pilgrim*, where I talked about the ancient primal figure of the Green Man representing the conscious human element in nature, and about there being something else out there that is pre-human, or of very ancient origin—a pre-human consciousness that appears to us as profoundly evil—a word we use because we don't know what else to call it. In fact, evil seems to me to be something non-human that has an entirely different set of values than we do. I have sometimes thought of this when I have had to deal with the horrors that human beings do to each other. On the one hand, there's the Green Ray: the human, accessible part of us. On the other hand, there's the Red Ray: the angry, violent, horror-filled, insane actions of people, which are somehow not human at all, but appear to emanate from a very savage and entirely inhuman and alien source.

Chesca is a natural psychic and an intelligent and caring woman. Perhaps her extreme sensitivity was the reason why she later withdrew totally from the world and disappeared from public life. What happened to her remains a mystery, and I've never had contact with anyone who knows where she went and what she is doing with her life. A close mutual friend told me that she destroyed or sold her pagan artwork and became a Born Again Christian.

I have made several personal efforts to locate and contact Chesca over the years (as have others), and she doesn't want to be found. I sincerely hope that wherever she is, she's safe, happy and secure in her new life. She is an incredibly talented and magical spirit and her insights and intense personal connections to the esoteric are profound and primal. Chesca's contribution to *The Greenwood Tarot* alone was highly significant to me and to my thinking, and I'll always be grateful to her for that.

Some might describe such interests as a form of intellectual displacement activity and a denial of reality, but I don't see it that way. There is no doubt that some esoteric practices can lead to various forms of self-medication. However, as I have never used drugs and have a moderate attitude to drinking, my friends working in the recovery field have proclaimed me a "normie." My place of healing, physically, emotionally and spiritually, will always be in nature. I can talk to the universal consciousness through a mountain, waterfall, a forest or a desert hot spring to receive divine healing. No priest, or other human conduit, is required.

While I respect and defend anyone's religious and spiritual beliefs and their right to express and practice them, it's always been a mystery to me why three of the five major religions of the world, whose God is (for all intents and purposes) the same, and whose spiritual creed and teachings comes from a common ancient root but with three different cultural prophets, have fought and killed each other throughout history under the misguided delusion that theirs is the only way. This did not make any sense to me as a child, and it still doesn't today. Surely if God exists at all, he/she is not this duplicitous or perfidious.

I've often said to people that if the Christian concept of God is to be believed, he gave us a mind to ask questions and the ability to make things happen, and that's what I always try to do. I just hope and believe that I make the right decisions, consistent with what would be ethically and morally right to do. I try to live by the J.C. Watts maxim: "Character is doing the right thing when nobody's looking. There are too many people who think that the only thing that's right is to get by, and the only thing that's wrong is to get caught."

If I ever get to those pearly gates, and some God or representative of a God is there, and he or she says, "You made really bad mistakes and did it all wrong," my response will be, "Why did you give me free will and the ability to do what I've done? I stand by the things I've done because I see it all as a path for me to create. If I was wrong, I'll take the consequences. Besides, all my pals will be "down there," so let's get this show on the road!"

This can help when you get things wrong, as I often do.

I've made many mistakes during my life. I've failed in areas that are critical in terms of relationships—with my children, with partners and with my family. I've paid for these errors. But I have this belief system that tells me if I can fix it, it will be fixed. It may take a while, sometimes years, but if I'm philosophical about it, if I keep moving forward—above all, if I keep on learning—at some point the universe will allow me the opportunity to tell my own story.

Part of the acceptance of my own human failings has helped me express this to other people and to bring them into that place and say, "Let's get the answer—let's find it even if it's a resolution that's unfavorable—let's go there."

I've been through situations when a mistake could have cost me my life, or the lives of others. You could say I feel protected; but not by gods or angels or anything like that. I try to mix having the right amount of native cunning and skill with the right amount of firepower.

Of course, it's also to do with physical presence, confidence and an understanding of human nature, as well as asking the universe to meet you halfway. I don't trust random factors completely. Having access to the means of defending yourself, such as a Walther PPK/S in your hotel room or an H&K .9mm locked in the trunk of your car, is also very important in certain situations.

So far, the "belt and braces" approach has worked. It allows me to function in a way that can do good. I may be a man of many parts—and sometimes all the parts don't function together seamlessly—but when they do, I know I can make a difference.

That's the other side of all of this: finding the balance between the discipline and spirituality of the sword, the concepts of being a protective force and a spiritual warrior, and bringing these ideas into your psyche as a practical and defensive tool.

5.
BLURRING THE EDGES

*"A small gun you hide is better than
a big one that gets taken away from you."*
~ Mike Grell

Wanderings in the Showbiz Otherworld

T**HERE'S A PART OF ME THAT REVELS** in show business and loves the entertainment and the creative side of things, and another part that wants to do something positive, healing and practical in the world that transcends these lighter endeavors.

I have lived a lot within the darker side of reality, but I seem to be able to walk through it and function there, and feel protected by whatever is out there looking after me. That is a gift; I accept it as a gift, and I accept the responsibility of what it means when it's applied practically in everyday life.

How do you make that function in such opposing worlds as showbiz and spookery? The two collide more often that you might imagine, and a positive attitude is definitely required to survive in both for any length of time. For me, it's all about blurring the edges.

When I was touring with *Don Giovanni* and *Figaro* in 1993, first in Germany and then in the U.K., something happened that brought the two halves of my life together in no uncertain way. The timing was difficult for me, as I was in the middle of the court case to win visitation rights to my children, but the job did mean I would be working in the U.K. and that the visitation rights could start right away.

I headed off for Germany with a whole new musical challenge. But it meant I was away for Christmas. I remember going into the great cathedral in Hamburg and sitting there alone while they were singing Christmas carols. I cried for what seemed like forever and wailed like a wounded animal, so loud that several people came over and patted me on the back or just sat with me for a while. It was a deeply cathartic moment and an outpouring of a massive sense of loss and inner turmoil. Somehow it was cleansing and healing and I managed to walk from the cathedral with a new resolve.

I had managed to buy and mail traditional German Christmas presents for both Daniel and Katherine in Hamburg and wondered if they would ever receive them, or if they would be left on the doorstep gathering snow, which had been the fate of other Christmas and birthday presents I had sent to them. Even so, I had mailed the presents with love from Germany and my heart broke at the thought of them never reaching my children, or my children not knowing that they were at least in my thoughts and prayers.

Back in England we ended up at the Nottingham Playhouse with Figaro and the Don. One day, before a performance, I had done a radio show interview with Gerard Casey to promote the shows, and we talked about what he called my "strange career." I remember he said that one of his favorite films was *Who Dares Wins*, and that we talked about some of the guys in the film being from "The Regiment"—i.e. the SAS. Afterwards, I thought nothing more about it, but it may well have had a bearing on what happened next.

We got to the theatre that night as usual. My mother and sister had driven down to see the show. We had just started the second half when the theatre manager walked into the middle of the stage, stopped the show and announced to the audience that we had to evacuate the theatre because a coded warning had been received—a bomb threat believed to be from the IRA.

Everybody got up and stated shuffling out of the theatre in a reasonably calm fashion. Then, two plainclothes guys appeared and started sniffing around. They came over to me and wanted to know if I thought the coded threat was real and what should be done. They clearly knew about my "other" life, and that I was likely to know what was going on. I said we should search the theatre and see if we could find anything. If anything was discovered, we should stay out, but if not, carry on with the show!

Then I ran around to the front of the theatre and found my mum and sister and told them to wait. I was damned if I was going to let a little thing like a bomb threat keep me from letting my mum see the rest of the bloody opera! Then, I went back to the stage door, brushing aside the stage-manager, who didn't want anyone going back in and was trying to evacuate the place, and went in search of the police.

I had my ID card with me (a real "get out of jail free" card) that allowed me to identify myself while on military duties. I approached one of the officers and insisted we search the theatre together. I think the plainclothes guys were still around, but basically this one policeman and I started searching everywhere—under the seats and in the toilets. We couldn't find anything that looked like it had been planted or left behind as a duffle-bag type bomb.

Eventually it was decided that the place was clear, everyone filed back into the auditorium and we finished off the second half of *Figaro*! The next day, I had to report the incident to the security officers in Nottingham. I drove down there and the guy I spoke to didn't seem that interested in what had happened. In fact, he seemed to think I was wasting his time and was very dismissive of the whole thing.

However, when I got back to London after finishing the tour I was summoned by my commanding officer, my section officer and my company commanding officer, and they all asked me to tell them what had happened. I told them my story and they said that the security guy in Nottingham had complained about me because I had identified myself to the police at the theatre, and because it turned out to be a hoax. Apparently I was going to be reprimanded over the incident, but I found out later on that my then-commanding officer (God love her) said that she thought I should be commended, not reprimanded, for volunteering to go into a possibly deadly situation without a moment's thought for my own safety. I had to admit to her later that I was so focused on getting back on stage that I didn't even think of any danger!

When it was all over, I was told that I would be neither reprimanded nor commended, but that I should keep a lower profile in future and try not to get blown up!

Aftershocks

On another occasion, I was invited to do a charity event with the Hammer Horror actress Ingrid Pitt and a bunch of guys from the Paras who were raising money for charity. One of these guys came over to me and said, "Come on, we're having a one-arm press-up competition for charity." There was one big, fit guy who had already done 20 or 25 of these one-arm press-ups and Ingrid told me I should have a go.

When I was really fit, we used to include press-ups in the training, and I could do a lot. Anyway, I managed 51, which blew the Para guys away—because at that time I had a beard and long hair and looked like a hippie! Ingrid was amazed and I think it was then she realized I was involved in something more than just the theatre.

Later, Ingrid and her husband Tony Rudlin introduced me to a guy called Nick Parish, who was quite a character. We got on well, and he told me he was ex-Intelligence Corps and had been seconded into doing civilian-type work. He owned just about every weapon you could imagine, locked behind a padded door that looked like a bathroom but had an armored steel door—a huge walk-in safe full of firearms, rocket launchers, assault rifles and stun grenades.

He once tried to test my nerve by showing me a flash-bang (stun grenade) and pretended to fumble and drop it. The arming lever flew off and he dived under the sofa screaming, "get down!" The grenade rolled ominously across the floor towards me but appeared not to be fizzing or smoking so I thought it was a dud! I waited a few seconds but it didn't go off and I looked at Nick under the sofa with a confused smirk. It turned out the grenade was an inert practice one he had acquired and he was simply trying to see how cool I would be under fire! The black sense of military humor prevailed and I jokingly said, "A booby trap is a savage practical joke..."

Nick later ran into some trouble during a TV investigation devised as an expose on the arms business. At the time he was supplying weapons to the QE2 and various other passenger liners to counter pirates and hijackers. Even in those days, piracy was big business, and there were armed security personnel on board most of the big cruise ships. Nick was supplying and delivering these weapons and ammo and got caught up in the investigation sting.

When I first knew Nick, he was a likable and happy-go-lucky kind of guy, but then things changed. He did some bodyguard work and spent some time in Beirut guarding a Christian military leader called Dany Chamoun, who had been Secretary of Defence for the National Liberal Party and also Supreme Commander of the NLP's military wing, the Tigers. When rival Phalangist forces massacred the Tigers, Chamoun escaped to West Beirut and went into self-imposed exile. Nick was looking after Dany's family, including his wife and three children, and had been living in the house with them. It was a very tense time, but Nick genuinely liked Dany and spoke warmly and happily about his life in Lebanon.

Sometime after the invasion of Beirut by Syrian forces, Nick came back to Britain to do a weapons delivery to one of the cruise ships, but on the twenty-first of October, 1990, Dany, his wife Ingrid and his two sons were assassinated in their home, and only his young daughter (who was wounded) miraculously survived the cold-blooded executioners.

I went to see Nick when I heard what had happened. He was devastated. He blamed himself for not being there and thought they would not have attacked the house if a bodyguard who was also a British citizen had been present. He poured over the pictures of the bloody scene and could barely speak. The pictures were indeed horrific and, from that point, he was a broken man.

In reality, there was nothing he could have done and, had he been there, he would probably have died alongside his friend and his family. But it was the death of Chamoun's sons that haunted Nick the most. Even hardened operators weep at the senseless slaughter of innocents.

My other life was to come to the fore again in late 1993, when I worked on a film called *The Doomsday Gun* for my old *Robin of Sherwood* pal and director Robert Young. The film was about an infamous case involving the murder of Canadian artillery expert Gerald Bull, who had been building a super-weapon for Saddam Hussein under the codename "Project Babylon." Bull had been involved in the secret testing of a variety of exotic weapons, including HARP (High Altitude Research Program), through his own company, SRC (Space Research Corporation). Bull was helping to develop the concept of launching satellites into low orbit from a so-called 'supergun'. The launch platform was a kind of crude rail-gun, using delayed and progressive charges within the barrel to build the gas pressure to extraordinary levels, which forces a SABOT-type projectile from the muzzle at hyper velocity. Bull was also reputedly involved with upgrading and modernizing Saddam's SCUD missile program, which threatened both Israel and Iran.

The film stared Kevin Spacey and Alan Arkin, with Frank Langella playing Gerald Bull. Robert explained he wanted me to do a cameo as the assassin who appears at the end of the film. I was very happy to help him out for old times' sake.

On arrival at the location, I was taken to the film's armorer, who was also in charge of firearm safety on the set. The nice young chap from Bapty Film Armorers (a place I have visited many times in my career) didn't know me and asked if I had ever handled a silenced Walther PPK before. I nodded and the nice young chap looked at me disbelievingly, having obviously had few actors respond this way previously.

He showed me the weapon, told me that it was safe and unloaded, and said, "Take it apart then!" I closed my eyes and had the little gun in pieces and reassembled again in about 10 seconds, including re-racking the slide and dropping the hammer with the safety lever. I opened my eyes and the nice young chap was red in the face. He looked at me and mumbled, "Okay then."

When Frank Langella arrived on set, we had a discussion about gun safety and silenced weapons and how they function. The armorer explained that no projectile or even flash would escape from the gun because the barrel was blocked with a hollow grub screw to keep the gas pressure up and recycle the weapon using a lower charge. Frank looked highly skeptical and wanted to hear the Walther actually fired. The armorer fired a blank round in the confined space of the hallway and it sounded like a cannon going off! This was partly due to the baffles in the silencer being worn out with regular use as a prop, combined with the blast echoing off the walls of the apartment hallway.

Frank was visibly uncomfortable and said he was nervous about another actor pointing a loaded firearm at him. I wondered what had caused this reaction, but he later explained that the famous martial arts actor Brandon Lee had been accidentally shot and killed recently while working on *The Crow*. Frank wanted us to find a way to film the scene without me actually pointing the weapon at him. The Bapty armorer patiently explained he thought I was probably more competent than most actors with a Walther and that Mr. Langella would be quite safe, but Frank still wasn't happy.

When it was all said and done, Robert managed to stage the whole assassination scene so that Frank did not feel threatened. I was simply credited as "SAS Man" in the movie, because one of the theories about the killing of Bull explored in the film was that British security forces, at the behest of Mossad, the Israeli intelligence agency, had eliminated him.

Bull's "supergun" was intended to fire a half-ton chemical or nuclear projectile into the heart of Tel Aviv, so they were understandably concerned. However, according to this theory Bull was a Canadian, and therefore a British problem. This meant that we had to take him out to stop the whole unholy endeavor from ever coming to reality.

Some years later, I spoke to Frank Langella at a BAFTA screening of the film *Frost/Nixon* in Los Angeles, and he remembered the incident very clearly. He again reasserted his genuine fear of firearms and said it wasn't anything personal about my acting ability that made him nervous. I just looked too menacing pointing a loaded and silenced weapon at him!

Extended Weaponry

During the early Nineties, I maintained regular visits to the Enfield Small Arms Depot, sometimes to borrow weapons for exercises with the group, and on other occasions just to keep up to date with new equipment.

My relationship with the place, which was both a museum and a repository, had begun in the early eighties, originally facilitated by a pal in the Diplomatic Protection Group, who wangled a visit to the Pattern Room, where they kept examples of every known weapon. At the time, only government people got into that place; it was a highly restricted area. Among the many exotic weapons I got to play with were the VZ-63 "RAK" machine pistol recovered during the Iranian Embassy siege, and various models of the then-rare AK-74 recovered from Afghanistan during the conflict with the Soviet Union. Also stored there were numerous specialty weapons designed for the SOE (Special Operations Executive), Winston Churchill's clandestine warfare organization ordered to "set Europe ablaze" during WWII. This equipment ranged from wrist-triggered, single-shot watchstrap guns to firearms disguised as tobacco pipes and fountain pens.

That was also where I first heard about the legendary "Castle" in Scotland, which was the origin of the famous TV show *The Prisoner* starring Patrick McGoohan. This was essentially the same story as *The Cooler*, a novel written by George Markstein, which I later discussed with him over lunch at the Gay Hussar restaurant in Soho during the shooting of *Who Dares Wins*. (George wrote the original synopsis for the film, which was later turned into the novel *The Tiptoe Boys* by James Follett.)

George explained the history of *The Prisoner* and his involvement in the show's creation, but he was reluctant even then to name the actual location of "The Cooler." I later found out it was the legendary SOE/MI6 training and detention camp at Inverlair Lodge, Inverness, known simply as "The Castle." It was the home of many secret and dangerous operations (and people) during WWII.

On one of my visits to the Pattern Room, I saw a beautiful Mauser C96 "Boomhandle" pistol, stripped down on a table, grip-stocks removed and firing mechanism lock-work gleaming and smooth. I asked why were they working on it and who had been its owner.

Herb told me that it was the "Mad Major's" gun, which I found fascinating. The Mad Major was an SOE operator, an assassin, who enjoyed his work just a little too much. He lived in the Castle after the war and had only recently died. His family gave the Pattern Room his weapons. I was very interested in the Mauser because I could see that it had been customized to slow down the cyclical rates, and showed various hand-tooled marks that resembled notches on the stocks—all this intended to make the action more smooth and reliable.

Some of these SOE/Baker Team operators were tasked by Churchill to hunt down Nazis that the British knew they were never going to be able to arrest and put on trial. They were told to either bring them back or execute them *in situ* after reading the *Nacht und Nebal* decree to them. This was Hitler's 1941 "Decree of Night and Fog," which gave license to interrogate, torture and try in secret Allied operators caught in occupied territory, thereby avoiding conventional military procedures for POWs or the conventions of war.

These "Baker Teams" hunted the Nazis down, and this is where the original Licensed to Kill/Double 0 concept came in, later made famous by

Ian Fleming in his James Bond novels. Fleming actually spoke with Peter Mason about his wartime work and learned that his favorite weapon was the Walther PPK, which of course became Bond's. Famed real-life firearms expert Geoffrey Boothroyd, who later appeared as "Major Boothroyd" in Fleming's novel, *Dr. No*, also blessed this choice of weapon.

Mason wrote his own book called *Official Assassin*, which was suppressed. The British authorities also took away his pension for saying too much. Strangely, as I recently discovered while shooting the trailer for a TV series on occultists, it was John Dee, the Renaissance magician, who first had the code-name 007!

For the most part the Baker Team operatives used German wartime weapons (except for the British made Welrod silenced pistol that was left unmarked) so that they could not be traced back to a British source. There were stacks of boxes of old weapons that remained unused, which I saw for myself in the Pattern Room. Mason and his guys would choose one and use it. They would then bring it back and it would go into a furnace, so that there was no actual weapon left to trace from any rounds that might be recovered from a body.

On another visit, I spotted a modified Browning GP-35 with various customizations, including an extended magazine, a modified suppressor and custom skeleton stock that looked a lot like the original *Man From U.N.C.L.E.* gun. It also had a kind of early laser sight. This made the weapon bulky and impractical. I asked Herb, who ran the place, whose it was. He shrugged and said, "Oh, some spook off to some shit-hole somewhere or other." I asked him why he had it, and he answered, "I took it off him and gave him a Makarov. Much more practical."

It was a lesson I never forgot. I still carry a .32 L.W. Seecamp in an ankle holster when needed. To quote my old friend, the great comic book artist Mike Grell, "A small gun you can hide is better than a big one that gets taken away from you."

Rockets in Streatham High St.

Working with weaponry can be a very tricky thing, and you always have to keep in mind what they signify to other people. Sometimes, however, their presence can have bizarre and ironic consequences.

Some years ago, while I was still with 24 Company, I used to write and run various training exercises to which I would bring the foreign weapons, take them apart and re-assemble them again. The MOD wanted to repeat a particular Bosnian exercise we had done, because a lot of guys were rotating through Bosnia at that time. I volunteered to go and get the weapons, which were sitting in Nottingham. I headed off to the Pattern Room and picked up two AKMs, two AK74s and some MP5s—a whole bunch of kit, including an RPG-7 rocket launcher and a Dragunov sniper rifle.

I had a Peugeot 205 at the time and I loaded it with all of these weapons and, because the traffic on the M1 was so bad I was late getting back, and the armory in North Hampstead where we were based was closed. So I brought it all back to my apartment in Streatham.

Being a dedicated chap, I had to sleep with the weapons. I could not just put them somewhere and walk away and go out for a pint! I couldn't leave them in the car, so I took everything up the stairs into the apartment, which was on Streatham High Road.

We were going to be doing the exercise in Bramley, Surrey, an old 21 SAS training area. So next morning I got up at 4.30, took everything downstairs and loaded it back into the car—right on Streatham High Road. Now the thing you have to know about Streatham, if you don't happen to live in the U.K., is that it's one of the most densely populated areas of London, with maybe as many as 4 to 16 people living in every house. Not at all the kind of place where you play with high-powered arms and rocket launchers.

As I was methodically and carefully loading up the car, I noticed some lights flashing and looked up and down the street. I saw that there was what we call a jam-sandwich—a white and orange police van—parked about fifty meters away with two uniformed officers inside it. They were just looking, and I thought: *This is going to be interesting.*

As I put the last piece of kit in the boot they got out and walked over. I was wondering what was going through their minds, but I left the boot open on purpose. One of the two young coppers said, "Excuse me sir, did you just put into the boot of this vehicle, what we think you put into the boot of this vehicle?" And I said, "Yes," quite calmly. They then asked what exactly was in there. I said, "Several AKMs, AK47s, some HK-MP5 sub-machine guns and an RPG rocket launcher."

They stood looking for a minute, and then asked, "Have you got an explanation for all this?" I replied, "Yes, I'm actually going on an exercise and I'm in charge of the weapons. Here's the paperwork!"

So, I got out my papers and they looked them over and looked at me, and looked in the boot of the car again. Then they asked for some identification. That was when I pulled out my MOD 90 pass, which will get you out of most problems of this kind. They looked at it and asked what unit I was with. I replied, "Intelligence Corps." They asked again, "What did you say you have in there?" I told them again, and they asked, tentatively, "Can we have a look?" I said, "Sure—help yourselves."

So there we were at 4.30 in the morning in Streatham High Road with two uniformed policemen and their white and orange jam-sandwich, behaving like kids as they pulled out the weapons and looked closely at them! Finally, they asked what time did I have to be at my destination, and which route was I taking. I told them I was going through Hammersmith and then onto the A3 and they said, "Okay, we'll give you an escort." So they escorted me all the way through Wandsworth onto the A3, then waved a jaunty farewell and went off!

This seems funny now, but it really only makes sense long-term if you look at it as a kind of spiritual lesson. I lived for so long in two worlds—one of espionage, darkness, interrogation, weapons and death—that it seems almost impossible to understand how at the same time I was doing acting jobs, working as a stunt director and a swordmaster on various films, then disappearing off to this alternative universe.

I'll always be grateful for the faith "The Group" had in me, because getting back into that side of the business saved my sanity. After the ugly court case in which I successfully won visitation and parental rights to my children, I was in a pretty sad and lost state emotionally. Being in *Figaro* and *Don Giovanni* helped, but the next stage of recovery came from the military giving me new goals and a sense of self-respect. It focused my head and my will. I was depressed to the point of thinking that my life was pretty much ruined and in a way that was motivating for them as well as for me. I remember my boss actually said at one point, "We could throw anything at you and you'd come back in one piece!" I felt that literally, I would take on any attachment, anywhere. Whatever they said, I did it, because it was a cathartic clearing out of all the ugly, negative and unnecessary legal turmoil that had happened just before.

During a later security vetting review, MoD officers visited Clive Mantle, my old mate from *Robin of Sherwood*. He was working in his vegetable patch in his beautiful house in Wiltshire when there was a knock at the door, and this chap with a Ministry of Defence ID Card showed up and started asking him about me. Clive sat with this chap, who recognized right away that he was "Dr. Mike" from the hugely successful TV show *Casualty*. Apparently this threw the officer into some kind of spin. It was certainly a strange situation: Clive having another version of "Messrs. Brown and Green" from the MoD at his door, and the men from the Ministry "interviewing" Dr. Mike. What he said to them I don't know, but it was clear that they wanted to keep an eye on me.

To give some idea of just how surreal this life could be, one of the classified training exercises I did is a good example of life during this period. You never really knew where you'd be sent next: you would simply get a call that might say something like, "Go to Hereford. Two guys have been kidnapped in the Congo. Off you go." I would arrive at Hereford and they would say either, "You're going to the Cayman Islands" or "You're going to Pontins." We would, however, usually be deployed on domestic exercises from Stirling-Lines, driving out across country to the target location, doing 70 mph through little villages with a police escort—what we call "full-disco" with lights and music (sirens). In case the local boys wondered who the hell these idiots in unmarked Range Rovers were, disturbing their patch, all the vehicle IDs were tagged. If anyone called in the number plates, they would all come up as "do not apprehend this vehicle."

You never knew what was coming. Every year there is a special type of exercise, which is basically a re-enactment of the Iranian Embassy Siege. This type of exercise was described in details in Andy McNab's (real name Steve Mitchell) book *Immediate Action*. It can be set anywhere—on a plane or a boat—that will test the reactions and responses of the emergency services and other crisis management elements of the government. On this occasion it was supposed to happen at a house in the middle of the Fens. That might sound strange, but if you think about it, it poses an interesting set of problems. How do you get close enough to assault a house in the Fens? There's not much cover, and you can't just drive directly up to it, which would be what the IA (Immediate Action team) might do. The

Agusta 109 choppers would be heard long before they got close. This was going to be yet another interesting and challenging knot to unravel.

When we arrived in Hereford to be briefed before we deployed, everything suddenly slowed down. Now we were told we'd deploy next day, so we all ended up in the Sergeant's Mess at Sterling Lines. There we were in the bar, representatives from all the different agencies involved with these things (Box 500—another name for MI5—as well as Special Branch, etc.); people turning up from everywhere to deploy. Of course we were being careful and not drinking too much, because we knew we were off in the morning. Then all of a sudden my cell phone rang.

In those days, back in 1996, the phone was a sizable black brick you couldn't exactly hide. Anyway, it was my old friend Ray Winstone, who knew about my other life. The conversation went something like this:

Ray: "Marky. Where are you?"
Me: "I'm in the West Country. What's up?"
Ray: "Can you talk?"
Me: "Well, let me just step outside."
Ray: "The ceasefire is over, the IRA have just blown up Canary Wharf."
Me: "What! How do you know?"
Ray: "I'm looking at it—it's just happened."

It turned out he was in an apartment filming, literally, just across the river from the Wharf. He said there had been a bloody big bang, an orange flash and next minute the whole thing was ablaze. He literally called me a matter of minutes after it had happened.

I walked back into the mess and said: "Can we have the telly on in the TV lounge please?" As the guy at the bar grabbed the remote and went to press the switch I took a quick look at what was on and there was a newsflash and shots of Canary Wharf ablaze. I walked back into the mess and said, "Excuse me chaps, a little announcement—the ceasefire is over, the IRA have just blown up Canary Wharf."

You can imagine the scene. Everybody piled into the TV area and my boss came over and said, "How the hell did you know?" To which I replied, "I've got a source." He asked who it was, and I said, "I can't tell you that, Sir—it's need to know!" I didn't tell him it was Ray. So the way the SAS and about half the U.K. crisis management intelligence apparatus in the country found out about the ceasefire ending was because Ray Winstone told them!

Sadly two people died in the explosion and another thirty-nine were hospitalized. The bomb caused one hundred million pounds worth of damage.

This was indeed no game.

6.

PLAYING WITH SWORDS

*"Good swordplay is like good sex.
It's all about balance, leverage, timing and passion!"*
- Bob Anderson

I HAVE ALWAYS ENJOYED WORKING WITH SWORDS. There's something about the science and elegance of the blade that makes all other weapons look clumsy and inelegant. Also, you are face to face with your opponent and fighting on equal terms. Working as a swordmaster on several movies and TV shows was a unique opportunity to express and explore this dynamic discipline of the blade and there's nothing quite like it. Watching two actors having a dramatic "conversation in steel," a passionate dance of tactical lethality, is exhilarating and artistically very satisfying.

I actually started making a range of wooden swords and other weapons in the cellar of our family home in Yorkshire from an early age, mainly prompted by Michael Moorcock's imaginative and evocative series of novels based around the character of Elric of Melniboné and his vampire-like relationship with the demonically possessed sword, Stormbringer. Later, in school, I fashioning a bokken-style katana in woodwork classes and even a large Bowie-style hunting knife in the metalwork room!

My first stage combat experience came with the doomed West End show, *Dean*, a rock musical based on the life of the legendary screen actor James Dean. I was playing all the bad guys who featured in Dean's life, including his movies; one of those was the character "Buzz" from *Rebel Without a Cause*. (Famed *Phantom of the Opera* singer Peter Karrie was also in this production). During the staging of the show the dance choreographer was attempting to show us how to "sell" the famous Griffith Observatory knife fight from the film and casually tossed the stage flick knife from hand-to-hand, in mock intimidation, telling us that was what a real knife fight looked like.

As we rehearsed and blocked the fight, the choreographer moved around me threateningly and kept tossing the prop knife through the air. I waited for the right moment and flicked the flying knife across the stage before he could catch it. That was the end of that daft effort and he handed over the staging of the fight to me!

Other than attacking a police officer in *Who Dares Wins* (staged by the original Bond stunt-coordinator, Bob Simmonds) and being shot in the face by the late stuntman Terry Forrestal, my only other interactions were with basic archery, some Karate moves and throwing knives around the garden. That was the total sum of my experience with stage combat until *Robin of Sherwood*.

My first real sword coach was famed Twickenham Samurai and British Airways 747 pilot, Michael Jay. Mike was the first foreigner ever to be invited to take part in Japan's ancient Soma Nomaoi Samurai horse festival, and he generously shared the basics of the graceful and balletic Iaido Japanese sword discipline with me. I also got acquainted with the distinctively limbed Japanese longbow, called a Yumi and Kyudo, or Way of the Bow. Thus, by the time *Robin of Sherwood* came along I had at least been acquainted with the basic skills required for the character Nasir and, under the ever watchful eyes of the stunt coordinators Terry Walsh (the eighth Merry Man!) and Steve Dent, I was able to practice and hone those skills to a workable "film-practical" level. This early experience and daily training opportunity in all three disciplines (archery, swordplay and riding) served me well, both for three seasons of *Robin of Sherwood* and also throughout my entire acting career. It was also preparing me for a unique opportunity, one that came my way almost by accident.

First Knight

You never know when a new project is going to appear on the horizon.

Things can happen via the more usual route, such as when your agent sends you for an audition, or it can just come right out of the blue when you're least expecting it. That was the way I got involved with *First Knight*, a big budget movie directed by Jerry Zucker that retold the age-old story of Arthur, Lancelot and Guinevere. It wasn't the only time I was to work on this subject, but that's a story for later.

This was 1994; Richard Howell, a friend of my brother Nigel, had started a company called Foxtrot, which supplied the TV and film industry with firearms, uniforms and action extras—mostly ex-Territorial Army guys who had been trained to tackle pretty much anything that was thrown at them. Foxtrot had been asked if they could supply action extras for a big production, and Nigel asked me to speak to Richard Howell about the guys he had working for him and to find out whether they were any good. Richard himself was a member of the Special Forces Reserve and a certified firearms holder. He also ran an armory, supplying all manner of weapons, equipment, tactical advisors and uniforms to TV programs like *The Bill* and movies like Michael Mann's *Heat*.

The politics between stunt guys and action extras can be quite difficult, so Richard asked Nigel if I would go along with him to help open the doors between them. He told me that we would be dealing with Greg and Dinny Powell, whom I knew well from both *Robin of Sherwood* and *Who Dares Wins*. We were also going to be meeting up with Steve Dent, one of the foremost stunt coordinators in the country. The Dents were a film and TV equestrian dynasty, and Steve's father, Reg Dent, had trained the horse for the TV version of *Black Beauty*. They also had a world-class collection of carriages and wagons that had been used in various films. Steve had been the horse-master on *Robin of Sherwood*, and I had done most of my training at Dent's farm during that time.

When we arrived, all the stunt guys were lined up on one side of a field and all of Richard's guys on the other. I saw Dinny Powell almost at once, and he greeted me like a long lost son. We chatted for a while about what I was doing and started looking at the stunt horses. I noticed a very tall, distinguished-looking chap with silver hair who was also walking around and talking to people. Dinny said, "Come on, I want to introduce you to someone." So we walked over to this tall fellow and Dinny said, "Bob, Mark here is the man you want." Bob looked me over and said, "I hear you've done a bit with swords?" I said that I had, and he produced a couple of swords and said, "Okay. Come with me."

He told me he was going to make two or three moves and that he wanted me to parry them. So I did that. Then he went through a sequence of another six or eight moves and I parried those. Then I repeated the cuts to him and he parried the attack. He seemed pleased and we went through a further sequence of parry cut, parry cut—all very safe and controlled. Then he said, "So you do speak the language!" He asked who had trained me and I mentioned several people—including Michael Jay and of course Terry Walsh, whom I'd worked with on *Robin of Sherwood*.

"Okay," said Bob, "Now let's try this." He had a sword with a blade-catcher near the underside of the cross-guard and he wanted me to do a move where I slid my blade down into the blade-catcher. We tried this and Bob levered my blade up so that it was almost rising out of my hand. But he wasn't quite satisfied. He decided that to make the move work I needed to rotate the sword as it left my hand. We practiced this a couple of times until we got the sword to rotate 360 degrees in mid-air and Bob actually caught it in mid-flight. We practiced this a few more times and then he said, "Great. Stay there."

I went around with Richard Howell, who was introducing everyone and setting out exactly what the stunt men and the action extras would be doing. We went through some moves, and everyone got on really well. This was the first time I worked out the process I used later on Jerry Bruckheimer's *King Arthur*, where you put your principals in the middle of a fight, the stunt guys around them to act as a blocking force, and your action extra guys and re-enactors on the outside—so they don't get caught up in the middle of the fight scene with the main actors and the background is full of action.

Greg explained all this to the stunt guys and the extras, and they were all happy. At which point Bob came over to me again and said he wanted me to come with him to the studio. I looked over at Dinny and he just nodded.

At that moment, I had no idea at all where we were going, but we drove straight to Pinewood Studios. I asked Dinny what was going on and he told me to wait and see. Once again, my ability to "take the journey" and go with the flow kicked in, and I decided that confidence in my own sword skills and my ability to adapt would once again come in handy, and that I'd be able to handle whatever was thrown at me.

We parked at Pinewood Studios and walked across the parking lot. At that moment that I spotted Richard Gere walking towards us. Bob shouted across to him and said he wanted to meet in the Band Room (where I had rehearsed some of the fights for *Robin of Sherwood*) in fifteen minutes. We did another quick practice with the blade catching sequence and after twenty minutes or so Richard Gere came in and Bob said, "Richard, this is Mark. He's going to work with you. This is what we're going to do."

We went through the sequence of sword moves Bob and I had practiced and Richard managed to flip the sword exactly as Bob and I had done, with me rotating the sword as it left my hand. Richard managed to catch it the first time, although it took several more attempts to make it look fluid and graceful. We practiced a few more times until Bob was satisfied. Then he sent Richard off to work on something else, and we walked across to the main building.

Bob went in first, while I waited outside. Then he called me in and introduced me to the director, Jerry Zucker, famous for directing *Ghost* and writing and producing the *Naked Gun* movie series. Bob told Jerry that he and I were going to be working together, with me as his assistant, and that he also wanted me to play the part of "The Challenger" in the early part of the film. Jerry didn't even hesitate. He just said, "Okay!"

I still felt like I was in a weird kind of lucid dream, and it still hadn't hit me that not only had I just landed a role in a major Hollywood motion picture, but that I was about to become the assistant to one of the great legends of the stunt world. Because, what I had not realized until that moment, was that I had just done an audition with Bob Anderson, who had coached Errol Flynn in swordplay and was acknowledged as the doyen of stunt guys. With regards to swords in motion pictures, he was the master—the best there was. I was about to become his assistant—all because I had done my brother's friend a small favor!

This accounted for the next eight months of my life, working everyday with Bob, choreographing sword fights and working with all of the actors, including several I had known from *Robin*. A couple of them asked why I was doing the assistant job (even with Bob) and not playing a knight. But I was learning so much more with Bob about working on the other side of the camera that I didn't mind at all. I was involved with scheduling, rehearsals and special effects—the whole thing. For me this was the most fascinating aspect of the film to be involved in.

Because of the intense and intimate demands of modern screen acting, when you're in front of the camera you live in a very narrow focus—trying to deliver the lines and be in that reality—you're not really aware of what's going on behind the camera. You can see and are aware of everyone doing their own thing back there, but you have to push that out of your vision and be in the moment as an actor with other actors. Working with Bob taught me to see things from the other side.

During these many enjoyable and demanding sessions, standing in the sun and working out action beats, I was continually impressed by Bob's remarkable stamina and physical coordination for a man of 72 years, his silver hair flowing as he put Richard Gere through his paces and pushed the younger man to ever increasing speed and style. I put his resilience down to the fitness demands of training for Olympic fencing competitions and his wartime service as a Royal Marine Commando. Indeed, his ship had been sunk twice during the war and he began his bladed weapons sojourn as a naval bayonet-fighting champion. He still cut a very impressive figure, as both a fencer and a man, and over dinner one night I jokingly referred to Bob as "The Silver Blade." Pearl (Bob's long suffering, knick-knack collecting wife) laughed and liked the name. Bob "The Silver Blade" Anderson stuck, and he was referred to by that handle forever after by the stunt community.

Later on, when I came to work on *King Arthur*, one of the things Steve Dent said when he introduced me to the stunt team was that I had been on *Robin of Sherwood*, but has also worked with Bob Anderson on *First Knight* because Bob had chosen me—so they had better treat me with respect!

Working Knights

Doing what I did on *First Knight* taught me more about the politics of the movie business—both good and bad—than I had ever learned on *Robin* or anything else. It was a real eye-opening experience. I also learned about dealing with major stars like Richard Gere—who was an absolute gentleman to work with, very dedicated and a great actor—and Sean Connery of course, who played King Arthur. I also got to witness the gentle genius and beautiful presence of Sir John Gielgud.

Because I was a close friend of Sean's son Jason, who had played Robin in the series, he used to call me with messages to give to Sean, so I had a good deal of interaction with him. Let me say now that Sean Connery has an aura the size of an oil tanker—when he comes into view, there's a wave of morphic resonance that goes before him; he has the most amazing charisma. He's a very powerful presence and when you talk to him it's almost like talking to a force of nature. Quite extraordinary!

Richard Gere was an absolute professional and a really nice man: charming, easy-going and always calm. We trained for as long as four hours a day, every day, just to keep the muscle memory for the big fight sequences. Sometimes I was allowed to be the opponent; but Bob, even at the age of 72, wanted to do it all the time. He would be running all the fights with Richard while I stood there asking when he wanted me to take over, when was it my turn? It was a really enjoyable couple of hours everyday—we all got on well together and it was great fun.

One day I was in Richard's trailer working out the fight sequences for the week and there was a loud thumping on the door and an easily recognizable Scottish voice said loudly, "Richard—get on the set! I'm playing golf at four o'clock, and I don't want to hang around all day. Let's get this thing in the can!"

Richard looked at me and said, "Who is that?" I said, "I think it's Sean," and Sean's voice said, "I can hear you whispering in there—get out here and get on the set!" Richard looked at me as if to say, you go out there and talk to him. I shook my head and said, "It's you he wants."

I peered out of the window and there was Sean thumping on the door. Richard said again, "Go and talk to him." I said I couldn't. After all, they were the Hollywood stars. But Richard didn't want to go and face a large, angry Scotsman, so we both hid inside the trailer, giggling like naughty schoolboys and pretending we weren't there until Sean went away. When it was all done and dusted, we did manage to get the scene in the can in time for Sean to get to his golf game.

Richard was so calm that nothing much fazed him. One of the actors, who was in most of the big sword fights, was having personal issues. He was a chain-smoker and so wasn't particularly fit; he would get very frustrated during rehearsals because he got out of breath quickly. When he and I were training he actually bent an aluminum sword blade into a banana shape he was swinging at me so hard! Then one day he lost it completely and ended up throwing a sword at Richard.

Bob and I stepped in immediately and asked him what he thought he was doing, but Richard just said, really calmly, "It's okay, I'll deal with this." He took the hyped-up actor to one side and said, "Look, we're both professionals, we need to work together on this because it's dangerous." After that the other guy calmed down and we got on with the scene.

Sadly, when they did do the big fight at the end, the same actor punched Richard in the mouth, chipping a tooth. The guy was just so tight and I don't know where his head was at the time, but these things can happen. It's usually great fun doing these stunts until someone gets hurt—I should know because I was one of those who did.

It happened while we were rehearsing a big fight scene involving a few of the stunt guys. I was in the middle of the field watching everyone's angles and Richard had done a move. Then one of the guys did another move that did not look safe to me, so I stepped in to tell them to hold on for a second. As I did this, I turned my head for a split second and Richard caught me right in the corner of my left eye socket with his sword. The blade literally hit bone and split the corner of my eye wide open.

I staggered back and had both my hands over my face because the blow had stunned me. Greg Powell came over and said, "Take your right hand away from your face." I could see him through my right eye and he said that looked fine—but then I took my left hand away and all I could see was a mist of red. Greg said, "Okay, someone get a car. You need to get to hospital right away."

As I sat in the back of a Mercedes a few minutes later, bleeding all over the back seat, I realized it didn't matter whether it was a big budget film production or a small budget one—I might just have been blinded in one eye. Luckily what had happened was that I had got blood in my eyeball from the cut in the corner of my eye socket and it was this that had obscured my vision. The doctors checked it all out and I had microsurgery and stitches to repair the damage. I returned to the set that afternoon and carried on working. You can hardly see the scar now.

Later Richard came to see me. He was very upset, but I was back on the set literally within a couple of hours—I had a black eye for a few days and couldn't see much, but other than that I was fine. When the filming ended Richard gave me a miniature golden Excalibur pendant—King Arthur's sword—engraved simply with, "Thanks. R.G." I still have it and wear it often.

Bob's reaction was typical of the man. When I got back to the set he came over to ask if I was okay and I told him I was fine. I said it was really my fault because I had come onto the middle of the set during the action and more or less walked onto the edge of Richard's sword. Bob just gave me the typical "Silver Blade" look of disdain and said, "Why didn't you parry?"

Three Stuntmen Went into a Bar

Some of the best nights on and off the set were spent sitting around with Greg and Dinny and the stunt guys—listening to their stories and learning about their early histories and backgrounds. Most of them came from the East End, and were ex-boxers, ex-military or sometimes workers from the East End fish and meat markets!

I first met another great young stunt man—Gary Powell, who now coordinates the *James Bond* films—on the set of *First Knight*. The film features a weird machine that has all these blades and spikes flailing around. Richard Gere's character has to run the gauntlet through it. It was an amazing piece of machinery and we all tried it and everyone got knocked off—except for Gary, who was doubling for Richard. The director wanted him to go through it so they could inter-cut with Richard. He did it in one. Then they asked him to do it backwards, holding a camera, so they could film Richard going through the machine. Gary did that as well, without once falling off. Everyone said they had never seen anything like it; it was a balancing act that showed amazing physical prowess, timing and control, and signaled the assured future that Gary would fulfill as a world-class stunt coordinator.

It was during these long rambling sessions sitting around talking that I first heard the story about Nosher Powell and the dog, a story that is now legendary and one of the most hilarious I have ever heard.

Nosher, who was Greg's father, had been asked to bring peace to a notorious London nightclub-come-restaurant called Jack Iso's, which was frequented by various villains and gangsters. The owner wanted to bring the fighting and feuding under control because it was bad for business. Nosher was asked to manage the door and take care of any developing aggravation before it got out of hand. Nosh suggested that they hire a dog and handler that everyone could see as they arrived at the entrance. This was designed to ensure there would be no more fighting, and future trouble would be handled very differently with swift four-legged action.

Nosh had the place under control after about a week of fighting and throwing people out, and he decided to made pals with his new canine guardian and partner, taking the dog for regular walks and bringing in steak and other treats. They soon became very comfortable with each other and the dog-handler felt more secure as well.

Inevitably the night came when various rival gangs decided to have dinner at the same time, and it soon became obvious that trouble was brewing. Nosher had placed himself strategically at the top of a long narrow staircase that led down into the restaurant so that he could lock the door and control the exit if need be.

Suddenly an ashen waitress came running out of the restaurant and shouted that it had "all kicked off" and various parties were fighting and smashing the place up! The manager had been rendered unconscious after presenting the bill to one gangland faction and various weapons were now being brandished and the blood and snot were flying liberally!

Nosher sprang into action and ordered the door chained and locked, telling the dog handler to get the dog ready. The waitress screamed for him to come down and "sort it" but Nosher told her wisely that the door was locked and nobody was leaving unless it was through him. He had the advantage of being in a tight space and could take them on, "like the Spartans," one at time as they ascended the narrow staircase. The dog could also be turned loose on them. If Nosher had gone down stairs he would have been at a disadvantage, outnumbered and possibly surrounded.

After a few minutes of screaming, smashing and crunching, the angry gangsters arrived at the foot of the stairs, snarling and threatening all manner of violence. Nosher calmly informed them (in his distinctive and iconic vocal style) that they were completely "out of order," the door was chained shut, the dog was ready and they should pay the bill and calm down. This did not provoke the hoped-for response and the gang started menacingly to climb the stairs, brandishing steak knives, shattered chair legs and broken champagne bottles.

Nosher responded in kind and prepared for a fight, ordering the dog handler to ready the dog to be loosed on the gang. After shouting more warnings and demanding that the men pay the bill and behave themselves, he once again asserted that the doors were chained shut and the dog was about to be let loose on them! The gang continued marching up the stairs with various curses and threats and Nosher realized there was no way to avoid the coming confrontation. He ordered the handler to let the dog go and the snarling and barking four-legged tornado tore into the fray!

Nosher was immediately bitten in the right calf and suddenly realized the dog was in fact attacking *him* ferociously and had sunk its teeth into his leg! Pulling the dog off as best he could, he simply had no option other than to knock it out and prepare for single combat with the gang!

As he was trying to rise, fists raised and ready, the dog handler, believing Nosher had in fact killed his dog, began throwing punches at him and screaming in anger. Nosher pulled off the enraged handler and knocked him out with one punch! Now he had an unconscious dog, and unconscious dog handler and an angry tidal wave of London gangsters rushing up the stairs! This was going to be nasty!

After steeling himself for the inevitable blood-letting, and feeling thoroughly frustrated, Nosh turned to stand his ground, unconscious dog and handler at his feet and blood flowing down his leg—only to see the now apparently stalled gang convulsed in hysteria in the stairwell, totally incapable of further violence as they were all laughing and falling about at the bizarre spectacle they had just witnessed!

I asked Nosher, after hearing this story from Greg and Dinny, what happened after that so I could hear it from the original source. Nosher replied in typical laconic style that not only had the gang settled the restaurant bill (stating they were paying for the entertainment) but they also gave him "a score [twenty pounds] to get a new pair of strides!"

I cannot claim to write this story with as much glorious color, flavor or humor as Greg, Dinny or the late, great Nosher Powell himself could tell it, but this and many other tales brought waves of laughter and merrymaking during the shooting of *First Knight*; I even became a part of one such story myself!

Towards the end of filming I invited Bob, Greg, Dinny and his wife out to dinner at the Savoy Grill as a way of saying thank you for all the fun I'd had on *First Knight*. On the day Bob said that he had a long drive back to Bognor Regis, where he lived, and that we should do it another time. So Bob drove off and I went to meet Dinny and Greg at the Savoy. We had champagne, wine and a lovely meal, and towards the end of the evening Greg told me that Nosher was looking after a pub in the Elephant and Castle. He suggested that we go down there and finish off the evening in style; so off we went.

We parked and walked to the pub, which was hard to see because all the windows had boards across them and the outside walls were painted black. It didn't look like a pub at all, but more like a Goth Club—which in fact it turned out to be.

We went in and there was Nosh. We said hello and ordered our drinks, but as we were standing at the bar I got a feeling that there was a bit of an atmosphere. Dinny and Greg and his wife were looking around and said they recognized some people in the corner who were not good news. Then, as I was standing at the bar with Greg's wife, Dinny and Greg disappeared for a few minutes. The next thing we knew there were bodies started flying everywhere in the middle of the dance floor. Then there was the unmistakable waft of tear gas. I remember thinking, *Christ, we just came from the Savoy Grill and now this has kicked off in a dodgy boozer in the Elephant and Castle...*

I stumbled out, towing Greg's wife with me, and got a blast of tear gas in my eyes. Inside, a riot was happening, and outside a full-scale punch-up was going on between and Dinny and Nosher and two or three guys I didn't know. There was blood and snot flying in all directions.

As I came out, my eyes streaming, trying to get Greg's wife out of the way of the fight, I saw that Greg had someone pinned up against the wall. He still had a cigar in his mouth and seeing me, took it out and said, "Mark, hold that for a second."

He handed me the cigar, and went back to pummeling the bloke.

After a while it all calmed down a bit and at this point a police car pulled up and the officer inside wound his window down and asked, "Alright Nosh? Is there a problem?" Nosh said, "No mate, I've got it all under control." The officer said, "Alright mate. But it looks like there are a few walking-wounded." Nosher said, "No mate, it's all under control. Honest!" The young officer wisely wound his window up and drove off into the night.

After about 20 minutes, once the tear gas had cleared, we went back into the bar, which was pretty much empty, and just stood looking at each other. I remember Greg asking me what had happened to his cigar, which I must have dropped in the mêlée. Then he said, "It's a shame Bob's not here—he would have enjoyed this." I couldn't help smiling. Bob Anderson was Mr. Elegant—a real gentleman: tall, well-spoken, distinguished looking, very gracious and always smartly dressed. Greg was right though, he would probably have laughed at the irony of the whole situation, and maybe even joined in.

My warm respect and affection for the stunt community and their stories has remained undiminished over the years, and is as fresh as yesterday. The undying and fond memories of my days on *Robin of Sherwood*, *First Knight* and *King Arthur* still make me chuckle to myself and feel grateful for the friendship, mentoring and company.

THE POSITIVE INTROVERT AND THE NEGATIVE EXTROVERT

Unlike the world of stuntmen, there's a weird and sometimes viciously destructive relationship that can exist between Hollywood personalities and the media who feed off them. This has become even more personal and intrusive over the last few years, but nothing is sacred, and Richard Gere had been the target of ugly rumors and negative press.

Before we even got under way on the set of *First Knight* Greg Powell had gathered all the stunt guys, including me, together and said, "Just a warning to you guys—if I hear anybody talking about chipmunks, gerbils, stoats—anything like that—you're fired, off the picture; we don't need any of that crap on this shoot!"

Everyone understood that this was a reference to a particularly nasty, hurtful and ridiculous urban myth involving Richard and, because we all liked and respected him, it was probably redundant anyway, but we understood the seriousness of the warning. The tale about Richard illustrates the daft dynamic of stardom and media feeding frenzy.

There's a particular hospital in L.A. where, whenever they have people come in with strange afflictions, parts of their anatomies stuck in vacuum cleaner pipes, or things wedged in places they don't belong, they'd give them a John Doe name instead of using their real name. And if patients looked a bit like someone famous they would give him or her *that* name, like John Wayne or Errol Flynn.

It happened that someone who looked like Richard had come in with a particular creature wedged where the sun doesn't shine, and they called this guy Richard Gere. Of course, that leaked out. Richard reacted; he took an entire page advert out in the *New York Times* denying that it was him and saying that his wife was not a lesbian, that he was not gay and that this was not a marriage of convenience. Unfortunately, this just made it worse because everyone assumed he was protesting too much. He realized too late that the best way of dealing with these lies would have been to let it go, but he was personally affronted that people would run with a story like that.

Later on during filming Richard and I were getting ready for our first fight sequence. We were chatting away, having become easy and relaxed with each other by then, and he asked me how much time I spent in L.A. and where I liked to hang out when I was there. I told him I had a lady-friend in West Hollywood and that we used to go to Barney's Beanery for a bite to eat or a drink. Richard said "Oh, Barney's Beanery—that's where the gerbil story started..." I looked at him in astonishment and told him how we had all been told not to mention it, out of respect for him. He smiled and said that he had been initially hurt by the bogus story but really didn't care anymore because it was all completely manufactured by the gossip industry within the media. He had let it go and moved on with his life.

I believed him because his composure and professionalism on the set was exemplary. As far as he was concerned, it was in the past and that was the end of it. Richard is a sincere Buddhist—a supporter of the Dalai Lama and the people of Tibet, and is a supporter of all human rights. He practices what he preaches and has an amazingly calm aura about him. He's gracious and positive and I felt honored to have crossed swords with him.

First Knight taught me several great lessons about the movie business. When it was released, two other very successful historical action flicks, *Braveheart* and *Rob Roy*, came out; for some reason the critics liked them, but didn't like *First Knight* and gave it a critical pasting—including Richard's performance and the whole look of the film; costumes and everything. They kept comparing it with the others, which were set in a historical period. I didn't understand this because *First Knight* was a mythical story about King Arthur. As such, it was well made and well performed, although some of the sword designs were a bit crazy like the one used by Ben Cross, who played the strangely named Malagant, and which we nicknamed the "Buick-Slayer" because it was such a big and unwieldy piece of crap; it was virtually useless.

Bob had tuned Richard's sword so that the blade, which was made of aircraft grade aluminum called HE-30, floated and balanced perfectly. I was fascinated by this and talked to Charlie Bodicom, the guy who made it. He told me that it had a trace of copper in the blade to help the flexibility of the aluminum and prevent it from being brittle. The hilt-set was held in place by a three-eighths of an inch screw-bar, which fitted onto the tang of the blade and fastened with a top-hat hex nut to enable the hilt-set to be removed quickly should the blade need to be replaced during filming. That fitting was really useful because otherwise swords can end up rattling as things work loose. I watched Charlie make the sword and hilt set, with Bob asking him to change the balance. They actually made some bronze hilt-sets so that the sword would have more weight at the pommel end to lift up the blade. It was bloody marvelous. I still have one of those swords, given to me by Richard Gere. There's nothing quite like it—it balances perfectly—literally floats in your hand. I've used that sword many times since both for training and for other films.

Working on *First Knight* was an amazing experience. I took away many things of enormous value for the future from it. Everything I know about choreographing a big film fight as drama I learnt from working with Bob Anderson. He was an artist who understood the ebb and flow of a fight. I watched the way he handled people and his understanding of their sociology and psychology. It was he who explained the four major sports personalities to me—something that he had been taught when he was doing Olympic fencing years before. There is the introvert, the extrovert and two different yin-yang aspects: the positive extrovert and the negative introvert. Most sports personalities are positive introverts. Bob said that most of the best actors he had worked with were stable introverts who were able to project a personality outside their own through their acting. It was ideas like this that made me realize that being a fight director is an art form of its own.

All of this was to stand me in good stead in the future. I would not be doing what I am now if it were not for Bob Anderson and the experience of working with him, which taught me the technical mechanics of a big set and the political and business forces that sometimes clash there.

7.
ADVENTURES WITH JULES VERNE

What Doesn't Kill You...

Conventions In Space And Time.

AROUND THIS TIME I started to get TV more work on shows like *Peak Practice*, *The Bill* and *Casualty*, and as a result received offers to attend fan conventions. It was at one of these that I met my wife to be, Robin Curtis. It was already a surreal experience because the guest of honor was Arthur C. Clarke. I remember standing in the artists Green Room with Jon Pertwee and Patrick Stewart. Patrick looked at Clark and said, "Well! You're Doctor Who. You're Nasir the Saracen and I'm Jean Luc Picard, Captain of *The Enterprise*; but that's Arthur C. Clarke, author of *2001: A Space Odyssey* and inventor of the communications satellite!"

Robin was also on that panel, having played Lt. Saavik in *Star Trek II & IV*. We had an instant and intense attraction to each other, which was apparently obvious even to the audience! It was also very obvious to us both that if the newly formed relationship was going to survive the trans-Atlantic distances involved, as well as the pressure of our professional careers, something was going to have to change and one of us was going to have to make a big commitment and a life-changing decision.

Because I knew people in Los Angeles and already had an open-ended visa to visit the U.S. we decided it was I who should make the leap of faith.

It was a decision that would have far-reaching and profound repercussions on my future.

After several weeks of flying back and forth around California, Germany and New York we decided that our relationship was strong enough to make a stronger commitment and begin our lives together. I was determined to keep up my strong contacts with the U.K. military, as ordered by Major Mich Barking, but despite this I moved to California in 1997.

The only way I could keep my specialist qualifications up to date during this time was by going back to the U.K. at regular intervals to take part in training and exercises. Being newly married was not very conducive to this kind of life, however, and was a matter of some understandable friction between Robin and I.

At the time I was still a member of the Intelligence Corps and in a section that answered to the Director of Special Forces (DSF)—not just the SAS, but also the SBS (Special Boat Service, the Royal Marines version of the SAS) and SIW (Special Intelligence Wing). There were eight of us in that Section, all whom held a DV (Developed Vetting) security clearance, a Top-Secret clearance, which meant that they could call us at any time and that we were cleared to work at that level.

The famous 22 SAS Regiment is a regular army unit; but they never had enough intelligence support personnel, which is why "part timers" ended up doing so much work with them. The British regular army simply cannot function efficiently without extra volunteer backup from the reserves. There was a grey area whereby, with cross training and "S Type" engagements, guys working for SOCA (Serious Organized Crime Agency) who are also in the TA (Territorial Army) could deploy with the regulars. We had people working for defense contractors like "Network Security," which was sort of a commercial spin-off of MI5 (or Box 500 as it's known in the trade) and corporate intelligence businesses like Hakluyt. You can go online and look up a company like Hakluyt, which acts as a commercial spin-off of MI6 and is apparently staffed by retired members of the SIS (Secret Intelligence Service, or Box 850).

The requirement to return to the U.K. kept my military qualifications current and active. This included weapons and first aid qualifications, as well as fitness and NBC (Nuclear, Biological and Chemical Weapons training—fearsome stuff I can tell you). Because of my security clearance, the powers that be had invested a lot of money in me, and so I promised to go home as often as I could. It took a lot of work to clear me and I was honored to have the security vetting status. Even Robin was vetted and had to fill in a pile of U.K. forms about her family and background going back two generations.

However, it soon became physically impossible to keep jaunting back and forward all the time between the U.S. and U.K. So, although I didn't really want to, I came back to the U.K. and finally handed in my kit—uniform, combat boots, respirator, "Noddy (NBC) Suit," sleeping bag and MOD90 ID Cards and papers. I actually wish now that I had kept some of it, but there was a £50 fine for not handing stuff in, and at the time I thought, *I'm going to get married and settle down to a new life in California; it's time to make a clean break with the clandestine world.*

OUT AND ABOUT WITH THE NATIONAL GUARD

After some 25 years in the film, TV and theatre industries, and a rather unique position in that curious twilight universe as actor/writer/spook, it felt like my secret life was finally coming to a close. As my old boss said, "You've had the best of it. What you did will probably never be allowed to happen again." Although I was officially out of 243 Section my old CO got in touch with me and said, "Considering your vetting status we'd like that you find a local unit to work with, so we can keep and eye on you."

That's probably why they suggested I work with the U.S. National Guard when I got settled in America. In fact, I had already worked with various U.S. intelligence units, so I went down to the headquarters in Glendale with all my identification and papers and explained the situation. The very polite officer I talked to said, "Well, you're not an American citizen, so we can't really take you on, but considering your background we'd love to have you along as an observer. You can wear your own uniform and do whatever you want." So I turned up and did a couple of exercises with them.

One of the first things they did was have what was called a "bounty weekend," which is where they have all kinds of tests. On this occasion they were holding a class in map reading and orienteering and, as I was watching them do this, the girl taking the class asked if I wanted to have a go. She gave me a six-figure grid reference and I went through the eastings and northings etc. and gave her the position spot on—but she said no. I said, "What do you mean, no?" and she said I was not in the right box. I asked for the grid reference again, did the same procedure and got to the same box. I thought, *maybe I'm making a mistake*. I actually had a silver compass with me to check my bearings, so I pulled it out, worked out the grid references again in front of her, and said, "There."

She still said no, it was the wrong box. So I went through it step by step again and she still insisted it was wrong. Then, I asked her to show me how *she* had worked it out, and she did it backwards—northing and then easting, which is not the way it's done at all. I told her she was doing it backwards. "Look," I said, "I don't know whether the American Army does this differently to everyone else in the world, but you do not find a six figure grid point like this." Eastings are always first, read from west to east; Northings second, which are read from south to north. I asked her to show me where she thought she should be and she was completely in the wrong place.

I told her, "Can I just say that if you were looking for a helicopter rescue, or are about to call in an air-strike, you've a) just missed the helicopter because it's in the wrong place, or b) bombed the snot out of somebody you didn't mean to!"

That was a bit of a shock for them, but on the following weekend we went out to a camp where we were going to spend the night on the top of a hill and do some night navigation. The first thing they did was set up their chow tent and cook house, a little way up the hill. Then, somehow, they set fire to the hill. There we were up a hill in the mountains above Los Angeles and they set fire to the grass. I took one look at the fire spreading around and said, "Listen chaps, I think we need to get off this hill before the wind blows round and cuts off our escape." When it was all over, they had to call in a helicopter to put the fire out and to stop the camp and the rest of the equipment going up in flames.

That was my experience with the National Guard. But I have to say good luck to them; I don't envy them wherever they are. They have been very badly misused in the war in Iraq, and probably out of all the psychological casualties the Americans will have, the National Guard will be the biggest supplier of people suffering from PTSD [Post Traumatic Stress Disorder] because they're not hardened professional soldiers; they aren't trained like regular soldiers, and some of these brave people are on their fourth or fifth tour with little real aftercare in some cases or psychological support from the undermanned, under-resourced and politically beleaguered V.A. Most signed up for two weekends a month to get a better education or make some extra cash, not spend three years in a warzone like The Sandbox.

There's a book we used to study called *War On The Mind*, which says that the longest a man can stay in a combat environment, as a general rule of thumb, is 55 days. After that time, anybody will become psychologically incapacitated and might suffer PTSD. For example, if just about anyone is kept in a fire zone in the middle of a battle they are going to begin to crack up eventually. Some of these guys have been going out there for six or seven tours!

I respect their enthusiasm, but the experience on that exercise made me decide it was really time to extract myself from all this and just get on with a quiet normal life. So that's what I decided to do.

Or at least, I tried to.

On the Island

I thought I had done pretty well to establish myself in L.A. in a short time, and I saw this as one part of being a good, supporting and loving playmate. I was a now a SAG performer and had a Green Card. I had found a respectable agent and was going for more work while pursuing my writing career. I'd chalked up episodes of *Frasier* and *Conan The Barbarian* as well as various music videos and convention appearances. I thought I was doing my part as a good partner and husband.

But all was not well. I began to realize that Robin and I had married too quickly, and that I really had no idea who she was. Nothing seemed to quiet her internal demons and issues, and my misunderstanding of the reality of this was no doubt a source of some of our biggest problems. I fully admit my failure to comprehend the depth of some of these emotional undercurrents. I had no idea how to deal with the complex emotional minefield I had walked into. All I could do was keep moving forward, hope for a break in the storm and try and see if repair and recovery were possible during the counseling and marital therapy we had agreed on.

Relief came in April 1998, in the shape of the offer of the play: a four-hander called *Neville's Island* that had been performed in the U.K. very successfully. I had actually seen it there, and now it was to be performed in the round at the Globe Theatre in Balboa Park, San Diego, a famous venue for Shakespeare and other serious artistic endeavors. The offer included the use of an apartment in San Diego for the whole rehearsal period and the run of the play. This was a huge relief, because things were pretty tense at home, and I was really just looking for a way to extract myself with some dignity left intact and to buy myself some space and time to think.

I liked that the producers had come up with the idea of doing it in the round with the Island set in the middle of the Cassius Carter Center Stage auditorium, with misty water spraying out over the audience! The play is a very funny comedy about four guys and their very human natures. At the beginning they are on an outward-bound course, and they get stuck on a little island in the middle of Lake Windermere, in the Lake District of Great Britain. The character I was playing, Gordon, was a wickedly sarcastic bully—very much a forerunner of the David Brent character played by Ricky Gervais in *The Office*. The play started with me swimming up a river, soaking wet, onto this island. I was actually splashing about in a trough of water, so we started with both the audience and me wet and cold. They actually handed out rain hats and coats in the auditorium.

The wonderful cast included Curtis Armstrong, Don Sparks and James Winkler, and it was directed ably by Andrew Traister, who kept the comedy moving and the satire sharply honed. It was one of the most originally staged theatrical presentations I've been involved with.

My part was wordy and comedic, and timing and reacting physically to the audience were crucial. It was a full-on task and one that demanded total commitment. When we opened in May 1998 I got some nice notices and enjoyed my time in San Diego as a buffer to clear my head and deal with the issues that now faced me regarding my failed marriage.

We had a great, sell-out run, and in the process it gave me a base to re-center my life, which had be thrown into a complete tailspin by what had happened with Robin. I had lost faith in the whole idea of marriage, because I didn't get married to get divorced: I got married to stay married. I was forty and believed I was doing the right thing with the right person. As it turned out, I was totally wrong.

Robin actually came to see the play, and we sat there and tried to communicate, but it was difficult because the trust had been totally shattered by her actions and previous avoidance of an open and totally honest dialogue. The lesson I learned from this, as well as other relationships I've had, is that if somebody does something wrong, expending energy on getting back at them doesn't make it any better. The best thing to do is put it in its box, look at why it happened, what my part in it was, and then move on. Moving on is almost always helped by outside circumstances, in this case the play, which forced me to refocus and re-ground my emotional energy.

Looking back—because there are really no such things as coincidences—one of the strangest things about being in San Diego was that they have a big aerospace museum in Balboa Park. Outside, on a great big metal spike, is an SR-71 Blackbird spy plane. On the way back to my apartment after the show I would often pull over and walk across to ogle this amazing piece of machinery and the wonder at its design, which is really quite extraordinary. What I did not know then was that a decade later I would be doing the voice of an SR-71 in the second of the *Transformers* films. I remember how, when Michael Bay told me there was going to be a Blackbird in the film, I was so pleased and excited I started telling his about the one at Balboa Park. I think he was surprised that I knew so much about it!

Adventures with Jules Verne

By the end of 1998 I knew the marriage was over. Filing for divorce began and I had to deal with the fact that I had failed in my attempts to keep the relationship alive. At about this time Michael Praed, my old chum from *Robin of Sherwood*, called me from Montreal. He was filming a new TV show called *The Secret Adventures of Jules Verne* and asked me if I would be interested in choreographing the sword fights on the show. He told me I would have to fly myself up and do an audition for the producers by actually running a fight.

I thought about it. My marriage was over, I had enough money for a flight and Michael said I could stay with him, so I decided to roll the dice and got on a plane to Montreal that night. I met the producers and we started working on the sword fight. I remember saying to one of them, Neil Dunn, that a sword fight is really good value in terms of screen time, because usually it's only two people with swords and you can fill in two or three minutes of really dramatic screen time if it's shot and edited properly. He got that and asked to see what I could do.

We did the sword fight in the middle of a huge iron foundry. I ordered swords and had them shipped in from Bapty & Co. in London so that they were made the way I wanted and properly balanced. I actually brought in the alloy small-sword blade that Tim Roth had used in the film of *Rob Roy* and had it fixed to a genuine 19th Century 1822 Pattern British Infantry Officer's sword's hilt from the Victorian era. Michael liked it very much.

Neil also liked what I did with the fight and I got the job, but it would prove to be more than a bit of a headache. The idea for the show was a great one. It took the notion that Jules Verne, as a young man, had actually lived through some of the stories he later turned into fiction, and that one of his best-known characters, Phileas Fogg, was a real person. The balloon, in which he had travelled *Around the World in 80 Days*, was real. It was one of the earliest shows to feature steam-punk elements, a genre that has since become hugely popular. Every week the heroes would sail off in a big dirigible and encounter a range of villains from history and science fiction.

However, there were problems from the start. I think the producers started with one idea and then changed direction. Neil Zeiger, who had been responsible for the U.K. TV detective series *Ruth Rendell Mysteries*, had been brought in to try and sort it out. I remember having discussions with others about Neil and saying that Jules Verne, as a science fiction show, was very different from a British detective series. Eventually Neil came in and gathered heads of departments together and said, "For those of you who were wondering, we are not making a science fiction show, we are making a drama show." I remember saying, "Can I just point out that the show is called *The Secret Adventures of Jules Verne*. We have an airborne balloon carrying a gondola around the world, we've got vampires, robots, underground mole machines and aliens—but you're telling us we're *not* making a science fiction show?" He didn't want to hear it. Neil was a very nice guy but a round peg in a very square hole.

There were definitely people on the show who didn't like me, probably because I noticed when things went wrong and said so. For example, the wardrobe department was completely out of control. I would stand outside a studio door with a red light on—meaning "no entry, filming in progress"—and they would just go through the door anyway and slam it behind them! I said more than once that if they did that in a London or Los Angeles studio they would be fired.

There were other, petty things that happened on a regular basis. One day, the costume designer came down and said, "Can I talk to you?" She told me that she had heard I was telling people I had designed the heroine's fighting corset with knives hidden in it. I looked at her astonished and said, "Are you seriously coming down here and disrupting a rehearsal to ask me a such a ridiculous question?" I asked her what on earth would make her believe I would even think of claiming that; but even as I said it I was thinking that there were members of her crew who hated the English and didn't want me there. So I said to her, "I'll tell you what we're going to do. You tell me who said that, and let's go upstairs, sit down with the producers and discuss it like adults." But she refused to tell me or take it any further.

There were many issues like that and I knew I had ruffled some feathers, but for the most part I got on well with everybody. Sometimes you get a show that just had these elements running through it, and there's pretty much nothing you can do about it but keep your head down and get on with the job.

I got on well with all the producers and writers including the show's creator Gavin Scott and consultant Rick Overton. I also worked closely with Pierre de Lespinois, Richard Jackson, Michael Huffington and art director Normand Sarazin.

However, despite having some good directors, including Ian Sharp (who I recommended, having worked with him on both *Who Dares Wins* and *Robin of Sherwood*) and Mark Roper (with whom I had done *Conan The Barbarian* in Mexico), *The Secret Adventures of Jules Verne* had technical problems from the beginning.

As with any big series, we didn't shoot the first episode first. The idea is to shoot out of order because it gives you a chance to make mistakes and learn what works and what doesn't. For example, on *Black Sails* in 2013, we shot episode three, and then two and then one. That way, by the time you shoot the first episode you've got it down—the relationships, the set, how things work mechanically—so that the first episode looks like a well oiled machine and you have time to go back and re-shoot anything from the third episode that didn't work so well.

Some of the early directors on *Jules Verne* were weak technically and overshot the episodes, so editing became a nightmare. The green screen and digital special effects were still in their infancy, and it became obvious that some effects were simply not viable using the technology available at the time. This was because the footage was actually recorded on old style VHS tape cassettes rather than on film. VHS was cheap, and so the directors could reshoot various takes over and over. This overworked the crew, so people were prematurely tired and bored.

I knew we were in trouble when it became clear, during the shooting of a special-effects heavy, split-screen fight scene directed by Tom Clegg, that after asking repeatedly for input from the special effects and visual effects departments nobody seemed to know how to do it! Everyone was "on holiday" the day we shot the fight, so Tom and I were on our own. We worked together to sort out a complex encounter between twin brothers using two doubles and a split frame format, and the scene worked without any help from either visual effects expert being present on the day.

Once a cell phone rang on the set for some time during a take involving Rick Overton, and everyone was surprised when the soundman finally realized that it was actually his phone. I was even more surprised when he answered the call and had a conversation in French as the take continued! That would have got most folks fired from the set immediately in London or L.A., but Quebecois rules are different, as I discovered. Rick made of joke of the incident and said it was his agent calling, but it was a sad reflection of the attitude and professionalism of some of the Montreal crew.

There's no question that a lot of the concepts and ideas for the show were brilliant and some of the writing was very good, but there were too many times when the writers were asking, "How are we going to do this?" However, ultimately the biggest problem was Michael Praed. He was the star of the show, but there were issues right from the start with what he wanted to do, what the directors wanted to do and what the other actors wanted to do. Even during the first fight we worked on, Michael was trying to dictate how he wanted it to go. The actor he was rehearsing with turned to me and said, "Who's choreographing this fight—you or him?" So I had a talk with Michael and told him I would make it look as good for him as

I could, but that he had to take a little step back because he was going to get a bad reaction from the other actors if he started dictating to them.

I had experienced similar things when working on *First Knight*. Of course our fight director then was the great Bob Anderson, and no one argued with him. If Bob said something, it was set in stone, and whoever it was did it that way. Bob kept a tight control over the way the fights went and what he wanted to happen. I was determined to do the same but it became a problem from the beginning. Michael was so invested in the show being a vehicle for him that he let the control issue take over. It would cause serious problems later on.

On-Set Clashes

Tom Clegg came to me quite early on in the filming and asked what was going on with Michael. When I asked what he meant, Tom said, "He wants to do all these things that are not in the script—there's one sequence where he wants to stamp on this guy's head and kill him." I agreed that I didn't think we needed that, but Michael said that artistically he hates the League of Darkness (his adversaries in the show), and felt the motivation is that he wants to kick this guy to death! Tom had said that this wasn't heroic, but more like the actions of a football hooligan and that Phileas Fogg (the part played by Michael) was a gentleman. I decided to ask the producers and see where they were on violence and get some direction from them.

The guidelines were clear standard TV guidelines, and I attempted to carry them out. I had a discussion with Michael and used the James Bond argument, saying that James Bond always ended up fighting the main enemy, who is always bigger or stronger than him, and that he's seen as a hero, not a bully.

By the time Ian Sharp arrived, there was already a serious rift between Michael and myself and other members of the cast. I was simply trying to carry out the instructions and guidelines given to me by the producers and get the show in the can, but Michael had his own ideas and began to see my role on set as some kind of artistic intrusion into his characterization of Fogg. It got to the point where Francesca Hunt, the girl who played the female lead, came to me and said she was terrified of Michael. She never knew what he would do next, even when they had rehearsed a scene.

There was sadly also a strain on my relationship with the stuntmen, to put it mildly. They were so closed-minded that, when I wanted to bring some sword guys up from Toronto for one episode they wouldn't have it. This was Montreal, and they were fiercely independent. Yet for all of this, I loved my time there—Montreal is an amazing, multi-cultural city with lots of different influences and I was enjoying that—so I tried to keep out of the arguments as much as possible.

Finally, things came to a head during the filming of an episode called *The Victorian Candidate* (set up to echo the famous Frank Sinatra film, *The Manchurian Candidate*). Here, the character of Phileas Fogg literally loses his mind, having been brain-washed into trying to assassinate Queen Victoria. He ends up having a sword fight with his sister, Rebecca, played by Francesca Hunt, as well as every other lead in the show, and I had to choreograph it! It was inferred by production staff that this was a symbolic attempt to send a wake up call to Michael about his behavior.

I asked Ian Sharp what he wanted. He told me he wanted the fight to move around the room in a specific way. So one night after we had been rehearsing and Francesca had gone home, I had a stunt double standing in for her and wanted Michael to do a clockwise move so that the camera could follow them around the room the way Ian had requested. Michael made it clear that he did not want to do it that way. We stood there for maybe half an hour talking about it, and Michael kept asking why we didn't do it another way. I told him we were trying to do what Ian wanted. The argument with him went on and on and then he said, "Why isn't Francesca here to rehearse this? Why the stunt double?"

It was late in the evening and we had people waiting around for us to finish, but all we were doing was standing around arguing. So I said, "I'm going to call an end to this rehearsal, Michael." He turned to me in a rage and said, "Why are you such a coward? Why won't you talk about her?" There was an insinuation in this that I was somehow involved with Francesca—which was definitely not the case.

I had not told Michael that she was scared of him, which was the real reason she had left early, so I just said, "That's it, I'm done for the night, we'll come back to this tomorrow." To which he replied, "Are you cutting my rehearsal short?" I said, quite reasonably I thought, "It's not just your rehearsal, Michael, it's my rehearsal and the stunt guys' rehearsal as well."

At which point he started shouting that I couldn't do that. So I said, "Look, we have to be back here at seven tomorrow morning and it's eleven pm now. There is a turnaround and overtime issue for the drivers and other crew. We're finished for tonight."

As I was walking away there was another provocative confrontation as I packed up the swords and other props. Michael ran around me and blocked the doorway. There was then a childish challenge that shocked and saddened me. I decided I was at the end of the process and was no longer willing to be put in this position and I looked across to Michael's driver and said, "Would you please take Mr. Praed home because this rehearsal is over."

When he finally left I went straight up to my office, and wrote the first of what would be two letters of resignation. I told the producers this was only going to end one way. I had tried discussing things with Michael, tried to persuade him gently and reasonably, but it hadn't worked. I didn't know what else to do. I knew I would probably end up losing both my job and my friend. I did not want this to happen.

The producers contacted me the next morning and said, "You can't resign. You're the only person who has any kind of influence over Michael. He ignores the directors, he's undermining the other actors and now he's in the editing room wanting to edit the episodes—it's all crazy."

We met and talked and I told them I thought Michael had some control issues that had become compulsive, to the point of bullying everyone involved. They were still insisting I should not resign, so I asked them what they wanted me to do? They said, "Stay on. Handle this. We'll back you up. We'll be there on set."

It had reached the point where we had to have rehearsals with both the producers and directors present. I told Francesca how we were going to do the fight, but she was still nervous. Sure enough, during one of the rehearsals, Michael smacked her on the forehead with the sword. He changed what we had rehearsed and hit her. It was exactly what I had been worried about. She gamely agreed to carry on and the producers said I just had to try and manage Michael through this—we had to make it work!

Consequently, we were taking almost a day to shoot the big fight scenes. Somehow we managed to shoot everything, but I left at the end of each day feeling heartily sick in my soul, because I knew where it was all going. I think I stayed on for another month, and I remember working on one of the episodes that had John Rhys-Davis as guest star.

It got to the point where there was another incident, totally unrelated to any of this but with one of the other lead actors, who had a serious substance issue and had been the subject of concern for the producers. He had been up all night with Michael and some of the stunt guys and got loaded. He wrecked his trailer and I was somehow the focus of his anger. So, I resigned again.

This time the producers said, "This is all going sideways. Maybe it would be best if you went." So I left and spoke with them a couple of days later on the phone. They promised to work out a settlement for me—which they did. I knew they were worried about finishing the show, which at the time they had not sold. That was the sad thing about it. The show had a lot going for it. The production and sets were fantastic, and it was the first television show to use the cameras from the new *Star Wars* films—shooting in high definition digital format. But it wasn't enough to save it.

As part of my final personal agreement with the producers I helped them select and hire a new stunt and fight coordinator, making sure that the new hire was clear of any political and social links to the previous cabal and hoping he was strong and independent enough to maintain a neutral and professional position and not be bullied or cajoled into one individual camp.

Soon after my resignation, I talked to one of the producers and said I hoped he could get the show finished and sold, and I told him that I was sorry if my presence had caused problems. He said, "It wasn't you—and it has got worse since you left. Michael believes he got you fired and now he thinks he can tell everybody what to do." He added, "When we finish here it's done, it's over. There will be no more episodes, we will probably never sell this show and Michael will have to take some of the blame for that."

In some ways, this had been signposted earlier. I had become friends with Michael on *Robin of Sherwood*, but at the end of the day, he left the show in the lurch, announcing half way through the middle of the second season that he was leaving. This understandably made Kip Carpenter, who wrote the shows, very angry because it could easily have killed the series. Only Kip's brilliance as a writer and Jason Connery's screen presence saved it.

Michael was leaving to do a Broadway show called *The Three Musketeers*, and hadn't told anyone. He had flown to New York on Concord to audition at the weekend and flown straight back to continue filming *Robin* on Monday. The production company had not signed him for a third year contract, so he was free to go.

Kip was furious but wrote a final episode, *The Greatest Enemy*, which is one of the best episodes in the whole show, to accommodate Michael's leaving. I remember him coming to me saying he had an apology to make. He had written an episode for me—everyone had had his or her own episode and this was going to be mine—but because of Michael's departure he had to re-write it a different way. They compressed the story of the assassins, which would have explained more of the back story of my character, Nasir, into the opening few minutes of the episode, and the rest was about the death of Michael's Robin.

Kip wrote that episode and killed Robin of Loxley off. Then, by one of those slights of hand that are always amazing, he brought him back by suggesting that Robin Hood was an archetype that could manifest in any person. It was a stroke of genius. Robin returned in the shape of Jason, who played the character of Robert of Huntingdon to the end of the show.

Even after everything that had happened, we all wished Michael well. However, I had my doubts about this move to Broadway: I thought it was too early in his career. I believed he should have waited until he was really established in Britain as a leading man in a successful TV show, but instead he went off to do *Musketeers*.

I went to see it with Paul Knight and Kip Carpenter and it was awful—and so were the reviews. When you do a show on Broadway you do the first night, have the party, and then wait for the first reviews to come out just after midnight. If two or three of these reviews are bad, it means the show is done for—it won't last a week.

We stayed for the party. Michael had a table for his friends and the rest of us had their table. The first critics came in and they were very bad. People started to leave, and the old story of the band packing up and leaving actually happened. They were gone by quarter past midnight. Half the place was empty, and even the cast of the show had left; the only people remaining were we Brits. We sat there reading the notices, and one of them absolutely tore the show apart.

The show began with the entrance of a character on a horse, which rears up and then gallops off. This particular critic started off by saying that the only good thing about this show was that at least one performer—the horse—had the good sense to walk on, do its part and ride off, never to be seen again. He then tore everything apart: the costumes, the lighting—everything. Michael was playing D'Artagnan, the lead of the show, and he did not even get a mention until the last paragraph, which said, "And finally, Michael Praed as D'Artagnan is the black hole into which this show finally disappears".

Michael thought this was screamingly funny.

While we were all still in New York his agent got the offer of a part in *Dynasty*. At that point Paul and Kip had been talking about the possibility that if *Musketeers* was a flop Michael should still come back to *Robin*. Paul wanted him to come back, but Kip said, "I've killed him off. This Robin is not coming back." I believe there was some discussion with Michael's agent, but Kip was adamant, so Paul told Michael to go with whatever else he had been offered and he went to *Dynasty*.

After the sad events in Montreal I did not see Michael again for several years. When we met up in London recently at a wake to honor the memory of Kip, who died tragically in 2012, it was like talking to the same person he had been ten years before, and who genuinely believed in the righteousness of his own cause, and just did not want to be told differently. He still believed I had been fired from the show and was stunned when I explained some of the back-story, and that I had actually been trying to protect him.

I do not wish Michael any ill will—I put this story here because the fans of *Robin of Sherwood*, with which Michael will forever be associated, know about this already and have probably heard different sides of the story from different people. It was Michael who instigated the sit-down at Kip's wake. I would have been quite happy to leave it alone and greeted him like an old pal. As far as I'm concerned, karma has taken care of it.

Michael had the potential to be a big star. He had everything going for him; but he took some really bad advice, and in Montreal he let the demons out of the cage. The lesson for me was that this could happen to anyone. I witnessed the implosion of a friend's ego and control issues right in front of me and it was one of the saddest and most heart-wrenching events in my career. I lost a close friend to the "Monster from the Id." It was difficult to watch and deal with, and I wish I could have reached him. Sadly I could not. I took this as a life lesson, and I hope that if ever such a thing happens to me, someone will tell me in a way that I'll be able to hear and take a different path

8.
SWORDS, SONGS, AND SPARKLY DRESSES

"We're shooting outside! What do we need the lights for?"
- John Morrissey

Getting Back in the Game.

IN 1999 I PRESENTED a couple of workshops on *The Greenwood Tarot*, one at the late and much lamented Goddess Shop in L.A. (After the shop closed I was given a couple of custom built shelving units made for the store and used them as a bedroom bookcase and living room TV and VCR unit!) Ramona Reeves, one of the lovely ladies who ran the store, told me she was involved with an indie film and that the production might be looking for a fight and sword coordinator. I told her I was always open to new opportunities and that she should keep me in mind.

As things tend to happen in Tinsel Town, I almost immediately got a call from the film and theatre director Brad Mays, who was putting together the project. It was based on *The Bacchae*, an Ancient Greek tragedy by Euripides, and he wanted somebody to do the extensive fight sequences.

Brad's 1997 stage production of the play had been a surprise hit in L.A., drawing big audiences and earning excellent reviews. It was ultimately nominated for three *LA Weekly* awards. It had got people talking, not only for the use of full-frontal nudity—especially in scenes portraying ritualized pagan worship and the violent killing of one of the characters—but also for its use of movement and dance. An independent film seemed inevitable after the success of the stage production.

The idea fascinated me, so I said yes and headed up to the location where we intended to shoot, at a private ranch in Topanga Canyon. I went there with Brad and his lovely wife Lorenda Starfelt to look around. It had everything—a reflection pool, glades of trees and paths and a ridgeline we could film on—plenty of varied locations we could use in the film. Brad offered me the swordmaster job on the film, which I took; though my remit extended quickly to directing the second unit.

One of the things the film is still famous for is having a bunch of semi-naked girls in a huge sword fight. I had plenty of volunteers from the stunt community to be involved with this battle, but being mindful of reverence for the original play and the spiritual aspects of the whole *Bacchae* concept, Brad was very protective of it, as were the actors. So I gathered the sword-slingers and stunt guys together and said, "Look, these girls are running around semi-naked and maybe feeling pretty vulnerable. These are very intimate scenes, so I don't want any of the girls coming to me with a complaint. If anyone does anything inappropriate, they are off the picture." I had to say this because, literally, there were bare boobs and arses everywhere.

The girls were actually great about it all and really got into the fights, but very early on T.J. Ratolo, who was one of my main stunties and a good actor, came to me and said, "How are we doing this? No matter where you look there are breasts and everything all over the place. It's getting difficult to rehearse the fights." So I said, "Do what I always do and keep eye contact. Whenever you're talking to the girls, just look them in the eyes. Nowhere else."

T.J. went off and must have told everyone else what I had said, because for the next week, all you could see was stuntmen and sword guys almost eyeball to eyeball with the girls and glazed looks everywhere. Eventually T.J. came back and said, "It's not working." I had to admit he was right and that actually all the staring looked very strange and intimidating. So I said, "The other technique is to look up at the sky. Start with eye contact and then look up towards the sky and sort of look around as if taking in the set."

For the next few days we literally had stuntmen crashing into each other and tripping over things because in between keeping eye contact they would be looking up and around and anywhere but at the girls. It was very funny, but it didn't help.

At one point Robert "The Bob" Chapin, who was playing the lead swordsman, came over to me and said: "You know, we should write a book about this film—because nobody would believe the way things are going." He told me he had just heard the strangest thing. We had a lighting truck full of equipment at the location in the hills that was brought in by Kelly Molloy, who was acting as Unit Production Manager as a favor to the production. One of the producers, John Morrissey, had gone up there and said, "Why have we got this? What do we need it for?" Bob had said, "It's a film, John, we need lights." To which he got the classic reply, "We don't need lights! We're shooting outside. What do we need lights for? " I have never heard a producer say anything quite like this, but John actually sent the truck away. Even though you're shooting outside, in certain situations—under trees, background and shadows—you need lights. The book Bob and I were going to write, which never got done to my knowledge, was going to be called *We're Shooting Outside, What Do We Need The Lights For?*

In the final days of shooting I was given charge of the unit to shoot the big battle scene. I had just two days to do it. Everyone really did well for me. We shot a lot of good material that I am still proud of. I had cameras up trees to get overhead shots of the two sides coming together, and the fights all went really well. It looked good.

The high spot of this was a big whip and sword fight between "The Bob" and Melissa Hellman, the main female action lead. Thinking about it now, this was probably one of the best fights I've ever choreographed, helped greatly by Roberta Brown, who arranged the whip-work and polished the fight. I had first met Roberta in 1999 at a sword convention and we got together soon after. Melissa was a tall, athletic girl and they did this very sexy sword fight where Bob is trying to chop her up and keeps moving swiftly from side to side. Every time they get into a position where it looks like he's about to kill her, she kisses him or touches him or does something that completely phases him. It was really interesting to watch and very well done, and I was proud of it. Brad was very happy with it as well.

Towards the end, one of the stuntmen, Alex Van Amburg, a gentle giant who everybody liked, had to pretend to knock a girl about in the fight, and then one by one these little girls would run at him and smash him in the ribs, behind the knees and on the head, until eventually he was dragged down and beaten by this swarm of whirling and howling girls. I copied this idea later in *King Arthur* in the scene where Keira Knightley and her posse of girls pull down a huge Saxon warrior.

We did all kinds of stuff in that battle, including swords being thrown through the air—everything I could think of—and we finally got to this last shot, the last shot of the day, and I just let the girls beat big Alex for three or four minutes, until somebody—I don't know whether it was Bob or the stunt guy himself—called out, "Are you going to shout cut?" I said, "Not yet, I'm enjoying this way too much!"

It was a lot of fun making *The Bacchae*—though it has the reputation of being a "troubled" picture. The making of the film was unnecessarily complicated by some sidebar issues, but gathered a small cult following in the genre anyway. Whenever people talk about real L.A. independent "Guerrilla Filmmaking" *The Bacchae* gets mentioned.

After shooting wrapped there were some legal problems concerning the editing of the film, and it didn't see the light of day for some time. It did get a limited release eventually, but I don't know who saw it or reviewed it. I don't think I've actually seen a final cut of the film but I know Brad worked very hard to get it completed and released at festivals.

Once it was over I was established back in Los Angeles with a film credit, another swordmaster credit and a second unit director credit. I was very pleased and proud of the fights and the folks who did them.

Being Stabbed in the Chest (repeatedly) by Lucy Liu

In late 1999 Roberta got a job choreographing a fencing match on the big budget movie based on the TV show *Charlie's Angels*. It starred Cameron Diaz, Drew Barrymore and Lucy Liu. The film was being directed by Joseph McGinty (McG). The action and second unit was being coordinated by legendary stuntman Vic Armstrong of *Raiders of the Lost Ark* and *James Bond* fame, ably assisted his brother Andy. The opening sequence called for Lucy Liu to be seen fencing fast and furiously with a male opponent; Roberta would double Lucy for the complex fencing parts and I would be the opponent.

We had discussed what could go wrong on set with swords and how to make the scene visually interesting (which modern fencing usually isn't) while still being technically correct. After working on various moves and counter moves we settled on several routines and moves to show Andy Armstrong. Then McG came along to observe and all the preparation went out the window. He wanted something very simple and pretty slapstick, and Roberta had to rush off to put on her chest protector. I was wearing a standard white fencing jacket, and thought the thick chest padding would be enough protection if I needed to take a hit… Or even several hits.

What I hadn't accounted for was the idea that what was really required was Lucy to actually bend her blade on my chest so the hit looked very comic-book-like, and that it would be repeated over and over again until the chosen arching of the blade was captured on film! We shot the reverse with Roberta doing the slap-stick moves and then Lucy stepped in to deliver the final hit on my chest before flamboyantly removing her fencing mask and tossing her beautiful hair in the golden sunlight!

We did this at least two dozen or more times and Lucy didn't hold back, firmly driving the point of her epee into my chest and bending the steel until the blade arched artistically into a classic fencing pose. This is much easier, of course, with a lighter foil blade, but we weren't using one. We finally got the shot and I went to get released and then changed. At that juncture I only noticed a general soreness and ache in my now battered pectoral muscles.

Over the next couple of days however, many deep blue points of bruising started to appear on my chest until I looked like a human pincushion! A couple of days later, while changing for a sword training session, my pals wanted to know how the hell I had acquired the now lurid purple pinpoints of bruising on my chest. I casually explained that Lucy Liu had given me the multiple chest contusions in the heat of the moment.

Not many "swordslingers" can claim that.

Touring with a Python

After this, while I was hovering about L.A. not sure what to do, I got a call one Friday afternoon from my then-agent, Brian McCabe. He told me that famed Monty Python star, Eric Idle, wanted to meet me the next day. Brian said he didn't know exactly what the show was about—it was confidential—but Eric obviously knew who I was and wanted to meet for a chat. The next day was Saturday, which is an unusual day to meet up for a professional job, but I went along to the Hudson Theatre on Sunset Boulevard, and when I walked in there were Eric Idle and the composer John Du Prez. Before I had even chance to speak, Eric looked at me and said, "Mark! I didn't realize you were a Yorkshireman. We can do the Four Yorkshire Men sketch!"

So just like that, and without a word of explanation, we went into the famous sketch. We just started with the famous line, "We used to live a shoebox in't middle of't road…" After that Eric wanted me to have a look at a couple of songs he thought I might not know—one of them being the now famous Always Look On The Bright Side Of Life. John played the piano and I sang. I followed it up with Brave, Brave Sir Robin from *Monty Python and The Holy Grail*. Eric smiled and thanked me for coming in and said he would be in touch.

I left wondering what on earth it had all been about! No one had actually given me any real details; they just asked me to sing and that was it. The next day (Sunday) the phone rang and Eric's then assistant Samantha Harris asked me if I wanted to go on tour with him! I told her I wasn't sure exactly sure what I'd auditioned for and she explained the show was called *Eric Idle Exploits Monty Python* and that basically there would be me, Peter Crabbe, Eric, herself and two other girls in the show. John Du Prez would be running the band and everyone would be playing different roles taken from classic *Python* skits and new material written by Eric.

Samantha told me that we would be starting at the Universal Amphitheatre in L.A., touring the west coast, San Francisco, Seattle, down to the Midwest, through Chicago and back up to Canada, where we would play Vancouver, Toronto and Montreal. The whole thing would end up at Carnegie Hall for two shows, possibly followed by a final one at no lesser venue than the Hollywood Bowl.

It took me a few moments to take in what Samantha had said. I was hardly going to say no to this, so I said I'd do it. First thing Monday morning I got a contract to go on tour all over America with Eric Idle.

We ended up touring for five months and I had one of the most memorable experiences of my career. We started with warm-up shows in Phoenix and Tucson, and then returned to L.A. for shows in Anaheim and at the Universal Amphitheatre. We then set off on the western leg of the tour performing in Salt Lake City, Portland, Vancouver, Seattle, San Francisco and Sacramento. Everywhere we went the audiences were enthusiastic and often ecstatic.

In San Francisco, the late, much missed Robin Williams threw an amazing party for us, which also included a glittering crowd of Hollywood elite. At one point in the proceedings Eric introduced me to two gentlemen, George and Francis. After a while I realized one of the men I was talking to was George Lucas. As we chatted I told him that I had worked with Bob Anderson and what a gentleman he was. George looked at me as if he had no idea what I was talking about, so I went into detail about Bob and *Star Wars* and lightsabers. Still, George looked confused. Eric looked at me as if to say, *you're on your own*, and so I started talking about my friendship with the great stunt guy Martin Grace. George looked even more confused and obviously had no clue who Martin was! As I started explaining about Martin's famous stunt work on *Raiders of the Lost Ark,* Eric looked at me, shook his head and headed for the bar.

At this point there was an awkward silence and Francis also headed for the bar. George looked at me conspiratorially and whispered, "What's it really like being on the stage with Eric Idle?" I leaned in close and whispered, "Fucking surreal!" George smiled broadly and slapped me on the back.

He was just about to utter another comment when Francis, whom I had finally realized was none other than Francis Ford Coppola, broke back into the group and grabbed George saying, "Eric's buying! Quick! Let's get some champagne!" So the only thing I ever got to say to George Lucas, or that he actually responded to was, "fucking surreal" before Francis Ford Coppola interrupted me! I'm not sure what that says about me as a raconteur, but I told Eric the story the next night before the show and he was very chuffed at being revered by these two Hollywood legends. I'm still not sure why George Lucas seemed to remember nothing about

Bob Anderson and Martin Grace, but there you are.

We were treated really well wherever we went on the tour and hit just about every major theatre in the country. Eric was very kind to me, giving me a lot of new material to perform such as "I'm a Man," wearing an ill-fitting toupee, a blue frilly shirt and very tight, vinyl leopard-skin pants. We also performed classic Monty Python skits including the famous *Spanish Inquisition* and *Nudge-Nudge, Wink-Wink* sketches, which Eric and I did together at most venues. It was great fun and Eric was very good to work with. Peter Crabbe remains a friend to this day. There were several times when great comedy stars like Robin Williams, Steve Martin and Tim Allen joined us, sometimes just getting up on the stage and joining in—all wanting to be a Lumberjack or a Mountie!

At Carnegie Hall, Art Garfunkel joined us on stage and took the lead singing Always Look On The Bright Side Of Life. I looked across the stage and thought, *You look familiar, but you're not supposed to be in this song!* Terry Jones made an on-stage appearance, and Salman Rushdie and Eddie Izzard both showed up.

Eric had been adamant that he would have us all in frocks by the end of the tour, and Peter in particular was very enthusiastic about getting into ladies' underwear. I should mention that he's six foot six tall with a shaved head and goatee and looks a bit like "Stone Cold" Steve Austin the wrestler. But he could do the heels, which is more than I could. I couldn't even stand up in them!

During the tour we decided that we were going to do a send up of country and western singers with Eric calling himself Dolly Taylor. We called ourselves Wynonna and Wyessa, and Eric decided we should all be in frocks for this. Eric had a red sparkly frock and Peter and I had green sparkly frocks. I have to say I was probably the ugliest looking woman you've ever seen.

My eldest son Daniel and his girlfriend came to see the show in New York, and at the end of sitting through two hours of Monty Python, we all went for a meal. I remember him saying, "One of the greatest gifts a father can give his son is seeing him in a green sparkly dress on the stage of Carnegie Hall, singing "Sit On My Face And Tell Me That You Love Me." He was not sure he would ever be able to get that image out of his head.

It's a source of great personal pride that not only did I get to perform on the stage at Carnegie Hall, but that I was one of only three men who ever dressed in a green sparkly dress to perform on that stage. It remains one of my major claims to fame, along with getting the word "bollocks" into the *Transformers* lexicon and the fact that I still own the record for killing the most people in one hour of family viewing in the U.K., in an episode of *Robin of Sherwood*.

When we returned to Los Angeles Eric invited us to join him at a special performance at The Hollywood Bowl. He was being inducted into the Hall of Fame at the famous venue where he had performed with The Pythons in 1982. At the show Bonnie Raitt would also be performing, and Stevie Wonder would be topping the bill. We would be singing a medley of Eric's famous Monty Python songs, excluding "Sit On Face And Tell Me That You Love Me," as someone from the Los Angeles Philharmonic thought it was inappropriate.

Robin Williams opened for us and introduced Eric to an ecstatic and sold out Hollywood Bowl audience. As usual he was screamingly funny and in brilliant comedic form, his energy and manic creative genius in full flow. As we finished the medley and marched off the stage to thunderous applause we all sang *a cappella* the forbidden "Sit On My Face." Unfortunately it was unheard by the crowd as our microphones had been turned off.

It was wonderful to be asked by Eric to share a stage with him once again and I was very proud and pleased to be involved in honoring his amazing and unique talent.

From 1776 to 9/11

As soon as the Python tour was over, I came back to L.A. and auditioned for the part of John Dickinson in the musical *1776*, which I landed. This classic, Tony Award winning American musical was based on the story of the Declaration of Independence. It had one of the longest dialogue sequences in any musical, driven by Dickenson and John Adams, played by RSC member Roger Reese in this production. Roger and I got on very well, and I really enjoyed the intense interaction of our verbal battles during the show. Also in the cast was Orson Bean, a legend of American TV, film and theatre. Orson was a gem to work with—quietly funny with a wry and ironic sense of humor, which was often needed when trying to work with director Gordon Hunt's limited comedic range. This was so bad that we nicknamed some of the direction "Gordon's Book of Comedy."

For some reason that I never understood, Hunt, who was the father of Helen Hunt, decided he didn't like anything I did, and made it obvious to the cast that he didn't like the way I played the part. This added even more stress to a situation where Roger and I had a lot of dialogue to deliver while fending off the intense scrutiny of the director. At one point I toyed with quitting the show entirely, because it was obvious I wasn't giving Gordon what he wanted. However, because there were no understudies and only two weeks to stage and learn the show, it would have been unfair to the cast and producers, Marcia Selegson and Ronn Goswick, who were both lovely people; so I decided to stay.

On the opening night Gordon had me repeatedly going over the big speeches in the front of house because he wanted it more charming and gentile. I don't remember how many times we went over it, but by the time I was done I was totally addled and despondent. We ended this final and confrontational coaching session with angry words exchanged between us. I was left struggling to regain my self-confidence and focus on what was going to be a tough evening on the L.A. stage, without thinking about the angry little man barking like an arse-stung whippet and whining constantly.

I stood at the side of the stage before curtain up and Roger came to see how I was doing. The entire cast knew what had happened and Roger was supportive and I soon rediscovered my sense of humor as we decided to hide every time Gordon came backstage. We actually did this several times so Gordon couldn't deliver any more of his comedy and dialogue notes as they only confused and distracted us. The show is so well written it really doesn't need polishing or embellishing. Maybe that was the problem.

The cast kindly came up with several curious explanations for Gordon's unnecessary pressure. It was even suggested that it was all about Peter Hunt (Gordon's half brother who directed the Broadway, Tony winning production of the show) and how he wanted to prove himself equal to the challenge. He could hardly mess with Orson or Roger, so I was next in line.

What should have been an enjoyable rehearsal period turned into a nightmarish and artistically frustrating two weeks and, in the end, I just wanted to get through the run and get on with my life without further directorial attention from "The Gordon," which, unbeknownst to Hunt, became the label (based on Cockney rhyming slang) for him during the remainder of the production. Roger and I continued to hide backstage like naughty schoolboys every time he came in to give notes.

On the other hand Peter Matz, who also worked with Barbra Streisand, Noel Coward and Marlene Dietrich and passed away in August 2002, was Musical Director. Peter was a gentleman and a true professional, as was Kay Cole, the long suffering choreographer who patiently got me to walk in step with the other "Cool, Cool Men," even though the song wasn't my favorite in the show and had been cut from the movie because of it's right-wing and somewhat fascist leanings. Kay continued to work with us in a manner that got us all goose-stepping and singing in time as the finale of the first act.

Once we opened, things settled down and we got into a well-oiled performance rhythm. The notices were posted and were, for the most part, good for this type of staged revival. Working with Peter, Roger, Orson and the amazing cast were the redeeming elements of this entire production and I began to really enjoy the individual performances.

Then it happened...

It was early on a Tuesday morning when the phone rang at around six-thirty in the morning. We had not performed *1776* the previous night because it is customary in L.A. stage productions for Monday to be dark. Somewhere in the back of my sleepy mind I heard the voice of my old friend Mike Grell on my voicemail saying I should to get up and switch on the TV. The World Trade Center had been attacked and it looked like an act of terrorism. He wanted me to turn on the TV right away.

I must have drifted back off to sleep for a while, but a voice in the back of my head told me Mike wouldn't have called unless it was important. I suddenly thought he might be in trouble so I crawled out of bed and listened to Mike's serious and urgent message.

Then I switched on the TV and tuned to CNN.

It took time for what was happening to sink in. By this time both the Twin Towers had been hit, and then news of the attack on the Pentagon was coming in. Coverage was switching back and forth between New

York and Washington, D.C. Throughout the day, as the horrific details of the 9/11 attack unfolded, I bounced though all the TV news sources with disbelief. Very early on, as the film of the second tower falling was played over and over, I remembered with shock that I had eerily considered this very scenario during the early nineties.

Sometime in 1991, I wrote a scenario for a novel called *The Asset*, which I gave to my then literary agent, Barbara Levy. I don't know if she even read it because when I contacted her sometime later, having written it on my old Atari computer, and being unable translate it into a new format Barbara couldn't find it.

In the storyline, Saddam Hussein hires a professional group of terrorists based in Afghanistan to attack the United States in revenge for his defeat by the Coalition forces gathered by George H.W. Bush's administration in 1990. I had explored the idea of Saddam attacking the World Trade Center with a commercial aircraft, but didn't think it was a viable plot because I believed that there would be strict air traffic control over New York and Combat Air Patrols (CAP) and fighter cover if a rogue aircraft was hijacked and tracked on RADAR heading directly for Manhattan at high speed and low altitude.

I didn't have suicide bombers in the story, but I had been to Washington D.C. and was aware that Dulles Airport was a few miles west of the Pentagon. In my scenario a hijacked 747 cargo aircraft, carrying a modified shipment of fuel-air explosives, was flown to Washington. The terrorists then dispersed the special explosives undetected over the Pentagon and detonated it, flattening the building and making their escape in the confusion and fog of war.

The idea of attacking the Pentagon and other public buildings, using commercial airliners as weapons, had been discussed between various elements when I was in the Intelligence Corps. I remember that we discussed what our role would be now that the Berlin Wall had come down. We were already beginning to do joint exercises with the Russians, and knew that now the Cold War was officially over, professional and radical terrorist organizations were going to be one of the next big international problems the world would have to face.

With the growing financial muscle and ruthlessness of South America narco-terrorist groups and drug dealers, corrupt political powerbrokers and politicians too corrupt or fearful to resist, it could lead to the takeover of a whole country, causing a lot of people some serious trouble.

People smuggling was also becoming a huge business, as was the issue of "black money," the product of various illegal activities flowing through the banking system. Counterfeit money was also discussed. It was known that the Iranians were printing $100 bills that were just as good as those the Federal Reserve was printing, and it was feared this would destabilize the world economy. Astonishingly, the Americans had given printing presses, paper and ink to the Shah of Iran so that he could print his own $100 bills. After he fell from power, Iran was quite happy to continue printing bills by the billion. It is rumored there are still banks holding substantial reserves of this funny money that were actually not printed by the Federal Reserve, but by the Iranians.

An ex-member of the U.S. Secret Service, whose job it was to hunt down counterfeit money—because after guarding the President they are charged with guarding the currency—confirmed the story to me. I even talked to one of the Secret Service agents who were sent to Iran to try and get a handle on the situation. He added that not many people knew about this strange story, and that even if they did, nobody really believed it.

All of this Iranian skullduggery happened well before 9/11. But this was definitely a chilling and profound new paradigm in mass terror and the destruction of innocent human life as an act of revenge. As I watched the unfolding horror with a deep foreboding of what was to come, I realized, as did most people riveted to the TV coverage that day, that the world had just changed forever.

I called Mike Grell back and we spoke briefly, too shocked to really comprehend what was happening. It soon became clear that the place where I had once stood with my brother in 1979, looking out over New York from the viewing platform atop the World Trade Center, was gone. It seemed impossible.

I called my pal Jay Larkin, who lived in New York, but the cell phone network was jammed. I left a message for him at home on his family voicemail and asked him to call me back. I attempted to call various other N.Y. pals but could not get through.

Later in the day I received a call from the *1776* producers saying we would obviously not perform that evening but would probably open the following night and perform the show. While still stunned by the images flowing through the cable news outlets, I understood that this was probably going to be one of the most important performances of my career. *1776* was a show that underscored the complexity and stoical resolution of the American people, and it was going to have a far deeper reach and profound meaning than ever before.

As I stood on my balcony in L.A., listening to the chillingly eerie silence, made even more surreal because of my proximity to Bob Hope Airport, I realized this was a fight, one way or the other, that I was probably not going to avoid, even if I wanted to. In fact I didn't want to avoid it. If my new homeland needed anything that I could provide, I would volunteer to serve in any capacity I could. For now all I could do was watch in deep sympathy for those lost and pray for those who might never be found.

That night, after several concerned and personal calls from family, friends and colleagues and various conversations with contacts, an uneasy night's sleep was haunted by thoughts of people jumping to their deaths to avoid the flames and smoke in the towers. This thought alone was grim enough and terrible to comprehend. I believe America went into a collective state of psychogenic shock as the cold-blooded facts unfolded numbingly on our screens. I knew we were at war and I knew it was going to get bloody.

The next day, as I drove to the Ralph Freud Playhouse on the UCLA campus, I steeled myself for what was to come. The main dressing room, which all the male cast shared, was quiet and focused. We were all in shock. The auditorium was about one fifth filled with scattered, shocked and still faces as we slowly worked out way through the dialogue about New York and the arguments about democracy and responses to the threat of losing it. Slowly the audience began to respond and we got the odd, awkward laugh at the terrible irony of the show's dramatic core.

At the end of the performance, as we sat in our individual worlds and absorbed what had just happened, Stuart Pankin, who played Samuel Chase in the show, asked me what I thought would come next. Without thinking I responded, "Afghanistan and then Iraq." Stuart looked at me and said, "What will you do? What about your son Daniel?" He knew that Daniel had followed me into the military. I answered, "I don't know what

Daniel will do. He's had enough of the military anyway, but I'll call the British Embassy in Washington tomorrow and find out what the situation is."

As we sat there, still and quiet, it became clear that some folks had friends and family in the audience that night, and we all gathered in the small atrium next to the theatre entrance. Somewhere in the crowd someone started singing "God Bless America," and within seconds more voices joined in.

There, in the lonely and quiet stillness of a ghostly, abandoned UCLA campus, a growing and haunting chorus grew and rang across that still surreal evening. I found myself filled with overwhelming emotion as we joined as human beings and sang in faltering, trembling voices. It was one of the most moving and profound events of my life and I knew that a new chapter had begun, both in my life and that of my adopted country.

After speaking to a representative at the British Embassy in D.C., I was informed that no decisions had been made yet as to the mobilization of U.K. ex-servicemen with reserve status and clearances. I had a conversation the following week with some colleagues from the Chameleon Group, who informed me that thirteen of the nineteen hijackers were picked out by CAPPS (Computer Assisted Passenger Pre-screening System I) but were still allowed to get on the planes. One even had no picture ID of any kind. It was a stunning and chilling admission of incompetence, or conspiracy in my view, and a foreshadowing of more involvement with the intelligence world.

I've often wondered what really went on in that strange time. There was so much that took another three to four years to come out in the 9/11 Commission Report. It's known, for example, that all the members of the Bin Laden family that remained in the United States were rounded up, put on a jet and flown out of the country the next day—without being questioned, interrogated, debriefed or anything. It was the only plane that flew on that day, and Dick Cheney authorized it.

That still seems way too strange to me.

9.
PRIVATE INVESTIGATIONS

"When you have eliminated the impossible, whatever remains, however improbable, must be the truth."
~ Sir Arthur Conan Doyle

A Case of Cartels.

FOR THE PAST TWELVE YEARS I've been the proud owner of a California Private Investigators License. During all that time, and interspersed between acting and writing commitments, I've worked in the many various and eclectic areas of investigation specializing in human intelligence, corporate security and threat analysis. It's encompassed counter-terrorism, gang-related homicides, organized criminal casino scams, multi-million dollar New York art frauds and the secret smuggling bridge-wire detonators used in nuclear weapons.

I've seen every aspect of human folly, greed, cruelty and deceit, and also many acts of courage, moral clarity, empathy and altruism. Though I can't tell all of the stories for reasons that will be obvious, I've collected some here to give an idea of the kind of work being a licensed PI involves.

This all began back in 1999. The ink was still wet on my divorce papers, and I had just returned from Montreal and *The Secret Adventures of Jules Verne*. I weighed my options and seriously considered returning to the U.K. Circumstance and opportunity offered a road less travelled, and once again I decided to strike out down that path.

I was talking on the phone with a friend, respected Hollywood actor Michael Monks, and when he heard that I was thinking of heading for home he said, "Why don't you stay on for a year? You've got a Green Card. You're a member of SAG and you've got good contacts here. Don't go back to the U.K. Stay in California and see what happens." At that point, I had nothing to lose. I felt like a blank sheet of paper. I had some cash from my work in Canada. L.A. would be a new challenge. I'd had twenty good years in London, but I had also moved on from that life so I thought, *Okay! Bring it on.*

Once again the universe saw the vacuum and decided to fill it. That was when I got a call from my friend Kelly Molloy who introduced me to Merritt Rex.

Some of the strangest jobs I have ever done are because of Rex. He trained with the ex-SAS Close Quarter Battle and Heckler and Koch MP-5 expert, Phil Singleton. He then trained with S.W.A.T. units (Special Weapons and Tactics) in L.A. We also had a mutual friend in Chicago, and when I was introduced to Rex we got on like a house on fire. He's a full-blown, bull-and-bike-riding, Wild-West-cowboy gun-nut; and also one of the funniest people I've ever met. He has several claims to fame—one that the Mexican Mafia had a "hit" out on him for years and painted his picture on a wall, complete with droopy 'tache and a notice to shoot on sight. The other was that he has unfortunately had to end more hostage shoot-outs using deadly force than anyone else I know.

Walter McKinney, who was to become my other regular investigations partner, and who was a Police Chief at Desert Hot Springs and various other CA locations, would talk about Rex's bull-in-a-china-shop tactics, "Rex is a nut. He can be crazy all right—but he's our kind of crazy." I've done two drive-alongs with Rex in Desert Hot Springs. This is where you sit with an officer and drive around a criminal war zone: both were colorful and unforgettable experiences.

Rex is a serious officer indeed, but also an incredibly funny, loyal and dedicated man. He's been both my business partner and my partner in the field, and has many times displayed a very dark sense of humor. One of his dogs, Iggy, a French Malinois, was well known for reputedly killing an armed assailant while in a deadly hostage situation. In fact, if Iggy was here now he might be lying quietly at your feet, looking at you, gentle as a lamb; but if you ran off he would be after you immediately. The great thing was that you always had to speak French to him because he only understood that language. To hear Rex talking French to a dog was hysterical. I used to joke about it all the time. These days he has a new dog, Roy. If you send Roy after somebody, he's going to bring something back—an arm, a leg—something. This dog will hurt people: it's what he's trained to do.

So, when Rex phoned me up and asked if I was looking for some work (by which he meant investigation and security work) my initial reply was no. In fact I told him I was retired from all that. He ignored what I said, and told me he was working for a company who mainly took care of worker's compensation surveillance. There was one specific a job that he thought was right up my alley. He explained that it involved money laundering and corporate blackmail.

I thought about it for about a minute,—and then said, "Okay,"—wondering all the while what I was getting myself into.

Adventures with Mr. X

Rex introduced me to a private investigator called "Theodore," for whom I did many investigations in those early years. Theodore had a case involving Daniel Petrocelli, who had been the lead lawyer in the civil case against O.J. Simpson. He explained the situation to me. Basically, the company they were working for had banking relationships with Mexico and Columbia, and they believed that one of their employees had cyber-attacked and mailshot the company, implying that they were laundering money for the Colombian cartels and Mexican mafia. Whoever had done this had done it quite cleverly, putting out mail and leaving no fingerprints or DNA on the paperwork.

Theodore asked me how I would approach it. I told him I would start by looking at three people who had been recently fired from the company, any one of whom could be the guilty party. I said that I would study their profiles, then take the "blunt instrument approach" and go straight to them, not as myself, but under the alias Michael Roberts—acting again! Theodore agreed; I was given the three profiles and put them all under surveillance.

There was one profile that stuck out. The guy (let's call him "Mr.

X," as in all the best PI stories!) apparently claimed that his father was in the CIA. We couldn't confirm this one way or the other, but the fact that he said it suggested a certain personality-type: someone who liked to be seen as important. I thought he was the mostly likely candidate, and that I might be able to get him to confess to what he'd done. So I got in touch with some old friends in the U.K. I had some fake letterheads and business cards made up using the false name so that I could pose as a journalist and researcher working for the *London Financial Times*.

Building a "legend" like this is usually a slow process that takes time and experience, but I'd done it so many times I knew that details that were critical to getting away with it; so I made sure that everything looked right.

I called the suspect, introducing myself as "Michael Roberts, financial researcher" and said, "I've got some information about this bank that I believe has been involved in money laundering. I'd like to talk to you about it because I've been told by someone that you might be willing to see me." Of course he asked me who it was that has said this; I told him I couldn't say, but that he would probably know whom. Of course I was bluffing, but I knew that I'd got his interest because he said he would think about it and that he needed time to check that I was really who I said I was.

I gave him a couple of references. One was to my old friend and ex-SBS, ex-spook, Brian Hamilton, whom I knew would confirm my cover. In addition I also got several others, including the American journalist Anne Moore, to confirm my cover story.

Two weeks went by, and then Mr. X called me and agreed to meet. We went to a coffee shop in Long Beach. I had paperwork in a file to help build my cover some more. Building cover is like a magician creating an illusion: it's called misdirection. While you look one way, you are directing the audience to look in another direction. In this case, the guy saw that I had financial, consultant-type paperwork and business cards. It was all misdirection, but it sold the cover story. I even went to the bathroom and left him alone to look through the sanitized materials on the table so he could look through them unobserved and see what I wanted him to see, the paperwork and other business trappings of a professional, financial media researcher.

I talked about England a lot; convincing him I had come all the way to the U.S. to research a particular company, the Olivia Corporation. After about three hours I had him convinced.

I should mention at this point that I wasn't doing this alone. There were other people with me, hiding nearby in case this guy lost it and tried to kill me. Because, although I still had no clear idea who or what I was dealing with, something had happened before the meeting that set off alarm bells.

One name on the company records had jumped out at me, Gustavo de Grieff, the name of the one-time Attorney General of Colombia. Roberta, my girlfriend at the time, happened to be in Bogotá, and while she was there had visited the UN offices where one of her relatives worked. Just before the meeting with Mr. X took place, Roberta called me. When I found out where she was I asked if she could find out anything about de Grieff. She did some research and called me back. There was a Gustavo de Grieff Sr., who had ordered the hunting and jailing of Pablo Escobar when he was the Attorney General of Colombia. He was now the Colombian Ambassador to Mexico. She thought one of the names I had given her, "Tutavo," might be connected to the case and was possibly a relative of Gustavo de Grieff.

I briefed the lawyers on this, and they asked what I thought about it. I believed there were three possibilities. One was that Mr. X had been planted by the DEA (Drugs Enforcement Administration) or DOJ (Department of Justice) to penetrate the organization, and that he had just gone "tilt" and decided to attack them. Two, that he might be an individual with personal reasons for doing what he did. Or three, what we had heard was true and that the whole thing was a money-laundering set-up linked to the Mexican and Columbian cartels. I was instructed to carry on and attend a meeting with Mr. X if I could arrange it.

So there I was talking to Mr. X face-to-face and he had some papers that he kept playing with. He was very, very cautious, but Theodore was hiding nearby with a load of high-tech surveillance equipment, filming and recording everything. A couple of other guys, including Rex, were there in case something went wrong. We were all very wary and on edge.

Sometimes the best way to get something out of someone is to show absolutely no interest in what it is they want to tell you. I could see that he wanted to tell me something, so I just kept talking until he couldn't help himself any longer.

Eventually, after three hours of drinking coffee and talking about various issues, he said, "I wasn't going to give you this, but I think you should put it in your article." He gave me a piece of paper that contained the exact wording of the document that was on the Internet; literally word for word. All he had done was change the typeface and layout. I went to famed lawyer, Daniel Petrocelli with this new evidence as he was the lead legal advisor on the investigation, and he said he thought we could make a case with this new paperwork.

Daniel Petrocelli is the formidable legal brain that had won the financial settlement against O.J Simpson for the Goldman family of $8.5 million in damages for the wrongful death of Ron Goldman. I was in no doubt Petrocelli could make a case and win it with this devastating piece of the puzzle.

The next day, Mr. X was presented with a subpoena and appeared at the Santa Monica Court House. I was outside, sitting in a car with a .38 Special + P Titanium Smith & Wesson Air-Lite revolver sitting next to me, wondering what would happen next. Theodore went in to bask in the reflected glory of Daniel Petrocelli's brilliant explanation of the case for damages against Mr. X to the judge and we had a surveillance team outside to see what Mr. X would do afterwards, just in case he decided to meet others.

This is where the seeds of how I came to have a PI license were planted. I had called Theodore that morning to tell him that I was done with it all because I was sure he would get me killed. If Mr. X spotted me anywhere in the vicinity of the courthouse he would know I was part of the case against him. My cover and all my U.K. contacts would be blown and who knew what he might do for revenge! This didn't seem to worry Theodore in the least and he insisted I lead the surveillance operation outside the courthouse, focused in the parking lot and in close proximity to where the case would be heard.

I sat in the lot and watched Mr. X come out and go to his car, where he sat for a while. I could see he was shocked. The judge had just told him that he had been served with a subpoena for a lifetime retribution order and that he had better get himself a lawyer because he was either going to prison, or was facing bankruptcy. He knew he had been trapped, and he must have known that I was the one who had done it. I watched and waited to see what he would do. Then, Theodore called me on the cell phone and I could see him walking across the car park calling, "Where are you?"

Theodore is a six foot four inches tall, three hundred pound man, whom you really can't miss. So I called him on the cell and said, "Theodore, you're standing about six feet away from Mr. X!" Theodore yelled loudly, "Where?" Then he called out, "Tell me where *you* are?" I said, really, really quietly, "Theodore, I'm in my car. If you just look left you'll see me but don't look!" Of course he called out, "Where? Oh, over there in the red car, I see."

By this time the whole notion of a quiet, covert surveillance was out the window. There I was looking at the guy I'd interviewed, wondering if he was armed. I knew I had probably just destroyed his life, and that he knew it. Then there were the bad guys, the ones he was probably be working for, or worse that *we* might be working for. I had no idea whether they would kill the guy or, for that matter, come after me. So, there I sat, thinking that this could all go horribly wrong, and there was Theodore in the middle of the parking lot shouting, "Oh, I see you—in the red car next to the blue car!" He actually said I should get out so that he could see me, and I was thinking the only reason I would get out of my car was to shoot Theodore!

Anyway, I did manage to creep out of the back of the car and tried to indicate to Theodore that he was very close to Mr. X, who could both see and hear him and now knew where I was. Mr. X got out of his car and walked over to me. He called over and said he just wanted to talk and I called back that I couldn't. I told him not to come any closer. "Just turn around, get in your car, and go home."

He said something like: "Well done. That was amazing!" I was backing away from him, trying to put Theodore between him and me, because if he was going to pull out a gun and open fire, I preferred that Theodore's three hundred pound bulk was between the subject and myself and that he would catch a bullet first and buy me time to return fire!

I managed to maneuver myself around so that I had some cover, and after a moment or two Mr. X turned away, got in his car and left. After that everyone was extremely happy with me. By going straight to the source as I had—challenging him, letting him respond and luring him into giving the evidence we needed—it had taken less than three weeks from the beginning of the job to actually get the guy into court. Sometimes the blunt-instrument, head-on approach beats all the forensic scenarios, which could have taken months.

Pulling off this case was what really kicked off my other life again. Suddenly I was in a world of guns and bad guys of the kind you'd normally only expect to meet in movies. Roberta, who had helped by getting me information about Gustavo de Grieff, was not happy about this. Some of her family are Jewish and come from Rhode Island, and some are from Colombia and live in Bogota, which is why she was there when the investigation was going on. I was carrying a weapon most of the time after this because I knew the situation could be dangerous, although I also knew that Roberta did not like having weapons in her house. We had discussed it, and I understood her point of view; but I had been around weapons for a long time. I had shot with a bow since I was fifteen years old, and have been around swords and firearms most of my life. It's something I understood and was very comfortable with, so for the time being we had agreed to disagree.

I'd like to make it very clear at this point that I'm not a gun nut. There are enough of those around already and I'm not one of them. Nevertheless I've always believed in the concept of creating your own reality and trying to live in a positive way, and since I was very young I've thought that whatever power and strength you have, you have to use it for what you understand to be justice. All my close friends to this day have the same philosophical outlook, which is don't do anybody harm if you can avoid it and do good if at all possible; but if you can't avoid injury, or there are others in harms way, do what you have to do and do it quickly.

I've always felt that sometimes the wolf must guard the sheep, but the ability to step in and out of shadow and light takes its toll. I have been able to take this stance all my life. I don't hate anybody, but I've always had a very clear sense of justice, which is why I want to tell the story of what happened next, because it's one of the most shocking parts of my life, and there is a lesson in it.

When Roberta came back from Bogota and asked what had I been doing. I said, "I've been doing a job for the Colombians, depending on which way you look at it." I could see she was unhappy, and then she told me that the American Post Office had just ripped open all her birthday presents. She had mail coming from Bogota, and gift packages that were clumsily taped together after very obviously being ransacked. Now she wondered if it could have anything to do with me asking her about Gustavo de Grieff.

I admitted it could be, indeed that it probably was, and that was the beginning of a downward slope in that relationship, along with the issue of me having a firearm around during the aftermath of the case. Because of that situation I often travelled with a firearm, and that was something Roberta simply did not want to live with.

When I was at her apartment one evening, something else happened which caused a further stress. In those days, when your voicemail was received, you would dial your own number, put in a code, and listen to your messages down the phone. I called my home number, and found myself wondering why all the messages were for Roberta and not me. I felt instinctively there was something wrong with this, and asked Roberta, who taught theatrical fencing, if she had got any messages about her work. She played all the messages on her machine, and found she had mine. Somehow all her telephone messages had got transferred onto my machine and vice versa. There was only one way that could have happened: somebody was listening to our phone calls and somehow had mixed-up her voice-mail machine and mine.

I made the mistake of saying, "I think you should listen to this." I gave her the phone and she listened to her messages on my cell phone and asked, "Are they listening to everything we're saying?" I said, "Probably." To me that was normal and I accepted that they were probably bugging my e-mails as well. You just have to be careful. If there is something you don't want them to know, don't say it.

This cost me my relationship with Roberta. I guess it was inevitable. Roberta was a nice, normal, sword-and-whip-wielding, Jewish-Colombian magician's assistant from Rhode Island, but she hadn't signed up for this!

Guns, drugs, gangsters, telephone wiretaps and nightmares that make you jump, sweating and weeping from the bed in the middle of the night, are not the usual relationship issues women in L.A. show business expect or are prepared to deal with.

I've lost quite a few girlfriends that way.

Chicago Death Threats and Rasta Wigs

After this excursion into the world of private and corporate investigations I started to get more bread and butter, slip and fall-type surveillance work which really wasn't my forte. I had some notable successes, but it wasn't what I thought was a proper use of my training and skills. Theodore also asked me to manage various workplace violence incidents, which was more of a challenge and less boring than workers compensation surveillance.

On one occasion I was flown to Chicago to unravel a death threat situation to a manager of a recycling depot who had recently terminated an employee for various reasons. The client was a large business that Theodore had a long and lucrative relationship with. The nature of the manual labor workforce was sometimes transient and included troubled individuals with substance issues and criminal records. Still, the company had both liability and insurance issues, and there was a seventy-two hour window that was accepted as the most critical time when disgruntled ex-employees might return to a facility and seek revenge or go postal on co-workers and managers alike. My job was to assess, manage, secure and resolve this sticky issue.

Not being able to monitor the subject, secure the location and make other inquiries all at the same time, I sought the help of two bounty hunters I knew from my travels in the Midwest.

Timmy "The Ink" and his trusted friend "Filthy" drove overnight to the Chicago suburbs, and we began to put the pieces together of how this situation had come about and how we could best defuse it. I had brought my .40 SIG P229 and trusty Walther PPK/S as well as various other bits of equipment that might come in handy.

After making various local inquiries it appeared there were some disturbing links between the subject and local drug dealing activity. I put Tim and Filthy on surveillance duty and talked to the facility manager and the Human Resources department of the corporation to explain the situation. We were given the go ahead to carry out further investigations and handle whatever arose.

That evening the subject left his home and proceeded to a local bar and restaurant where he and a female companion consumed at least a dozen beers each and various shots in a very short space of time. As I sat and ate dinner in a corner across from the bar I noticed somebody else at the restaurant entrance was also watching our subject. Tim called me to inform me that what appeared to be an unmarked police car had been parked outside and yet another subject was also present and appeared to be keeping watch outside.

What was going on? What had we stepped into?

Then, using an old trick, I felt eyes on the back of my head and used the reflection in the glass of water to see why my animal warning instincts had kicked in. I noticed another man standing casually behind me and concealed by a low white-lattice wall. I decided to take a trip to the restroom and sure enough the man behind me accidentally made eye contact directly with me.

I returned to my table and continued to finish my supper, acting as if nothing was wrong and no alarm bells were going off. I was simply going to have to let this play out and see where the dice rolled. I watched our subject down several more beers and he seemed pretty drunk at this stage. I called Tim and explained the situation and told him to stand by if the subject left and attempted to drive his truck.

As the subject weaved his way to the exit I went to the bar to pay my tab. That way I could also check to see what the couple had been drinking. It wasn't alcohol-free beer, so I evaluated our subject as being well over the limit to drive. As I exited I noticed both the other subjects were talking with a uniformed bike officer at the door and casually smiled at them as I left. Now I was even more intrigued by all the activity!

I told Tim to get behind the subject's vehicle and I would see if the cops stayed on me. Tim told me he was behind the subject's truck and he seemed pretty drunk. I had what appeared to be the unmarked Crown Victoria on me, so I made a quick detour through a gas station to see how they would react. Watching them drive by I believed they knew they had been made and did what I would have done and pulled off the tail.

I called Tim and told him to call in the subject's truck as a drunk driver and drop back off him. A few miles on Tim called again and told me the truck had been pulled over by a marked patrol car and our subject was out and talking to the cops. As I drove past the two vehicles our man was indeed going through the basic sobriety test regime, touching his nose and walking down a white line in a parking lot.

Whoever his criminal connections in Chicago he was going to stay in jail for the night at least and that would take the pressure off of us. Also, he would have cooling down time to reflect on his recent threats of violence toward the factory manager.

Tim and I kept our distance and watched but to our utter surprise the cops let the subject lock his car and begin the short walk home. We leap-frogged our way back to the subject's residence and watched the light go out once he had entered. We were both confused and concerned by this strange turn of events and met at the motel to discuss all the various possibilities.

Who were the other subjects in the bar? Why had the cops let our guy go from an obvious DUI? Was he that well-connected and who the hell was watching me?

Tim drew the short straw and began the early surveillance shift in the morning while I reported in and mulled over the situation with Theodore. The direction was simple. Keep the pressure on and if the subject even looks in the direction of the facility, inform the cops and call a lockdown to protect the workers there. We also called in Code 5 and vehicle IDs to the local law enforcement watch-commander, as is usual practice for PIs on surveillance work.

The next day passed with the subject walking his dog and showing no interest in going anywhere other than to recover his abandoned truck from the previous night. We arranged that I would take over the evening shift so that Tim and Filthy could get some sleep. I promised to call them if the subject headed out again. All was quiet for the remainder of the afternoon and into the evening, and I sat there wondering what was coming next. What transpired then surprised even me!

The subject did not appear again until the early hours of the morning, when he appeared to be wandering down the street with a purposeful stride. It's pretty hard to follow someone in the dead of night in a vehicle when there is no cover and the subject knows the local ground. They can dart down alleys, stroll into open ground or hide in bushes or doorways. The best I could do was parallel him on the streets in the vehicle and try and keep visual contact. Then he appeared to turn back toward his residence and slipped down an alley. He obviously knew he was being followed and was possibly preparing for a confrontation with me.

As I was driving around the block to see where he might re-emerge, a dark figure suddenly launched itself from the shadows and threw itself onto the hood of my hired SUV. The subject was obviously distraught and appeared to be pleading for mercy! He slid off the vehicle and seemed a pathetic and harmless figure, crouching in the road. I took the opportunity and drove away leaving the subject to wander back home shaken but unharmed.

The next morning I decided to visit the local police station to see if I could gain any insight into the whole strange situation. Talking with the officer on the front desk she seemed to be aware of the previous night's adventures and called a detective who came out and waved me into his office. I explained why I was there and my role in fulfillling the insurance and legal liability issues for the company, but expressed my concern that the subject seemed to be under surveillance by others and that he seemed to be getting assistance from other officers.

The detective smiled and declared his belief that the subject would not be returning to the facility and that we should not worry about it any longer. He also intimated that our subject was already being watched by officers and was acting as a CI [confidential informant] for local drug enforcement officers. His paranoia came from a belief that I had come to kill him and he had asked for further protection from the cops!

The picture cleared and now everything made sense! I explained that we would only be around for another 24 hours anyway, as that was the end of the high-risk period and we would have completed the insurance company's liability requirements for this assignment. In the meantime, I would ensure we drew back and let the subject stew a bit while not getting in the way of their operation. The detective was happy and we agreed to the plan.

While on my way back to the residence I thought a little lightening of the mood would probably be welcome by Tim and Filthy. I spotted a novelty shop on my drive back and pulled over to see what was there that might cause some amusement. I found what I was looking for and called Tim to tell him I was back in the area and he should drive up and jump in my car so that I could fill him in on my meeting with the detective.

Tim and Filthy drove by. The first time they stopped, stared and drove away again. The second time they drove slowly past, looking very puzzled, and again drove away. The third time they pulled up alongside my car and just stared at me. Then they began laughing hysterically! It seemed my Rastafarian wig, Rasta multi-colored woolly hat and full beard with huge gold sunglasses had sent them into some confusion, followed by fits of laughter!

On asking Tim what was wrong with my new disguise he expressed the opinion that considering the local drug dealing issues in the area and the Rasta links to marijuana, I was most likely to be shot by the local mob if they mistook me as someone selling dope on their streets! My disguise broke the tension and we were all relieved and what is vitally important more relaxed, if physically exhausted.

I explained the situation to Tim and Filthy and called in for further instructions from Theodore. As discussed with the detective we drew back and just kept a watching brief for the next 24 hours to fulfil the contract. I later explained some of the details of the situation to the facility manager who was relieved and got back on with the business of recycling cardboard.

I still have the wig, hat and beard but I'm more careful in what areas I wear it while chasing scallywags around other cities.

Oysters, Goodfellas and Nuclear Triggering Mechanisms

In 2010 I got a call from Lorenda Starfelt, the wife of *Bacchae* movie director Brad Mays. She asked me if I would do her a personal favor and meet with a friend of hers who had a rather convoluted and awkward series of issue that I might be able to shed some light on and perhaps help to resolve. I liked and respected Lori so, as I've done in many, many instances before, I said I would meet her friend, listen and help if I possibly could. Although there were no guarantees I promised I would do my best.

I met Francine the following week. Things had come to light in recent months that made her fearful for her life. The story that unfolded over coffee was truly worthy of a Hollywood film noir screenplay and was dripping in dark political intrigue, twisted psychological drama, vast amounts of illicit money and a chilling cast of very dangerous characters.

Her tangled web of stories regarding shady dealings, arms smuggling and organized criminal operations intertwined with covert U.S. intelligence efforts, trailed all the way back to Ronald Reagan and the Iran-Contra affair. I think she was genuinely relieved that I was unfazed by the strangeness of the tale she told and also slightly shocked that this all sounded like run of the mill political intrigue to me and very much business as usual.

One name she mentioned caught my attention immediately, suggesting that this might not be the usual kind of PI case. I looked at Lori, who seemed bemused but pleased that her suggestion that I would understand was correct. As the story unfolded, however, some of the political and crime family-related elements seemed to genuinely shock and worry her.

The name she had mentioned was Sidney Korshak, who passed away two days after his brother Marshall at the age of 88 in Beverly Hills. His was indeed a name from the annals of Hollywood legend. His history of Chicago wheeling and dealing, of fixes involved some of the most famous gangsters, producers, film stars, bankers, union leaders, Las Vegas players and lawyers, was a thing of legend and the subject of several books.

The many dubious and serious criminal connections attached to the name have been covered extensively in Gus Russo's well-researched book *Supermob*, and it is not my intention to delve into the history of Korshak's life, reputation and Chicago outfit connections here. His possible involvement in the current situation meant a certain amount of caution, strategic thinking and confidentiality was required. I took some notes and decided to do some quiet research and assess where to start unraveling this bundle of twisted and knotted dramas.

Over the next few months a deeply disturbing labyrinth of criminal influence, political intrigue and intelligence black operations began to unfold from Francine's story, which might have caused even the wildest conspiracy aficionado to have an apoplexy.

There were stories of CIA involvement in secret smuggling operations, facilitated by elements of organized crime during the Iran-Contra operation. This might sound shocking to some readers, but the story of "Freeway" Rick Ross and cocaine deliveries into South Central Los Angeles in exchange for financial support and arms shipments to the Nicaraguan

Contras have been well researched, investigated and reported. As I have stated many times, a conspiracy theory is not a theory if you know it's true. I should know: I've been involved in several.

Francine's story was liberally seasoned with names like Castellano, Franzese, Profaci, Messina, Kahane, Oppenheimer, Teller and Henry Hill, as well as Los Alamos, Groom Lake, Science Applications International Corporation and Sandia—all people and places which were the favorite haunt of conspiracy seekers. A colorful cast of characters and spooky entities indeed. It might all sound preposterous if you know nothing about the murky and convoluted waters and historical relationships that are ingrained in the "black" U.S. political system. Working these bizarre and sometimes sensitive correlations was my personal bailiwick, and one where I understood the realities and dangers very well.

There was enough material here for a dozen novels, several screenplays and an entire season of conspiracy theory TV shows, but all Francine wanted was to live long enough to enjoy her later life and legacy without further threats, intrigue and intimidation.

As I picked my way through the labyrinthine matrix of information, I decided to focus on one issue at a time, beginning with the ones that I could verify and where I could find documents that might reveal the reality of her situation. They didn't take long to find and what I uncovered shook me to the core.

This was going to be fun!

How To Detonate A Nuclear Weapon

During my many hours talking to Francine I asked her many questions that she couldn't reasonably have had detailed insights into without inside knowledge from her relationships. This analysis helped to give me a framework for seemingly random and unconnected points, and helped me drill down into the heart of the matter.

In my time in California I have met many forms of professional scam artists that roam L.A. Skilled and polished grifters claiming to be Chinese ambassadors-at-large, financial advisors "managing" funds for the Duke of Northumberland in Orange County, and deviant ex-monks claiming association with the SAS and MI6 and selling their exotic sexual expertise to rich Beverly Hills divorcees! I'd met them all, and thanks to the wisdom imparted to me by Bob Dick I usually saw through these sad if colorful folks with a somewhat weary and jaundiced eye. My first task with Francine was separating fact from fantasy. It didn't take long.

Her natural father was a bright, smart and a technically proficient gentleman who passed away in 1976 when she was still young. Her mother was part founder of a wire manufacturing business based in Burbank, and her close friend and scientific consultant was a man called Henry A. Walker. Henry's background included work with SAIC (Science Applications International Inc.), National Oceanic and Atmospheric Administration, EPA, NASA and a strange little wire manufacturing company called Permaluster Inc. Francine told me that her mother was involved with the daily running of the company. She had met and discussed various production issues with Robert Oppenheimer, and also visited Rocketdyne, a rocket engine design and production company headquartered in Canoga Park, regarding various secret issues connected to Permaluster's specialized products. This would be easy to confirm from online research. Francine also told me that her mother was involved with Livermore Research and Sandia Laboratory (now owned by Lockheed Martin), both at the center of rocket engine design. This seemed highly specialized and unusual for a woman with no technical or scientific background. It might be problematic to confirm, but I kept an open mind. Work with defense contractors during the sixties and seventies in California was not unusual for a scientist, but the detail and depth of Henry Walker's involvement was impressive to say the least.

Francine's stepfather Irving Korchak (note the spelling) had been reputedly associated with Sidney Korshak, and could have been a major bagman and runner for him. Her mother had indeed met Sidney in Beverly Hills, and confirmed many odd details about her second husband (Francine's stepfather Irving) that seemed related to money laundering and loan sharking operations. Indeed, the family owned apartment blocks in Beverly Hills and substantial properties in North Hollywood. As one highly creditable source told me, "Irving Korchak stole from everyone." This might be why he died under mysterious circumstances after attempting to change the primary beneficiary of his trust in November 2005.

For the time being all I had to go on was that the Permaluster premises in Burbank burned down in 1993 after some openly hostile visits from what was perceived at the time to be Iranian and German individuals, and there was a possibility that the arson was carried out by foreign agents who were seeking information regarding the material that the company produced and supplied to the U.S. Department of Defense, NASA and Sandia Laboratories. Francine's mother worked at Permaluster until the day the building burned down.

To explain some of the historic and technical issues surrounding the case, it's necessary to understand that a German freighter called the *Scheersberg A* vanished while sailing from Antwerp to Italy in 1968. It was carrying arguably between one hundred and two hundred tons of uranium ore that was probably later enriched and processed at Israel's Dimona nuclear plant and became the cornerstone of their nuclear weapons program.

Much discussion has been heard about how Israel acquired its nuclear capability, and it is still denied to this day. There is a reason for that. Israel has denied it has *any* nuclear weapons and has refused to sign a nuclear non-proliferation treaty. Their stockpile of warheads is unknown, but some estimates are around between one and three hundred types of tactical and strategic nuclear weapons.

With help from various governments and intelligence assets, including the French, British and South Africans, Israel produced plutonium and reputedly tested a successful nuclear weapon of it's own, all the time maintaining its stance of "nuclear ambiguity." Israel claims that revealing truth would be "contrary to its national security" stating only that "it would not be the first country to introduce nuclear weapons into the Middle East."

However, acquiring uranium ore and developing plutonium or other fissile material is only the beginning of the process of building nuclear weapons. Since their original design during the 40s, nuclear detonations have evolved from pure fission atomic bombs to fission-fusion hydrogen bombs, doped or salted thermonuclear warheads, to cold-war-era neutron weapons.

The Israeli intelligence service, Mossad, created a technical and scientific unit called LAKAM, dedicated to purloining, borrowing and sometimes stealing the technical expertise and material to begin its own weapons production program. It recruited and utilized not just professional and dedicated intelligence operators, but also sympathetic scientists and financial supporters around the globe, including from within Californian's scientific, business and even Hollywood's glamorous movie production communities.

If it hadn't been for the botched Mossad assassination of an innocent Moroccan waiter (mistaken for the terrorist Ali Hassan Salameh, responsible for the Munich massacre as detailed in Steven Spielberg's film Munich) in Lillehammer, Norway and the subsequent discovery of the *Scheersberg A*, now renamed the *Kirkira*, little would be known about some of these methods, and the resulting international repercussions. But having acquired the uranium and enriched it, they now had to build a trigger for their bomb. This was where Permaluster came in.

This may sound unlikely and fanciful, but recently declassified, heavily redacted FBI documents from the counter-intelligence branch, released under the Freedom of Information Act (FOIA) clearly show that efforts to acquire nuclear weapon-triggering technology was an on-going and high-level effort by LAKAM throughout the early 70s and 80s, particularly in Los Angeles.

A convoluted plot involving Hollywood film producer Arnon Milchan, (*Noah, 12 Years a Slave, Pretty Woman*) a glittering backdrop of Hollywood celebs, MILCO International Inc. of Huntington Beach, California, ex-Israeli PM Ariel Sharon, the Heli Trading Company of Tel Aviv and current Israeli PM Benjamin Netanyahu was revealed.

In November 2001, U.S. aerospace engineer Richard Kelly Smyth, business college and close friend of Milchan, was extradited from Spain under an Interpol "Red Notice" and pled guilty to violating U.S. weapons export regulations. Smyth was eventually sentenced to 40 months (later paroled and freed) for illegally smuggling Krytron cold-cathode, high-speed switches that can be used in EBW and "slapper" type detonators for nuclear devices. (Some of these operations are detailed in Milchan's biography, *Confidential: The Life of Secret Agent Turned Hollywood Tycoon*).

During the original development of nuclear weapons, a method was devised to initiate the critical mass reaction in implosion-type weapons. This required compression and lensing effects via a shockwave of detonated high explosive through the core to compress the uranium and begin the chain reaction in the plutonium. This required a type of detonation system called an EBW or electronic bridge-wire detonator, later developed into a "'slapper"-type detonator. With these, instead of directly coupling the shock wave from the exploding wire, the expanding plasma from an explosion of a metal foil drives another thin plastic or metal foil called a "flyer" or a "slapper" across a gap, and its high-velocity impact on the explosive delivers the energy and shock needed to initiate a detonation. Permaluster's specialized wire production had many uses in NASA missions and other missile development programs, and could have had another innocent explanation; but then the documents began to surface.

In April 1999, the U.S. Department of Defense published an obscure document entitled *Ammunition Manufacturers and their Symbols Handbook* (MIL-HDBK-1461A). The document was marked "NOT MEASUREMENT SENSITIVE" and was approved for public release, albeit you would have to dig hard through the files to find it!

Listed as "A" status, Permaluster Inc. had its own Department of Defense symbol code and noted address in Burbank, and was still apparently an official supplier to the U.S. military. This confirmed the connection between the company and the military that Francine had believed existed, and undoubtedly required a security clearance for both her mother and Henry Walker. This document officially confirmed that the sensitive nature of the specialized wire and other materials used in ammunition, missile and nuclear weapons production that were being developed by Permaluster.

Although I always took security precautions during this type of investigation and met Francine at various codenamed locations, it soon became obvious that my research and involvement had attracted the attention of somebody who thought I would be intimidated by subtle and not so subtle threats. On one occasion someone called my number and asked to talk to my then-girlfriend. On handing her the phone (because I thought she had given my number to someone in case of emergency) the caller made several lewd and insulting comments and hung up. I soon traced the origin of the number and the owner of the cell, and using subterfuge, confirmed the caller's identity. I then called him and explained that I knew where he lived. After further calls and exchanges, his angry wife threatened to call the police and the FBI. I offered to go with her to explain the phone calls, and advised that she should keep a shorter leash on her talkative, amateur spook husband, or I would fulfill my promise and "out" him. The calls stopped, though further intermittent surveillance vehicles were spotted, identified and confronted, in each instance causing the surprised "tail" to make a hasty retreat out of the area.

Francine was getting more information than she had expected about her mother's history. With a little advice and coaching regarding how to handle her situation, using tactics and methods that were both practical and wily, the situation began to settle down and various subtle approaches were made in an effort to begin some kind of dialogue. Francine was an excellent student and handled herself with stoical patience and practical operational and security disciplines. It was obvious that the tide had begun to turn in her life.

Then a vital piece of information came to light that cemented the connection between her stories and the issues they had raised. It gave me leverage in the evolving situation, and convinced other parties to back off and leave Francine in peace. After all, at least eight hundred Krytron tubes had been successfully, if illegally, shipped to Tel Aviv via Huntington Beach, California. Richard Smyth faced a lengthy prison sentence, but was eventually sentenced to only forty months and paroled with a twenty thousand dollar fine. Most of the others involved were either in prison, deceased or had quietly retired from public life. Maybe it was time to let sleeping dogs lie.

However, another document dated May 1975 surfaced from the Explosive Physics Division of Sandia Labs, which clearly showed that the research and development of EBW detonators was still being refined under a program to develop a computer code to "predict the behavior of electrical circuits in exploding wire elements." Los Alamos and Livermore Labs were on the distribution list, but also recorded as a supplier of various materials and a contributor to this research was Permaluster Inc. of Burbank, CA. It was specified that this specific document was to compare and tabulate the threshold burst current required to initiate an EBW detonator.

This research was vital for the successful detonation of the implosion type of nuclear warhead because the electrical pulse has to be so precisely timed to detonate the lensing pits and compress the plutonium. The wire used for this purpose must be predictable and reliable and explode within a millisecond (0.1 microseconds), otherwise the nuclear reaction does not take place and the fissile material within the core will be squeezed out of the casing under tremendous pressure and fail to detonate the warhead.

So it appeared there was a real possibility of links between Hollywood's most powerful lawyer, friend of the Chicago "Outfit" and deal maker (Sidney Korshak), a movie-producing LAKAM spy (Arnon *Once Upon a Time in America* Milchan), a small company in Burbank making components for EBWs and Krytron detonators (Permaluster) and a military export company in Huntington Beach, CA (MILCO) with business ties to an Israeli nuclear secrets smuggling operation in Tel Aviv (Heli Trading Corp/Milchan Ltd) - apparently associated with future Israeli Prime Minister Benjamin Netanyahu!

After consultation with various contacts, including Vince Messina and Larry J. Kolb, authors of two expose books, *America At Night* and *Overworld*, I was afforded invaluable and insightful information that allowed me to let it be known that any further intimidation or interference with the affairs of Francine and her mother would certainly attract the attention of both Federal and other intelligence agencies, and that the wisest path might be to step back, cease and desist and let bygones be bygones.

Following a period of peace and quiet I got a call from two FBI agents who I had previously had interactions with during another operation. They wanted to meet to have a "chat." My usual watering hole was The Robin Hood Pub in Sherman Oaks, and that seemed a suitable and neutral meeting place. Besides, they had good beer and fish and chips.

As I had suspected, it appeared the FBI had been monitoring some strange and bizarre information regarding possible Chinese, Iranian and even organized criminal activity focusing around historical attempts to acquire information and the materials utilized in nuclear triggering devices. Apparently, I was associated with some of these still surviving subjects and had headed-off something of a diplomatic and security "mishegas."

As close to a thank you as you will get from any federal law enforcement entity, the two agents listened to the background of the story and my involvement, nodded in agreement and bought me lunch. The issue was obviously handled quietly and with an economy of the truth. I never heard from them again.

In the murky, looking-glass labyrinth of private investigations and threat analysis, a successful result is often the one that doesn't make the newspapers, end in a county jailhouse, a civil or legal settlement or in the morgue. Sometimes the best outcome is that the situation is defused, evil intent is neutralized, and that calmer and more experienced minds prevail and nobody gets hurt.

I've walked away from many of these complex cases, and felt good in my heart about the end results. Sadly, Lorenda Starfelt passed away in March 2011 leaving her grieving husband, Brad Mays to celebrate her life and passion for filmmaking. I attended her memorial service and was quietly relieved that I had been at least able to keep my solemn promise to help her friend.

The Art of Fraud

My most recent—perhaps my last - serious consultation job as a PI was for a client caught up in an eighty-one million dollar New York art fraud case in which a woman called Glafira Rosales had colluded in the sale of some thirty-seven million dollars worth of counterfeit paintings claimed to be by abstract expressionist artists such as Rothko, Motherwell, de Kooning and Pollock.

This fantastical trove of "lost art" was sometimes delivered to various New York dealers in carrier bags by the attractive, dark haired if nefarious Long Island art dealer, and on one painting at least (a Pollock hanging on Ann Freedman's wall) Pollock misspelled his own name! According to *The New York Times* they were apparently painted in a garage by a Chinese immigrant named Pei-Shen Qian in Woodhaven, Queens, New York and paid for by various checks and wires from Rosales's boyfriend, Jose Diaz.

The fact that multiple N.Y. and European art "experts" involved had been genuinely taken-in by this obvious and transparent fraud was preposterous and a ludicrous malfeasance, but actually not that surprising to me.

I had explained the story told to me by Bob Dick about his art dealer days to various players in the case, and I wondered how the cream of New York's art elite could have possibly been conned by this petite, fraudulently married immigrant and her paper carrier-bags of apparently unknown and priceless masterpieces with no provenance or provable history whatsoever!

It's still amazing to me that greed, pride and hedonism will still override common sense and fair dealing, but I felt genuinely sorry for the victims of this massive and yet unsophisticated confidence trick and the damage done to honest brokers and historic art connoisseurs alike.

I had flown into JFK airport and headed straight into this arrogant, hedonistic and hermetically sealed world of New York art dealing, once again donning a cover story and protected by close friends and confidants on the Upper West Side of my old stomping ground on Manhattan Island. This would help me create the picture I wished to paint for my targets for the short-term of this latest sojourn into the otherworld.

There had been resistance from the beginning to my assertion that this had been a transparent and obvious confidence trick, and various expert noses were very much out of joint and offended with my challenge to their N.Y. sensibilities and world-view of art dealing. Some of these early contacts viewed me with the same distaste as I had experienced when first working in London's West End theatre. To them I was just an unwelcome amateur who was very much out of his depth in the complex morass of chic and highly lucrative N.Y. art dealing, and who would soon be heading for home with my tail between my legs.

Within forty-eight hours of cold contact debriefings on the Upper East Side, close quarters coffee-shop surveillance to assess body language and demeanor, snippets of furtive conversations and subterfuge business dealings with suspected could-be conspirators, I began to understand the whole sorry con-job and why it had happened.

The Emperor's New Clothes? Without a shadow of a doubt.

I was also warned that the FBI was hard charging in the same direction, obviously coming to the same conclusion that I had done and unfazed by the myopic and snobbish view that protected the whole fraudulent enterprise.

One of the many things I had learned about FBI operations was that when the Feds are in hot-pursuit of the same person of interest it's better to get out of the bloody way! After briefing the client three days later over dinner in a very expensive upper east-side hotel I headed back to JFK and closed the cold, emotional door on my active involvement in this whole bizarre affair and pondered my genuine personal loyalty and respect for the client.

Eighty-one million dollars worth of defrauded cash, more than sixty forged artworks by famous artists that were resold through historic and respected art houses to rich, urbane and gullible socialites. I shook my head at the foolishness.

Rosales faced charges of money laundering, tax and wire fraud and forfeited thirty-three million dollars in property holdings in her plea deal; she also faces eighty-one million dollars in restitution. More charges will follow, I'm sure.

10.

ON THE WALL WITH KING ARTHUR

"What place is there within the bounds of the empire of Christendom to which the winged praise of Arthur the Briton has not extended."
~ Alanus de Insulis, 1608

EARLY IN 2003 I got a call from old *Robin of Sherwood* colleague, Steve Dent, asking whether I would be interested in doing the swordmaster job on a big budget movie shooting in Ireland. The film was *King Arthur*, which was being made by Jerry Bruckheimer, a man whose reputation in Hollywood is as one of the major movers and shakers.

The subject interested me and it meant working in Ireland, where my grandmother's family originated. Grandma's family (my dad's mum—surname Geraghty) came from Co. Mayo originally, whereas my granddad's family (my dad's father—surname Hughes) came from North Wales.

The Geraghtys (my great, great-grandparents) were evicted from their home in the 1870s, after which the whole family came over to Liverpool. My granddad walked across northern England to County Durham to find work in the coalmines.

Interestingly, my great-grandfather Thomas Geraghty was a bare-knuckle fighter and his wife Sarah was the daughter of a man named John Martin, also an immigrant from Ireland (County Tyrone) who ran an Irish Pub/Sinn Fein Club in the North East at Seaham, County Durham. At that time Sinn Fein was a political party and an extension of the Republican movement. Thomas Geraghty worked in the club as a bouncer, and that's where he met and subsequently married Sarah.

I remember pondering whether to take the job or not because my connection with Ireland, and in particular its Republican sympathizers, had not always been comfortable. When I finally said yes to *King Arthur* I was aware that there could be a real and tangible threat because of my other life, so I took this possibility seriously.

Once the job was confirmed, I flew to the U.K. and went down to Steve Dent's farm. We did our preparation there, where I had stood with the boys from *Robin of Sherwood* years before working on our archery and horsemanship and then later again with the wonderful Bob Anderson on *First Knight*.

King Arthur was a radical new look at the Arthurian story. Scripted by David Franzoni, who had just had a fantastic success with *Gladiator*, he sold this idea as *King Arthur and the Seven Samurai*. Its premise was the idea that a second century Roman officer named Lucius Artorius Castus, who was a real person, had been placed in charge of a group of warriors drafted into the Roman Legions from Sarmatia, a country somewhere between the Red Sea and the Black Sea. The Sarmatians had their own set of legends regarding a semi-mythical hero named Batraz, who bore a strong resemblance to the later British figure of Arthur—even fighting under a dragon standard and carrying a magical sword as did the Arthur of myth and legend. Franzoni moved the action from the second to fifth century and added the Saxons to the original Pictish forces that Artorius had fought against. He set the whole thing on Hadrian's Wall, that extraordinary feat of Roman engineering which stretched from Wallsend on the River Tyne to Solway Firth and effectively separated the whole Northern part of the country (what is today mostly Scotland) from the rest of the British Island. It was a controversial theory, and got the Cornish and Welsh, who both claimed Arthur as their own, into a state—but the truth is *King Arthur* is probably the nearest thing to an accurate portrayal of the man and the time yet produced by Hollywood.

Two of the leading proponents of this theory were Linda Malcor in the U.S. and my old friend (and co-author) John Matthews in the U.K. John was signed up as the lead historical advisor for the film, and was often seen prowling around the set doing his best to ensure that not too many historical blunders got onto film.

My job was basically to come up with seven different fighting styles for the seven different knights—Arthur, played by Clive Owen, included—and to make them all look as different as possible. I also had to get Keira Knightley, who was playing Guinevere, into the fights if possible. This was an issue because she was so petite, but I argued the point, as did the historical advisors, that the Celts were famous for their women fighting alongside the men, or even leading them into battle, as in the example of the warrior queen Boudicca.

The challenge was to make Keira look real against these great hulking bearded Saxons. If I could do it, they would put her in. So I started looking for a style for her, and meanwhile began breaking down the major battle sequences—starting with the Saxon raid, which is the first action sequence in the film. I broke it down into a real battle strategy and choreographed it so that we could keep the little fighting groups on horseback separate so they weren't crashing into each other. We laid all these sequences out on Steve's farm, and that was exactly how it ended up looking on film.

Another part of my job was to assess the various actors playing the Knights. My old friend Ray Winstone was playing Bors and another Ray, big Ray Stephenson, was playing a knight named Dagonet. He was fantastic and wanted to be in everything. Ioan Gruffudd was playing Lancelot, Hugh Dancy was Galahad and the Danish actor Mads Mikkelsen was Tristan.

I had given Mads a fight scene to work on so that I could assess him, and he went into the middle of a field to work through the moves on his own. I could see he moved really well and after a bit I asked him if he had trained as a dancer. He told me he had trained for the ballet. Once I knew this, and that I had his natural skills to work with, I started creating a kind of almost Samurai style, in which he moved very correctly and in a controlled manner—using his sword like a Samurai instead of swinging it furiously as most Western fighters did. I also had an idea to make his sword look different—so we got a Chinese short sword called a Yang-Ling, and I set about converting it into something more elegant and stylish for the screen.

I went to see Tommy Dunne the armorer, a really lovely bloke and a real pro, and drew out a design for this sword. It was about seven to eight inches longer in the body than a normal Yang-Ling sword, and we reversed the handle so it had a cantilever effect, which gave it more leverage. The blade had a flamed-out end like the Yang-Ling, and looked strikingly beautiful. In fact, it was a very successful sword; it really worked well, looked unique and moved fluidly on camera.

One or two people were a bit unsure about the design, but I kept remembering what Bob Anderson had said several times on *First Knight*. When people said that there was never a sword like that, he would reply, "Were you there at the time? Do you know that for sure?" Bob talked all the time about duels and sword fights and how, in Shakespeare's plays, people couldn't talk if they had just been stabbed with a court sword or a rapier. It's well known that a wound from a sword in those days might kill you instantly if it pierced a vital organ, but if it was through a lung, for example, it could take quite a long time for you to die. Historically, we weren't there, so we don't know for sure about these things, but this was a great opportunity just to be in the middle of that creative mix, coming up with styles and fights and ideas for battle scenes.

I've been asked a few times If I had anything to do with the wedge formation adopted by the knights in a couple of scenes. I remember talking to our director Antoine Fuqua about how on *First Knight* Dinnie Powell wanted to do a flying wedge horse charge and we had almost three hundred horses at our disposal. They were looking for extra riders, and I said to Steve that I would jump on a horse if he needed me. But Steve said, "You really don't want to be in the middle of this, because if you fall off there's no way those horses are not going to stomp you into the ground."

We discussed the concept of the flying wedge and how if you are in a straight line you can't bring all your bows and arrows and power to bear because you are attacking on a very narrow front. However, if you are spread out in a wedge formation, all of the knights could loose arrows travelling forward without taking off the back of someone's head in front of them. That formation is true of an infantry marching order as well—there's a signal you can give if you're leading a patrol and you want people to spread out into that formation—you give an arrow signal by putting your hands up and pointing behind you. I know Antoine liked that idea.

One of the most important things we had to do was make sure our King Arthur, Clive Owen, looked good on a horse. He was a bit nervous about this and didn't strike me as a natural athlete in terms of co-ordination. Horses are intimidating enough, and the one thing that you can be sure about is that if you are nervous around them, they know it—they can smell it somehow. They know if you are not in control, and if you don't know what you're doing they will have you off their backs in a heartbeat.

This was illustrated during the filming of *First Knight*, when I was not the only person to get injured. An actor who was up for one of the parts of the knights said he could ride, so Dinnie put him on a horse and had it just trotting around the field. As we watched Dinnie said, "This guy hasn't a clue what he's doing—watch this." Dinnie shouted to him, "Okay, canter now, please—kick him on." Well of course the horse took off like a rocket down the field, straight for the corner without any sign it was going to turn. I thought it was going to jump the fence and said, "I hope he *can* ride because if he jumps that fence and comes off it could be a real mess."

As it was approaching the corner, the horse jinked to the left, threw its body to one side so it did not run into the fence and threw the guy right into a post. He went flying off the back of the horse and I think fractured his collarbone or arm. As the horse was leaving it just gave a couple of little kicks as if to make sure the guy was aware of what an idiot he had been. It actually looked around to see if we had seen what it had done, as if to say, "Sorry about that chaps," then plodded back to Dinnie and almost nodded its head as if to say, "Yes he's an idiot. He's got to go." We couldn't help laughing—after all the guy had said he could ride—but we went down to help him, and he had to go off in an ambulance.

I don't know if I told Clive Owen that story, but if I did it might not have helped the situation. I think he was just timid with the horses, which was funny really because he was very much into horse racing and spent as much of his free time as possible at the track.

We had a couple of extra weeks at the Farm because the set of Hadrian's Wall, which was being built in a field near the little town of Ballymore Eustace, about an hour out of Dublin, wasn't ready. That gave me some time to work with Keira Knightley on her archery. She was really good—very stylish. Eventually, we packed up the circus into various lorries and trucks and everything moved to Ireland and the giant base camp at Ballymore Eustace.

Once there, the fight training continued and I started work with Stellan Skarsgard, who was playing Cerdic, the leader of the Saxons and

Arthur's greatest foe. I hadn't met him before but had heard he was a nice guy and obviously he was a good actor, so I had no concerns about the fights. One of the first he did was very quick and very simple and we decided he would work with Mads, because Mads was good and I knew Stellan would be working with someone who was safe and would make the fight look good.

I remember Stellan coming to introduce himself and asking if he could have a chat with me in private. He said, "Look, I'm 53, I chain-smoke and I have never done a fight scene before. I've done car chases, but never a sword fight." Then he asked me how I was going to manage it and what my approach was going to be. So I stole a quote from Bob Anderson and said, "Look, Stellan, think of it this way. A sword fight is a drama scene where the blades have the dialogue—a conversation in steel. Instead of you speaking the dialogue, the sword has the dialogue. It has all the beats, the highs and lows and dramatic pauses. You're playing a chess game with a blade, but it's still a drama scene." Stellan looked at me and said, "I get it. I'd never thought of it like that." I said we would choreograph it as a little drama scene being acted out.

That's how we started and he was wonderful to work with. He's a big guy so we made his style very simple, very lethal. We were rehearsing a fight one day, where Stellan had to kill somebody for not following his orders. We were deciding how he was going to do this—whether to just stab the guy or slash him. As we discussed it, Stellan was leaning on his sword and looking at me and I asked, "What's up? Is everything okay?" He said, "Yes. I just wanted to say I've just got a really important insight into who this character is and what he is about." I said, "Really, what's that?" Stellan lifted his sword and said, "It's all about this. This character doesn't say anything that does not have weight behind it, and he doesn't draw his sword until he means to use it to lethal effect. When he does, it's over in a moment and the sword goes away." He said, "He's simple, brutal, business-like."

That's how we came up with that scene where one of the Saxon soldiers is attempting to rape a woman and Cerdic kills him with a single blow. Then, as the woman is thanking him desperately, he just says, "Kill her." Very straight-forward, very economical in the use of the violence and very chilling in his response to the woman's thanks. Cerdic never intended to save her.

Working with Keira Knightley was a real pleasure. She was one of the hardest working members of the team. When she arrived at the Farm we were still trying to work out how we could get her into the fights, and how to make her look different. There was a general concern that, because she was so petite, she looked too small to be in a fight and might even get hurt. In fact, they were thinking of not putting her in the fights at all and just having her use the bow. But when I told her this and that it would be historically incorrect because the women would have been in the fight she said, "What do you want me to do?" I told her that we were working on a style for her that was very fast, rolling and using the advantage of her speed and agility against the big hairy armored guys. I needed her to be able to move quickly with a knife and a garrote and it had got to look brutal.

Some people were concerned that making her look too brutal was a bad thing and would go against her for future work on *Pirates of the Caribbean*, where she played a quite different kind of character. But Keira was up for it—she wanted to be covered in blood and in the middle of the fighting, slashing people's throats. In fact, when John Matthews asked her if she liked what had been done to develop her character away from the more usual portrayal of Guinevere she beamed and said, in her wonderful cut-glass English accent, "I love it. I get to kick arse!"

We rehearsed various movements and various fight sequences that we thought would work, and she worked very hard indeed. When Antoine saw it and how it would look he said, "Go ahead. Get her in as much of the fighting as you can." The archery she got very quickly and was good at it and had a very graceful style.

There is one scene in the middle of the big battle at the end of the film—just before she kills the character played by the German actor Til Sweiger—when she is running through all the mayhem. I came up with the idea of a swarm of girls jumping on this one Saxon warrior and pulling him down and stabbing and strangling him, much as we had done in *The Bacchae*. They took it out of the theatrical release, but Antoine put back in for the Director's Cut, which I thought was a much better film. Keira wanted to be in this sequence, so we had her running through the fighting, ducking under things, stabbing people, throwing a spear and finally jumping on Til's throat. She rotates him through the air by stabbing him in the knee; rotates herself through the air at the same time, lands on his chest as they hit the floor, stabs him in the throat and then carries on. I told her that when she was rolling down and the guy was falling on his back to hang on but not to look down because the blood mortar, which sprays fake blood everywhere, would be going off. I wanted her to look up and find the camera as soon as she hit the ground and slashed him.

We worked it all out and rehearsed it and it looked fantastic. When we started actually shooting, Keira did the whole thing and it was great; she rotated through the air attached to this guy's throat and they hit the ground together and she slashed his throat... and then she looked down and the blood mortar went off right in her face... When she looked up she had blood in her teeth, eyes, hair and all over her face. She looked positively demonic.

I was standing next to Antoine at that moment and he said, "Did you see that?" He looked over at Keira and added, "Bye, bye, Elizabeth Swann!"—referring to the character she played in *Pirates of the Caribbean*, who was much more of a lady and not at all a bloodthirsty warrior queen!

The shot looked just fantastic, but it never got used. Luckily, Keira was not hurt. She practiced a lot with Alan Poppleton, who had been on *Lord of the Rings* and had also worked with Bob Anderson, and she worked hard every day. Alan was doubling as Cerdic, and every day Keira would drag him off to practice her sword fights. She was very dedicated to making it look good.

Keira was always poised on the set. I remember her standing there, watching some kind of mayhem going on, and I said to her, "You know, for someone as young as you are—and I hope you don't take this as offensive—you are one of the most poised, collected and focused actresses I have ever worked with. You have this amazing presence on screen as well as a wonderful all-work orientated attitude on set—you really will do well." Judging by her meteoric rise to fame after this I think I might have been right.

Originally my job-title was Sword Master on the film and Steve Dent, who I had first worked with in the long ago days of *Robin of Sherwood*, really got me the job. Steve is a very capable and experienced horseman, and one day on set one of the horses was playing up and Steve jumped up on it to calm it down. I'm not sure exactly what happened, but the horse bucked or twisted somehow and it broke Steve's pelvis. He was still up on the horse with a broken pelvis for some time and I don't know how they got him off, but I was summoned to go with him to the hospital and stayed with him while he was X-rayed.

When it was confirmed that his pelvis was broken he had to stay in hospital, which meant that he could not carry on for a while and had to make plans. He delegated the horse action to Pete White and the fight action to me. That's how I ended up with the title of Sword Master and Fight Director, with the authority to do that on the set. For Steve there were two options to fix his pelvis—one was to have a metal plate put in place to hold the two pieces together, which means you walk normally but not as easily because your pelvis flexes when walking. The other option was to let the bone fuse, and always walk with a strange gait, which Steve opted for. But that of course meant he would need six weeks to heal. We talked about what he should do while his wife was there and I said I would personally opt for the operation, because although he would be on his back for a few weeks, he was going to be able to walk properly at the end of it.

To me this was the most sensible thing to do. There was no pressure for him to get back early; we were just concerned for his health and wellbeing. But the stunt business is a very competitive one, and people always have a certain amount of paranoia regarding power. Steve opted to get into a wheelchair and come back to work a month after he had been in hospital. This was manageable—he could get around the set in a wheelchair and around the office—but he was physically unable to do much else; so a lot of the running around the set was left to me, which I was happy to do because I got on very well with Antoine.

Earlier on, when we'd been working at Dent's Farm for a while, Antoine came down surrounded by a gang of about twenty people—designers, producers, assistant directors—and I could see that he was uncomfortable. We did a sword fight for him and he watched it and I rotated it around so he could see it from a different angle and he watched it again. I could tell he was pleased with it, so I walked over to him and said, "Come and see it from over here, just come with me." We ran the fight again and walked around, and I showed him the camera angles and how to hide them. I told him, "It's all about hiding the angles so we can move slightly on a different axis so we can hide all these hits." He said, "I get that."

At one point Antoine was on the floor as if he was the camera and he called the DOP, Slawomir Idziak, over and said, "Come here and have a look at this." He was lying on his back and looking up into the sky with two men fighting above him. It was there that the idea of using all these different angles got started.

Overall Antoine and I got on really well, and I think that might have made me unpopular in some circles; but what really mattered was getting it all done. I remember how one day the Irish producer, Ned Dowd, came to me and told me that Dan Weil, the Production Designer, wanted to dig some huge trenches and fill them with fire. It was going to cost about £150,000 and no one really knew how we were going to do it. While he was talking about it, Ned looked at me as if to say, "Can you come up with anything else?"—although he didn't actually verbalize it. As we were walking around, Antoine came over and said, "Look, we're going to dig these trenches but I don't see why we have to." I said I didn't understand it either. "Why dig fire pits when you have a dry river bed over there."

He looked at me and asked what I meant. I said, "Well, you could make it an L shaped ambush, which is a real strategy, and instead of digging things here, just let the land do the fighting for you. There's a dry riverbed right here; set that on fire. Once half of the force has been drawn into a fight, you bring your archers out here and they start letting off fire arrows. They set the riverbed on fire. That way you split their forces and the Knights can attack head on into that force, whereas you have the rest firing arrows both into the forces trapped by the fire and into the other force." Antoine said immediately, "Right. That's what we'll do."

As I was walking away, Ned looked at me and nodded as if to say—you've just saved us about £150,000. Later on Steve told me that Ned had commented, "That Mark Ryan is a smart guy; it was a good idea bringing him along." At this point Steve was quite happy that I had got involved and saved them some money.

When it was all said and done, another problem arose when they filmed the scenes with the fire pits. Antoine wanted to make really black smoke, and to do that you have to pour thicker oil onto it. The discussion was—could they paint it in later to make it black enough with CGI, or should they make real black smoke. They talked about the cost of this, but Antoine wanted black smoke, so they started pouring whatever mixture it was to make this work, and it started to make people sick. We all ended up wearing masks, but I couldn't work and speak and do what I needed to do with a mask on, so mine ended up on my forehead. There was some concern that the smoke was toxic and a few people didn't like that, so eventually they used another mixture. But it did look good on screen.

Antoine was very clear about what he wanted throughout the filming. He really liked Slawomir's work on *Black Hawk Down*, and wanted the same juddery effect that Ridley Scott got on that film. Ridley had also used a lot of cameras on *Gladiator*, and for some of the action sequences we were using twenty-two cameras to get all the angles Antoine wanted.

But the problem is when you've got that many cameras, including some that were in shield bosses or buried in the ground, you end up either tripping over them or falling into them, or they are filming each other. This meant that on several takes, particularly during the big battle sequences, the other cameras were in shot. That was a lesson learnt very early on: there were just too many cameras. In fact, the camera team got a bit carried away more than once, digging holes in the middle of the battle ground and putting cameras in them. I was concerned that people would fall over them and said I wanted to know before they started sticking cameras everywhere.

I know this irked them. It came to a head when one guy almost got crushed by one of the carts because he decided to go and stand behind a horse with his camera. He was trying to get an angle between the horses looking down the length of the carriage, so he stood behind the horse, which was not the brightest thing to do because the horse was getting nervous. Pete White was walking past and noticed the horse pulling about and the guy who was sitting on the carriage holding the reigns said, "You can't stay there, mate, you're going to get injured. I need to move this wagon." As Pete was walking by he just leaned over and grabbed the cameraman by the shoulder and yanked him out of the gap behind the horse. As he did so, the horse bucked, kicked back, and pulled the carriage forward. If the cameraman he had been where he was moments before, he would have been kicked and crushed.

I think that's when the camera boys realized they should listen to us. Later on, during that first fight sequence with Mads, I got their respect because we were losing light and Antoine came to me as said, "Do you think we have time to do this?" I said, "I think we have—Mads knows what to do, so all you have to do is cover it."

Then they began laying the camera track on the opposite side of the fight I had planned for, and had wanted it done the other way around. I was thinking, *How the hell am I going to do this, because now all the hits are on the wrong side,* and I had no time to re-choreograph the fight. The stunt guys were wondering what to do, so I said, "Okay, this is what we're going to do; we're going to mirror-image everything—rotate this one hundred and eighty degrees. Mads is going to ride in from the other side."

The camera crew was watching me do this—and we rotated it one hundred and eighty degrees and I said, "Okay. Now let's do it."

The "A" camera operator, Ciaran Barry, shot it and everything worked. He looked at me and said, "You're a smart guy. That was magic!" To which I replied with an ironic and relieved smirk in the quickly fading Irish twilight, "That's why we get the big bucks."

It was shot like that, it looked great and everyone was pleased with it. That is how I grudgingly got the respect of the camera guys. Soon after that the camera package was cut down from twenty-two to sixteen, which became an easier crew to deal with.

Yet More Swords

In some ways working on *King Arthur* was like being back in the happy days of *Robin of Sherwood*. Ray Winstone was there, of course, as were some of the old stunt guys. My very good friend Martin Grace, who had been on *Who Dares Wins*, and was Roger Moore's stunt double and stunt coordinator for a lot of the Bond films—was there. Martin had suffered a very serious accident when filming the Bond film *Octopussy* while doubling Roger Moore on a dangerous train stunt. He had his pelvis fractured and his legs broken, but being a very fit and tough man he managed to get himself back in the game and again doubled Roger Moore running up and down the massive cables of the Golden Gate Bridge high above San Francisco during a fight sequence. He was knocking the holy shit out of the younger stunt guys on the set and loving every minute of it. There was also Gabe Cronnelly, who was my original archery teacher on *Robin of Sherwood*, and Graham Crowther, who had doubled for Jason Connery; but he had previously had also suffered a bad accident and had to leave the production early. Our collective knowledge meant that we had enough input that people would listen to.

However, I did have some serious issues with Dan Weil, the Production Designer. Some of his sword designs were frankly ludicrous—I don't know what other word to use. He wasn't very happy with me for saying that. The armorer wasn't very experienced either, so I had to take over and start breaking the swords he had made for Dan Weil into working parts and giving everybody their own weapons. We kept turning up at the armory asking where the weapons were—and they had masses of stuff laid out on a table as if we should look at it and love everything. What was *not* clear was who got which weapon, and there were *no* doubles or practical fighting versions of any of it.

I had already made some specific choices for the knights, but John McKenna (the alleged chief armorer) had done absolutely nothing about it and was eventually banned from the set by Antoine. Another of the stunt guys, C.C. Smiff, went along with me to the armory. We brushed everyone aside, broke down the weapon packages for each knight—the doubles of swords, axes and everything. Most of the weapons were unusable. We showed the armorer what we needed, and I said he needed to start making more swords and fast. He had bought loads of aluminum blades, stashed them in a corner and apparently forgotten all about them. So we pointed out that they were all potentially practical sword blades and that he needed to start marrying them onto sword hilts in sets because we are going to get through them really quickly—that's what happens once you start the big fight scenes.

These little petty sorts of things went on much of the time, and obviously Dan Weil was unhappy with the choice of the Excalibur sword design and tried to sabotage that. John Matthews came in on this because on the first day he arrived on the set they showed him the sword and he pointed out that it had Saxon runes all over the blade—which was a bit daft as the Saxons were Arthur's main enemy. John suggested using a form of Celtic lettering known as Ogham, and he and his wife Caitlín came up with an inscription that said *Defender of the Land*. They had to re-inscribe the blade on the other side and make sure it was only ever seen on camera from there.

Earlier, John had gone with a party that included Jerry Bruckheimer, producer Mike Stenson, writer David Franzoni and Dan Weil to visit the original of Hadrian's Wall, where much of the movie was set. John took them all around the sites of the Roman fortresses along the wall, and described how the original Hadrian's Wall would have looked and how tall it was. Finally, when the set was built, it was at least ten feet higher, and would have looked just fine in China.

In fact, the original design had called for the wall to be about three hundred yards long and they were going to CGI the rest, but the set kept getting longer and longer. One of the issues they had was that the Health & Safety people came along and said it was not attached to the ground properly. A strong wind or something hitting it could easily cause it to fall over and crush somebody. So they had to go back and re-anchor all of the scaffolding that was there into the ground, which cost a bloody fortune!

The wall ended up being nearly a kilometer long. There was so much timber and plaster and scaffolding involved that they actually ran out of scaffolding in Ireland and had to import more from the U.K. Ultimately, a lot of it was not used. They built the whole fortress area, which I thought was really good, but they didn't get much use out of that either. The wall cost a fortune—the figure of three million Euros was talked about. I remember, when there was a lot of discussion going on about the wall, looking at it and thinking—that's a lot of wood, plaster, paint and scaffolding—somebody somewhere is making a lot of money out of this. But I have to say it was without doubt absolutely magnificent—very impressive.

The Irish Question

There's actually another part to this story. I was sitting having breakfast one morning with Steve when a gentleman I knew only as "John" showed up. I had some idea who he was, but didn't know until later that he was actually a leading fundraiser for the Republican movement. He had a couple of very large Irishmen with him and they all sat down at the table. The big guy looked at me and said, "We need a favor from you." Steve looked at me and asked what they needed. We both knew the guy was something to do with the company that was running security for the set.

He said, "We'd like to bring some orphans from Tallagh—about thirty or so—and we'd like to give them a tour of the set and show them how the film is made and maybe do something with the horses and the stunt boys, like climbing onto a wagon and jumping off onto an airbag." He asked me if we had any rubber swords and if we could do something with bows and arrows. I said we could do a sword class and some archery, and that we'd work something out.

So we turned our stunt base into a fairground. We dragged Steve Relphs into it so we could do some archery, and had the older kids doing that. I had them doing swordplay and little sword fights with rubber swords. We did this entire evening of stunts and action skills for them and it was fascinating and very rewarding for the kids.

As I was leaving that night "John" came up to me and said, "Thank you, Mark. We know who you are and you are safe with us." I said, "Thank you, John, that's nice to know." There was a bit of eyeballing going on from some of the guys with him, but he had said it publically, and I knew they would not go against what he'd said. Every time after that if he saw me he made a point of coming over and having a few words. I knew who he was and he knew who I was, and we simply acknowledged that and got on with things.

Not long after this a couple of the stunt boys gave me a storyline for a film about the life of Francis Hughes, a ruthless Republican terrorist who went back and forward across the border and was involved in dozens of shootings, bombings and attacks on off-duty RUC and UDR officers. There was respect for Hughes in the Republic because he had pulled off operations that were both cunning and bizarre, and he had earned the dubious title "The Most Wanted Man In Northern Ireland." He escaped several shootouts with RUC and UDR patrols, and calmly talked himself through RUC checkpoints while delivering arms and explosives to other arms cache locations. He reputedly once escaped while surrounded by British soldiers by crawling through their lines, dressed in combat gear and carrying a rifle and talking to the soldiers who mistook him for one of their own.

Eventually, a team from Hereford was sent to help hunt him down. Hughes had crossed over the border into Ulster and the team was on his trail. Eventually, after a lot of running gun battles with the RUC and UDR, he killed one British soldier and seriously wounded another. Hughes was also severely wounded in the leg during the exchange of gunfire, but managed to crawl away and go to ground. Eventually he surrendered to British troops bleeding and weak from loss of blood after the RUC searched for him with tracker dogs. It was suggested that the RUC said he should be left to "bleed out" (i.e. leaving him to bleed to death), but the British team leader said, "No, he's coming with us and is going to stand trial and face justice. We are not going to let him die here. He's our prisoner."

It has been rumored there was a standoff between the RUC and the British team, but the soldiers managed to get him into a helicopter and out of there. He eventually stood trial in Belfast and was sentenced to eighty-three years for murder. He eventually died in prison in 1981 during the infamous "H Block" hunger strikes at the Maze prison.

I remember various members of the Irish crew saying to me that the British military and the SAS in Northern Ireland were just assassins, but this story showed that wasn't true. They would not have taken Hughes to stand trial if they were just assassins. They were soldiers and subject to the rule of law.

This was the basis of the storyline I had been given, and they wanted me to present it to Ray Winstone. Ray said he couldn't deal with it because it was just a storyline and not a script, and I said I had just done what they asked. Ray asked me what I thought and I told him, "It's a good story because it's true, but the ending is slanted." I said I didn't think it told both sides of the story evenly, and if a script were to be written, it would need to be written differently.

Later, at the wrap party for *King Arthur*, I was walking around and saw an arm waving at me from the corner of the club where we were. There was a kind of sanitized zone where "John" and some of his cohorts were sitting, and he was waving me over. As I walked over, the crowd of people around him literally parted, and as I got to the table one of the guys got up and pulled up a chair for me. "John" said, "So, Mark, have you enjoyed yourself while you've been here?" I said, "It's been wonderful, I've had a great time." He gave me a look and said, "Yes, it's been good for everybody." To which I replied, "It's certainly been good for you, hasn't it?" He gave me a funny look at that, so I said, "That wall probably cost a few quid—you must have made a bit out of that." He just chuckled, but I was serious. There I was sitting with a known fundraiser for the Republican movement, and there would have been a time in our lives when things would have ended badly, probably for me.

Finally he looked at me and said, "That storyline you were given...?" I told him I had given it to Ray and he said, "I hear you're very close with Ray." I admitted we had been friends for a long time. "So what do you think?" he asked. I told him that the first thing Ray had said was that it was only a storyline and he needed to see a script before he could make any decision.

After a minute "John" said, "If we get you a script, would he read it and assess it?" I said he might, but that the problem was that the way it was written was very one-sided. There was a whole other side to the story that could make it much better—about the hunter as well as the hunted, and how they get to respect each other.

I added, "Remember, I know the other side of the story." To which he just nodded and said, "We know you know the other side of the story." I told him that when he had a script to get it to me and I would make sure Ray got it. But I never did see anything.

I walked out of there feeling as if I was in a rather strange no-man's land. I think it might have been this that triggered another incident that was off-putting, to say the least, and which in many ways illustrates the strange connection I have with Ireland and it's often convoluted and complex social history.

During the filming I had started seeing a girl named Tamara Conboy, who worked in the art department. One evening we decided to go to the theatre in Dublin, and spent some time wandering about the city. Early in the day I noticed that we were being followed. This might sound strange, but you have to remember that I'd had a lot of training to spot this kind of tail. There were at least three guys that I noticed, and when we arrived at the theatre they were there as well.

There's a well known rule that you never make eye contact with the person you're following, but we were on an escalator, and there were two guys behind us and one in front. I got the feeling that someone was staring at the back of my head, so I looked around up the escalator and the guy a few steps above us made direct eye contact with me. I literally took a mental snapshot of his face and the same guy was at the theatre later on.

Later, when I was in the toilet, a guy in a blazer just started talking to me out of the blue, a perfect example of a cold contact approach. Once he had engaged me in conversation he wasn't going to let go. He walked back with me to where we were sitting, and started talking about the Parachute Regiment and the SAS and the intelligence war—just out of the blue, which immediately made me think to myself, *Why is this guy talking about this within seven or eight minutes of randomly starting a conversation?*

We went back to the table where Tamara and I had been sitting, and the guy ended up inviting himself to sit with us. He bought us a drink and kept on chatting to me. Finally he said something like, "Ireland is a funny place; you never know what's going to happen here. You could just be sitting chatting to somebody and someone could just come up behind you or at the side of you and…" He put his finger to my temple, and said, "Boom."

At that point I grabbed his finger and the collar of his jacket and literally dragged him off the chair. Then I escorted him quietly to an exit and outside, where I pushed him up against a wall and said, "I don't know who you are or what you want, but just watch it," or something like that. I told him, "I'm out of all of that. I'm not involved with you lunatics—not either side. So leave me alone!"

At this point he got defensive, and said he didn't know what I was talking about, but that he merely thought I might be interested in a business deal. He even gave me a business card and said, "This is the number to call and this is the code word and this is how you spell it."

I said, "What the hell are you talking about?" I told him again that I was not interested, and didn't want to be involved in any way. I said, "I'm here to see a play with my girlfriend and I'm done with all that." Then I walked away from him. I don't know to this day who he was or what he really wanted, but I never saw him again.

There was always this undercurrent going on, all the time I was in Ireland, all the time we were filming. On the very first night I got there, the entire stunt crew went down to Bray and I went with them. I was sitting outside, on my own, having a drink, watching the sea, and these two ladies, mother and daughter, came up to the table and asked if

I minded if they sat there. When I replied no, they started chatting. I told them how beautiful I thought Bray was, and what I was doing there and how wonderful Ireland was. Then, right out of the blue, the mum looked at me and said, "I have a question for you—why do the English hate the Irish?"

Her daughter almost went puce, but I said, "I think you'll find that the English don't hate the Irish. A lot of us, like me, have some Irish ancestry in us. You might think I'm English but that's not so, and two of my best friends on this film are Irish. I live in America and there are more Irish people there than in Ireland."

The daughter was horribly embarrassed, but it was obvious that that the prejudice was still there. At the time I think I said something like, "I know there's a history to all this, and that a lot of it originates with the Catholic Church. I have a lot of questions about the authority of the Church and how it defines itself here." I was quite shocked by the whole episode, but the same kind of thing came up again later a couple of times. Most people seem willing to forgive and forget, but not everyone is.

This was at the time when the Boston child abuse settlement had just been made. Millions of were dollars paid out, and they were in the process of working out the Los Angeles settlement and the Cardinal Mahoney scandal.

Tamara's own family had someone that had been molested, but it was still expected that if she had children they would go to a Catholic school and go to Church. I just did not get it. Irish society was full of beautiful, gentle, lyrical, poetical, fun-loving people, but under it all was a very deep underscoring of conflicted spiritual and societal drives. Tamara used to say to me when she introduced me to people, "Don't say you're British." I asked her why on earth not, and she said, "Because so many people here hate the very word British." I said, "So is it better to say I'm from England?" She said, "No, just say you're from Yorkshire."

I was shocked by this kind of prejudice, but it's so very deeply rooted. I got into lots of interesting discussions about who actually was responsible for the potato famine. Apparently it was not the English but the Irish potato speculators. I remember having a discussion with one of Tamara's brothers and trying to get to the bottom of this prejudice. I kept saying I treated people as I found them, but he kept saying there was too much history between us. After a while, I said, "Let's just go over this history. In 1916-17 you had a revolution against the British Empire or the English, whatever you want to call it. You followed the doctrine of the Russian Communist Revolution. So Communism is basically how this all got kicked off—you followed that concept?" When he nodded I asked, "How did that work out for you? Not too well, right...? And how did Communism work out for the world? Not too good...?" Then I asked, "What about the Second World War? Didn't you remain neutral? How well did that work out? As a nation, you made a moral decision to side with, or at least remain neutral with the Nazis—the most destructive and evil regime in history, simply because of this ingrained hatred of the British. What's more you re-fuelled German U-boats in Irish ports."

He got very defensive then, and said, "That's never been proved." But I said, "The fact is that people left Ireland to join the British Army to fight the Nazis, but as a Nation, you remained neutral. In fact, one of the founders of the SAS was Robert "Paddy" Mayne!"

Then, the Republican movement decided that they were going take weapons from Col. Gadhafi. Tons of Semtex and hundreds of AK47s were supplied to the IRA from that source. How did that work out for you?" In those terms it made sense to me, but there was no getting away from the primal feeling of injustice the Irish feel towards the British—which is very sad.

The interesting thing was that Tamara's father told me how much he loved the English, because he had made his money in Liverpool and said that the lifestyle he enjoyed was because of the business he had been able to do in the U.K. One of Tamara's brothers said that the worst mistake that had been made was joining the Euro because they realized that they had handed over their power to the German banks and lost their independence.

At the time, this was both a very interesting experience and a heartbreaking one to be in the middle of. It gave me an insight into certain aspects of spiritual belief. There was a time when I went into a Catholic Church to attend the wedding of Tamara's brother. I had never actually been into a Catholic Church for a service (they could not believe it!) so I had no idea when to stand up, when to kneel down and so on. In fact I did not want to kneel at all. So I was looked at as if I was some kind of alien creature. Later on Tamara's sister came to me and said, "Have you really never been to a Catholic mass?" She seemed quite angry with me, but I said I hadn't, and added, "If I can chose not to, I never will again—I only came out of respect for your brother."

Later that night things got a bit rowdy when some gypsies arrived and took over the pub where we'd all headed off to after the wedding. There was a bit of a stand-up fight outside—and guess who it was Tamara's brothers came looking for to help?

I had a cigar going and had bought them all cigars as well; then one of the brothers came over to me and started telling me about the gypsies outside and one in particular who was hanging about inside the pub. As we walked over to the door he said again, "You won't need the cigar—what are you going to do with it?" I said, "I'm going to put it out on that guy's eyeball." Tamara's brother looked shocked. He had the look of someone thinking: *Oh my God, what have I done!*

The guy at the door who'd been causing all the trouble saw us coming, or maybe he heard what I said, because he backed out of the door, got into his car and drove off. I learned that trick from Greg Powell—keep your cigar handy, just in case!

So that's the story of being in Ireland and working on *King Arthur*. On the whole I enjoyed myself a lot and had some exciting times. But I realized afterwards how much the history of sectarianism in Ireland touched me, how strong it all was, and still is, even though we are supposed to be at peace. Once again the shadow side of my life, even though I thought I had left it all behind, had raised its ugly head.

At the end of the day, I headed back home to Los Angeles in November 2003, wondering what fate had in store for me next.

11.
A LONG DRIVE INTO THE DESERT

"The detective... must be a complete man and a common man and yet an unusual man. He must be... a man of honor. He must be the best man in his world and a good enough man for any world."
~ Raymond Chandler

Lost Boys

AFTER THE COLUMBIAN Money-Laundering Case I became involved in several others, and ended up with my California Private Investigator's License. I never set out to do this kind of work, but somehow everything seemed to lead me to it.

Being a private investigator in Los Angeles is no simple or easy profession. It's more of a calling than a job, and it challenges you on every intellectual and emotional level, particularly what you believe about the human condition and the consequences of peoples' actions. These actions sometimes result in tragedy. PI work allows you to look deep inside other peoples secret lives in a way that they would never usually allow another person to see. This can be very rewarding sometimes, because I've seen people act with complete selflessness and generous humanity, and yet the most petty and bestial instincts arise more often than not to reveal the fetid underbelly of the glamorous lifestyle. It can be a real challenge to keep a moral compass in the midst of all this deceit, manipulation, wealth, abuse and bone-chilling violence.

By 2004, I was beginning to get a pretty solid reputation as a reliable and hard charging investigator. I had done celebrity stalker work as well as corporate terror assessments and gang-related homicide investigations in South Central Los Angeles. I had also been working regularly for the Chameleon Group, an Israeli company based in Los Angeles. They had a solid background in aviation and corporate security, based mainly on the security protocols and methods used by El Al, Israel's national airline.

Most of the company's principals came from the Israeli intelligence or military spheres, and we got on very well. Even with the odd joke about kicking the Brits out of Palestine and how late in life one can be circumcised, we had a strong mutual respect and understanding of our viewpoints on terrorism. Both of our countries had fought a real counter terror war on the streets, and this experience and revulsion at the horrific acts of violence had left both scars and resolution in our cultural psyches.

On February 13th, 2003 I got a call from Kosh Haimovitch, one of the partners in the company. He wanted me to take a look at a disturbing and perplexing case regarding two young Israeli men, Ben Wertzberger, who was also known as Ben Berger, and Adar Ne'eman, who the FBI had assessed as missing persons. However, many things in the situation seemed to not add up, and Kosh was working in conjunction with the Israeli Consulate on behalf of the mothers of the missing men to find out what had really happened to them.

So, I went down to the Chameleon Group office in Woodland Hills and studied the file about the missing boys. Adar Ne'eman and Ben Berger were childhood friends. They had apparently gone missing while on a road trip from L.A. to Las Vegas to do some "DJ" work and enjoy some partying. Berger had already been living in L.A. for some years and seemed to have got himself involved with some unsavory characters suspected of growing dope. Ne'eman worked at Ben Gurion Airport in Tel Aviv, but also loved the club scene and wanted to try his hand at becoming a professional DJ.

My initial reaction to the case was stark and concerned. I reviewed the known facts and noted several omissions, anomalies and unanswered questions in relation to the current FBI investigation. Two agents had been dispatched to the remote northern Nevada hamlet of Round Mountain, where they had assessed witness sightings of Berger and Ne'eman as accurate.

It appeared the boys had arrived in Vegas and then left the city immediately, heading for Round Mountain. The reasons for this were unclear. What we did know was that they had abandoned their unlocked car and precious DJ equipment at the rear of a local police station in Las Vegas, and apparently walked away. This didn't make any sense.

The FBI agents sent to Round Mountain concluded that the boys had simply run away together. They had been identified at a bar and motel in the area, but after that the trail went cold. As far as the agency was concerned, the case was simply a matter of two missing persons. I was not convinced.

I remember staring at the map of California and Nevada in Kosh's office. I kept being drawn to the vast expanse of the Mojave Desert between the two cities, and in particular to the area around Barstow. I knew the area well as I'd camped at Deep Creek Hot Springs many times and knew how easy it would have been to find a remote, quiet spot to bury a pair of bodies.

The information Kosh had gathered about the folks with whom Ben Berger had been associated gave me a looking glass view of the case. Given that they were known to have associated with members of at least one organized crime syndicate, I thought it was more likely that the boys had either been murdered in L.A. and hadn't got to Vegas at all, or were murdered in Las Vegas and their bodies disposed of somewhere in the desert.

We had some tenuous but promising leads to go on, and these needed exploring further. First, I had to prove that the FBI report was wrong so that we could go back to them again with our own suggestions. I mulled over the clues and the map, but my attention kept returning to Barstow.

Kosh said, "What do you think?" I ran my fingers across the map, along the edge of the Mojave Desert. "There's only one way to shake out some tangible facts. Let me go to Las Vegas, talk to my contacts and then go to Round Mountain. I'll leave tomorrow, but for what it's worth I think they're there." I tapped my finger at the general area of Barstow on the map not knowing how fateful that intuitive impulse would become.

"Okay," he said. "Keep in touch, and be careful."

I have a CCW (Concealed Carry Weapon) permit for Nevada, and as I drove over the border from California I pulled over and loaded both my personal weapons. In those days, I kept a heavier SIG P229 in the car and carried the Walther PPK/S on my person. The PPK (of James Bond fame) is, contrary to some popular shooting myths, a very reliable, accurate and compact pistol and is easy to carry and conceal. The SIG is standard issue to FBI and Secret Service agents and fires a heavier .40 caliber round. I usually loaded both weapons with potent and reliable Hydra-Shok ammunition. On this occasion the SIG was loaded with 135 Grain, Jacketed Hollow-Points and 90 Grain JHP .380 rounds for the Walther. These high velocity rounds added significant punch to both weapons, and were highly regarded by law enforcement and criminals alike. There are a lot of opinions about ballistics, bullet weight and actions. However, Mike Grell's often quoted dialogue from his James Bond graphic novelization of *License To Kill*, which I mentioned earlier and on which I advised, was "a small gun you can hide is better than a big one that gets taken away from you." I still have the original black and white frame from the graphic novel hanging on my wall in Los Angeles.

As I drove to Las Vegas I began ordering my thoughts and letting my mind explore the possibilities and probabilities. The immediate issue I'd be looking into was a signature on a receipt where Ben Berger was supposed to have shopped but which did not appear consistent with that on an official document he had signed earlier.

I also decided to talk to a roommate and friend of Ben's, "Enrico" with whom he had stored his DJ equipment. This friend had been expecting both Ben and Adar to show up at his house, but neither had done so. Neither had they contacted him to say that their plans had changed, which was highly unusual.

Another friend of Ben's was a girl named Rachel, who had also been expecting to see him. She had been working at one of the bars in the Bellagio Hotel at the time the boys went missing, but had apparently since moved on. The first thing I did when I arrived in Las Vegas was contact Kyle Edwards, VP Corporate Security for the MGM/Mirage Group. I asked him for help tracking down and interviewing Rachel. I also talked with him for access to hotel surveillance tapes to see if they could identify either of the missing men.

By far the most significant issue was the validity of the Round Mountain sightings. Considering the very isolated location, on a little used route, and with the young men's car abandoned in Las Vegas, this was questionable. I needed to talk to the witnesses myself and try and validate the use of a distinctive false name, "Elad Leshem"—apparently used by Ben Berger on a motel guest receipt.

I called Enrico and he confirmed that Ben had called him on December 1st and said he was coming to Las Vegas. Ben never arrived at the apartment and left several valuable possessions and expensive DJ equipment behind when he disappeared.

Another contact told me that Ben was reportedly seen at a nightclub location known to be associated with organized criminal elements linked to narcotics, but no reliable witness who knew the men could positively confirm that the persons seen in Las Vegas were actually Berger and Ne'eman. Confidential sources also confirmed several leads regarding organized criminal elements and drug trafficking that were associated with the various reported places where Ben Berger had been sighted.

I also spoke with officers from the Las Vegas Metro Police Tourist Safety and Las Vegas Missing Persons—both to no avail. They had no useful information regarding the missing men's activities in Las Vegas.

Kosh called and wanted me to check out two telephone numbers recovered from Ben Berger's cell phone around the 4, 5, or 6th of December. The first was to a call girl business. When I ran the number a guy calling himself Jesus answered. He was surprisingly helpful, and offered to take a look at pictures of the men. He gave me a fax number to facilitate this. He also offered to look at the website records and check for the two names. In addition, he gave me an Internet address to check out. He explained that there was no point putting up the pictures in his office, as the girls did not work from there.

Babes answered the next call. I explained the situation, and the voice on the line told me that she knew about the case. She told me she would get the management to return my call. Shortly after I hung up I received another call, this time from a man called Angelo. He offered to check his records for that week. He said that he didn't keep a record of phone numbers, but retained names and hotel room details. He offered to check it out and would call me back the next day.

Call back he did, but said that he could find neither the name Berger nor Ne'eman in his records. I asked him to check for the names Huang and

Kharmik, two unsavory characters with whom Berger had been involved, but no references to these names were present either. Angelo was very cooperative and checked the whole of December while I waited. No names matched.

Given the nature of the outcall business in Las Vegas, (which isn't illegal in the state of Nevada) it was unlikely that the management would have had personal contact with Ne'eman or Berger. As Angelo explained, the customer would call the office and book a girl with a credit card. The girl was then dispatched to the hotel from wherever she might be. There was no central point where they gathered. Only the girls would have actual contact with the client. Further investigations of the girls from both businesses produced no results in terms of the calls that were made from the cell phone in early December, or who made them.

The file that I had seen also told me that someone had attempted to purchase $8,200 worth of computer equipment with Ne'eman's credit card at a Best Buy store on December 3rd. The purchase had been declined. The signature on a payment slip for another purchase of $460.00 worth of clothing at a shop called Cat Walk was obviously not Ne'eman's. Both these purchases were inconsistent with known facts about the men, but nobody could positively identify who had used the card. "George," the manager of the Cat Walk shop, checked his records but could not confirm who had made the actual sale and or what was bought. Neither store provided useful information as both businesses were busy and had a high turnover of both staff and casual shoppers.

INTO THE DESERT

After a fruitless couple of days in Vegas trying to refute or confirm whether the men had actually arrived in the city, I decided it was better to go north and see what sense could be made of the missing persons theory.

I headed for Round Mountain, Northern Nevada, in an attempt to confirm or discount the sightings on January 13th. It was a long and eerie drive through the desert with warning signs throughout most of the wasteland, "DO NOT PICK UP HITCH HIKERS." As I drove for hours without seeing another vehicle on the road and without cell phone service for large parts of the journey, I realized how remote and empty the desert actually was. I also understood why picking up hitchhikers was not recommended. I passed several large and fortress-like correctional facilities, way out in the vast desolate landscape, and as the outside temperature was hovering around one hundred and twelve degrees I pitied any poor soul locked away for any length of time in one of these stark, white prison compounds.

I finally reached the small, one horse hamlet of Round Mountain and drove up to the single solitary guesthouse, The Jumping Jack Motel. I booked into it and a cheerful lady called Mary told me about the night the two missing men had checked into the motel and showed me the receipt she had given them in the name of "Elad Leshem" and the hand-written details in the register. She kindly promised to photocopy the receipt and the register page, and described the guests in great detail.

That evening I talked to various witnesses in Carver's Café next door to the motel. I talked with several people who had been in the bar on the night in question and got some possible leads for the following day. I was tired and slightly frustrated and settled down into the small, sparse motel room with my trusty Walther under my pillow and the SIG on the nightstand.

The next day I woke early and hunted down every witness who lived locally, knocking on trailer doors and walking up dusty driveways, sidestepping pit bulls and children's skateboards in one hundred and ten-degree heat. I interviewed everyone I could find about that night in the bar. As a matter of course, I recorded each interview with the permission of the witnesses. Descriptions of the men seen in the bar ranged from, "One of them was wearing a wig" to "It was definitely the men in the photos, although I'd been drinking all night and thought they were younger!" Accents ranged from German to Arabic, and one witness claimed that one of the men "didn't speak English at all!" Clothing and mannerisms were also all over the map, ranging from "hippy" to "furtively suspicious."

No reliable, consistent descriptions of the men observed in the motel and café could be confirmed and crosschecked with the known facts. Even a local police officer, who was present at the time and talked to the men while in the bar, could not confirm they were the subjects seen in the pictures displayed on the missing persons website.

Although I interviewed a total of twelve witnesses that day, no consistent physical description of the subjects or their clothing, accents, mannerisms, conversation or habits emerged. Contamination of the witness's memories was a major factor, and although 100% identification by several witnesses was offered, no two witnesses had consistent and convincing memories. Although well meaning, these witness sightings had to be regarded with extreme caution.

Later that evening I tracked down two other people who had been present in the bar—waitresses who worked at a rival restaurant some miles from Round Mountain. While eating and chatting with the girls it became clear there was possibly another angle on this whole mystery.

The waitresses told me that Round Mountain was on the main ecstasy smuggling route into Vegas, and that one of the people I had already interviewed was fully aware of this trafficking and was involved with it. Organized criminal biker gangs usually controlled this business.

Then, the girls told me something else.

Various people had been warned to be wary of talking to me because my presence in Round Mountain was unwelcome and had already ruffled the feathers of the drug-runners. They had been made aware of my nosing around in their town because one of the folks I'd interviewed earlier that day had tipped them off. The waitresses thought that they were concerned in case I stumbled on the business and might pass on the information to the FBI.

The girls seemed sincere, knowledgeable and uneasy.

I took their unsubtle warning seriously.

As I drove back to the motel, I took simple precautions to make sure I wasn't being followed, but on arriving I noticed two new and expensive SUVs parked in the lot. I noted the license plates and sat in my car for a few minutes, watching the area.

Unpredictable Strategies

I mulled over my predicament and weighed my options. I could pretend that I wanted to buy ecstasy and see who offered it to me. I could make up a story about the missing men and who they really were, as a ploy to see what else I might discover about that night. Or I could let somebody know that I had been warned off and was going to leave first thing in the morning.

Or I could just leave.

At the end of the day, I decided to do something I had often done before—use an unpredictable strategy to provoke a reaction. I returned to the local bar to see who flinched when I walked in. When I walked in I heard stifled muttering and smiles that were fixed like granite on confused faces. I talked generally to several folks in the bar and let it be known that I thought it really had been the missing men in the bar. I had to stay and find out why they had been there. Were they looking for someone or something special in Round Mountain? Were they running from someone in Las Vegas? Had they mentioned anything suspicious, anything drug-related, especially locally?

This was still a real possibility that, at this point in the investigation, and could not be totally ruled out. Much of the information gathered in both in Las Vegas and Los Angeles had a definite narcotics undercurrent and once again, right here in the middle of the remote Northern Nevada desert, the narcotics trade reared its ugly head.

If there really was a local drug connection to the disappearance of the men and these elements were really concerned at the questions I'd been asking in Round Mountain, perhaps they'd make their presence felt and confirm the theory.

It was going to be a long night.

I sat, chatted and joked with the locals until late, drinking tonic water, while all the time keeping my Walther snugly concealed, yet easily available, over my right hip. The spare, seven shot magazine remained easily accessible in my left pants pocket. This, with one round already in the breach, initially gave me eight rounds available. Then I'd have to reload, and quickly. A combat shooting technique I practiced seriously and regularly, with all my weapons, and with live ammunition.

A PPK/S and fifteen rounds of 9-mm K hollow-point rounds would not be considered a serious personal firearm choice by some self-defense aficionados. They usually prefer bigger and heavier .45's and .357 Magnums. These are reliable and effective firearms and great for killing mountain lions, rabid pit bulls and Buicks, but hardly concealable. Once the rounds actually start flying and chaos ensues, a cool head, firepower and well-placed shots of any modern pistol caliber usually end the discussion.

As Rex (a solid Colt .45 guy) once said about his undercover .22 hideaway pistol, "When you shoot somebody in the face with any caliber they usually just lose interest in continuing the confrontation." Now, sitting in the bar, I tried to appear relaxed and talked amiably to the locals, all the time trying to evaluate them and work out who my secret informant might be. I continued to pry information from them to assess the situation, while hiding my real intentions by talking about the club scene in Vegas, missing "pot-heads" and ecstasy. I had to be wary, because everything told me the two men were probably dead, even though I didn't yet know why. If this was their last stop on the road, their killer could be sitting right beside me.

I finally said my goodnights and walked slowly back across the parking lot to the motel. It was a cold, star-studded night and I listened to the desert breeze, gently waving the sage grass and considered the endless and empty expanse of desert, vanishing into the dark. Should I get in the car and find a safer place to sleep for the night? Was anyone watching this small human drama, playing out in this remote and lonely place? What if I had wrongly evaluated the situation and lethal danger was waiting quietly for me in the motel room. What if that angry and deceptive soul was smarter than I, and had actually talked to me this evening and evaluated *my* capabilities and was even now waiting for me to sleep with cold and focused resolution?

I looked up at the sky and said a silent prayer to any guardian angel out there who might be listening, *Watch over me this night. Be my eyes and ears in the darkness and know the danger before it arrives. Let those who would harm me, feel your presence, waiting for them also in the darkness. Let them see our eyes, fierce and just. And in the light, bring us all safely home to our loved ones with forgiveness, fortitude and wisdom. Let justice be done in this world, and in this life, with patience, pity and impartiality, but tempered with a terrible and implacable resolution.*

I sat in the car in the dark and dusty parking lot and called Rex, "I think I might have stepped in some shit here. If I don't contact you by nine in the morning, call Kosh and let him know."

Immediately Rex offered to drive out to Round Mountain. I told him that by the time he got there it would be 9:00 am anyway. So he agreed to let Chameleon know if I failed to call in. It felt good to know that Rex would have driven halfway across the southwest to face an unknown and possibly lethal danger in the middle of the night. That's why he's a true friend.

I decided to stay and wait it out.

I entered the motel room, Walther in hand, and checked to see if anything had been disturbed. Once I was convinced the room was secure, I wedged a chair under the doorknob and locked the windows. I looked for alternative exits, in case the place should be engulfed in fire, and tested the ceiling and floor for loose or weak areas. The floor and ceiling were impractical escape routes, but both neighboring walls offered a promising alternative way out. I decided that I needed to deploy my secret weapon—a Remington 870 shotgun with a mixture of breaching rounds and OO (double-aught) buckshot. If necessary I'd shoot through the walls (maybe several motel walls) and fight my way out from there.

I settled into a seat in the darkest corner and of the room, SIG on my lap, and waited.

I heard the footfalls first. Steady, rhythmic and deliberate. There was a moment of potent silence, then a sprightly knocking on the thin motel door.

I arose from the chair with a swift and deliberate aggression, now eager to confront the forces that had drawn us inexorably together, like a deadly clash or ethical imperatives, to this very moment. I was resolved to bring righteous and just retribution to these forces if I needed to. I ripped the door open as fast as I could, crouching and ready to bring my SIG to bear on the unknown assailant at the door without breathing a word, to avoid giving away my general position.

A wide-eyed Mary (the duty manager that night) stood there. Unaware of the .40 SIG held behind my back, she offered me the photocopies of the register she'd promised. I smiled and accepted the papers with as gracious a nod as I could muster under the circumstances, and wished her good night. Then, with my heart beating a swift tattoo, I settled down again and spent the rest of the night silently waiting for the rush of footfalls and blaze of gunfire that fortunately never arrived.

The next morning, after breakfast in the local diner, I headed back on the long and monotonous freeway to Los Angeles. I called Rex and let him know all was well and mulled over the information I had gathered in

Round Mountain. I began writing my report in my head. It was obvious from the spread of witness descriptions that it was unlikely the two men seen in the town were actually Berger and Ne'eman. That and the name in the register "Elad Leshem," was a telltale lead that might prove decisive.

Proving a negative is, of course, a very tough challenge, but I was 98% sure of the evaluation. I knew that Kosh would trust my judgment, but the problem wasn't Kosh. The problem would be convincing the FBI that their agents were wrong and that the two men weren't simply missing—that some possibly calamitous if not lethal misfortune had befallen them.

On the drive home I received a call from "Rachel." She sounded nervous and wary but willing to tell me what she knew. It was pretty obvious that she had been more than just a friend to Ben, and I guessed she knew more than she was willing to say over the phone. She said that she had also been in contact with someone called "Skittles" and her boyfriend, who also knew Ben. She told me that this girl would be working at the Light Club in the Bellagio Hotel and that we could track her down there. She also told me that she had found a picture of Ben in Las Vegas and a CD he had burned for her. She requested an address to which she could forward these items, and promised to keep in touch.

On the route home I made inquiries with the Tonopah Sheriffs Office and several motels, but none of these provided reliable witness sightings. All of which solidified my opinion that the Feds were barking up the wrong tree, and that the answers to this riddle lay somewhere in Los Angeles or in the desert.

Vital Clues

When I arrived back in L.A. I turned in my findings to Kosh. It was also now apparent that one of the mothers had received a mysterious and mocking call from an unidentified female who had told her that they would hear some "interesting" news about her son very soon.

This seemed an incredibly cruel and callous act, especially if the men were really dead, but it provided the FBI with a vital clue. The callers had hoped to hide the origin of the call by using a disposable calling card but it was possible the cell phone from which the call was made could have been owned by the girlfriend of one of the major suspects in the case.

We set up a surveillance operation to keep an eye on this woman.

Then, Kosh and I went back to Las Vegas to interview Rachel at the Bellagio. She told us that she had seen Ben in Las Vegas around the third week of November 2002. She confirmed much of the information reported previously, and revealed new details of his contacts while in the city.

She explained that Ben had tried to sell counterfeit diamonds while in Las Vegas, as well as a substantial amount of artwork—which she claimed he had created himself. He had asked her to seek out an art gallery for this purpose.

Rachel also said that Ben that had played at a club called BJ's and at Ra in the Luxor Hotel. He had also appeared at The China Grove in the Mandalay Bay and Treys in The Barbary Coast Hotel. The partner of her friend "Skittles" had helped Ben find these engagements. She said she would provide contact information for all these people.

It appeared that Ben had not been making much money. In fact, Rachel said that he was down to his last $20 at one point. He had also helped her decorate her apartment and given her a small TV. He had seemed reluctant to tell her a lot about his life in Los Angeles—only that he was unhappy and felt paranoid in the house where he was living.

Rachel seemed to know a lot more about the house and what really went on there, but was reluctant to go into more detail. From what I'd seen of the place and what she was telling us, I guessed that the house was probably a "grow house" used to cultivate marijuana. This is a very common practice in the drug business in California.

Such places grew out of the medical marijuana provisions in California State Law, and had turned into a flourishing criminal enterprise. The dealer rents a nice large house or apartment in a quiet suburban neighborhood and fills it with dope plants. With special lighting rigs and potted dope plants watered and tended by a trusted "associate" who lives in the house for free, these grow houses usually go unnoticed. A large house can literally be filled to the ceiling with dope plants producing their profitable crop without attracting any attention from law enforcement and, with the dealer living elsewhere, if the house gets raided only the associate would be arrested. The windows are all usually shuttered to thwart nosey neighbors, and a large dog in the back yard usually keeps out the kids looking for their lost soccer ball. This was just how Ben had been living in L.A.

Fake diamonds, dope "grow houses," ecstasy-running gangs and missing men. Things were beginning to fall into place.

Rachel had not seen Ben again after the November visit, but they spoke on the phone almost every day. She had then tried to reach him via his cell phone during early December, but an unknown male told her the phone no longer belonged to Ben Berger. She said that she would check her phone bill to confirm the date. She said that she did not understand why Ben had not contacted her if he had returned to Las Vegas. Rachel had no information about the attempted purchase in Best Buy, but said that the Cat Walk Shop was Ben's kind of place.

Kosh and I returned to L.A. with some new leads and insights, which were increasingly looking more like a possible double homicide than a simple missing persons case. He told me that the mothers of both men were coming to the U.S. to meet face-to-face with the FBI to find out what they knew. This effort was supported politically by the Israeli Consul General's office in L.A. and by charitable donations from well-wishers sending money to a website highlighting the case. It also became clear that there was another reason for the urgency regarding finding Adar Ne'eman. He worked as a part-time security guard at Ben Gurion Airport in Tel Aviv, reputedly the safest airport in the world and the jewel in the counter-terror crown for El Al and the whole Israeli airline business. If he had gone missing with knowledge of the methods and techniques used for keeping air travellers and tourists safe in Israel, I understood why finding him was a matter of some urgency for the Israeli intelligence community.

We met at the Chameleon offices to discuss how we were going to explain to the FBI that they had got it wrong, and that the culprits of this crime were living free and clear in Los Angeles after protecting their marijuana crop with lethal and bestial cruelty.

Kosh and I ran over our talking points and mapped out the best way to sell our theory to the FBI agents who would be present and whom we knew would resent our intrusion. In fact, we both knew that the only reason they were tolerating this visit at all was that it was fully backed by the Israeli Consul's office. For this, I still have total and undying respect for the Israelis. That any government office would insist on action regarding its missing citizens, whatever they had done or however they met their end, was extraordinary. We also knew that the Federal agencies were absolutely set against "outside interference," and our take on the case was going to be a tricky one to sell.

However, we had one thing on our side. By now we had identified the real "Elad Leshem." He was, co-incidentally, an Israeli student whose family confirmed that he was travelling with a companion in America. The family tracked him down. He had indeed been at Round Mountain. Finally, we could discount the sightings reported by the FBI as a case of misidentification. But the problem still remained: what had really happened to the missing men?

More bits of the puzzle began to fall into place as we pieced together the last days of the two men. We now knew that the phone call to the family in Israel was probably made by the girlfriend of one of the suspects, either at the time the men were still alive, or just before they were killed. It was possible she was trying to intimidate the men and did not realize they would actually be murdered. If that was true she would certainly not want to be charged as an accessory to homicide, and would be a vital witness if she could be made to "roll" on her friends.

A week later Kosh, myself and a feisty representative from the Israeli Consul General's Office made our investigation presentation to two senior agents from the FBI at their Wilshire Boulevard offices in Los Angeles. Also present was a very experienced Detective from the LAPD's Organized Crime Division. They listened quietly, taking in the points we raised. The Consul was insistent that the FBI should hear what we had to say and treat it with an open mind, putting aside the usual politics of cross-agency investigation.

Kosh took a deep breath and stood up to make his preliminary presentation. He ran through the situation as we saw it, and used a schematic mounted on a blackboard to explain the linkages and subjects involved in the case. I then had to brief the agents on the Round Mountain investigation and why the flawed identification of the mysterious "Elad Leshem" had been a totally misleading.

Without actually saying it or appearing to be critical, I had to convince them that the agents sent to investigate the Round Mountain sighting had missed a critical clue and made a mistake in their evaluation, based on a false premise. This was in fact an almost calamitous error as it had cost precious weeks of valuable investigation time in the immediate aftermath of the disappearance of the two young men.

We sat for a while, tensely waiting for the agent's reaction. To our relief, both Special Agents nodded in agreement and began to ask more questions. As Kosh and I answered it was obvious that the agents were taking us very seriously.

An officer from Organized Crime was brought into the meeting at this point and we ran over the details again for him. He seemed aware of some of the names brought up during the investigation, and jumped up to go and run these through the database to see if they had any criminal history. He returned shortly afterwards and before he said anything I could see by the look on his face that they had.

All of a sudden the pieces were beginning to fall into place.

The agents were obviously impressed by our work and openly happy to take the insights we had brought to the unsolved case. They looked at us both and said, "Thank you. Good work." They did have one question however: how did we identify all the players? Kosh was economical with the truth and said, "We have our discrete methods." The agents just smiled and said, "Obviously they're effective."

Kosh and I just grinned sheepishly, because we both knew this was true—and that even if the FBI did have the ability they would have been so buried in paperwork that it could have taken them weeks.

We continued to track the case from a distance, but as with all cases where the Federal authorities or Justice Department are involved, once they take over, it's better to withdraw and let them build a case that could stand up in court.

Consequently, it's nearly always best to let the federal authorities do their jobs and take the glory. They have to make the charges stick and have to do the legal legwork.

Much better to slip quietly back into the shadows and smile quietly when a press release from the L.A. County DA's office landed on my desk later on.

Man Sent to Prison for Life in Murders of Two Israelis 3 and 1/2 Years Ago

May 8, 2006. LOS ANGELES – A 32-year-old man was ordered today to spend the remainder of his life in prison for the murders of two Israelis, whose bodies were dumped in shallow graves near Barstow 3-1/2 years ago.

Deputy District Attorney Shellie Samuels of the Major Crimes Division said Benjamin Frandsen was sentenced to life without the possibility of parole by Van Nuys Superior Court Judge Martin Herscovitz. Judge Herscovitz presided over Frandsen's trial, which ended with a jury in November convicting him of the murders.

The jury also found true the special circumstance of multiple murder. The District Attorney's office had decided not to seek the death penalty against Frandsen.

Frandsen and two others were charged. One pleaded guilty to false imprisonment and was sentenced. The other, Shane Huang, 37, was convicted of the same charges by a jury in a separate trial a year ago. He has not yet been sentenced, although a hearing is scheduled for June 1. Huang also faces imprisonment for life.

Ben Wertzberger and Adar' Ne'eman, childhood friends from Tel Aviv, were killed sometime between Dec. 2 and Dec. 3, 2002, at a Canoga Park house rented by Huang. Huang grew marijuana at the house on DeSoto Avenue, authorities said.

Wertzberger, who moved from Israel to California seeking work as a disk jockey, had lived at the Canoga Park house with Huang's blessing. Prosecutors said he took care of the marijuana until he moved to Las Vegas.

In late 2002, Ne'eman came from Tel Aviv to visit his childhood friend, Wertzberger. The pair ended up in Los Angeles and went to the Canoga Park house. Huang, fearing they were trying to steal his marijuana, called two friends – Frandsen and Turner.

Wertzberger and Ne'eman were killed at the Canoga Park house, where they were beaten over a two-day period, authorities said.

The bodies of the men, both 24, were taken to a campground near Interstate 15 and Afton Canyon Road about 40 miles northeast of Barstow. They were buried in shallow graves. The bodies were not discovered until September 2003.

At the time the bodies were found, it was believed that Wertzberger and Ne'eman were kidnapped from Las Vegas, where they were last seen. The FBI investigated the case initially. A federal indictment charging kidnapping was returned against Huang and Frandsen on Sept. 26, 2003.

Further investigation showed that there was no kidnapping and the murders occurred in Los Angeles County. The case eventually was pre-

sented to the District Attorney's office, which charged Huang, Frandsen and Nicholas Turner, 31, on June 22, 2004.

Turner pleaded guilty in January 2005 of two counts of false imprisonment. He currently is serving a probationary term.

In my heart of hearts I had known that the young men were dead. When the time came to go into the FBI offices to explain how they had made mistakes in their investigation, I already felt that I knew what the outcome would be.

As I had walked out of the room at the end of that difficult interview one of the mothers, who had been waiting to hear about the fresh evidence in the case, followed me into the corridor and looked me in the eyes. She asked if I thought her son was dead. I tried to avoid saying what my eyes obviously showed. She touched my arm and said, "Thank you. I just want to be able to take him home." I said, "I understand. And I'm deeply sorry."

As I walked away, already knowing what the outcome of the investigation would be, I felt greatly moved by her stoic, heart-bruised resolution. Looking back now all I can think is that we had at least we had played our part in given their grieving families some sense of closure and maybe even a feeling that justice had been done.

As I said, being a PI is far from easy, but at times like this at least you know that you've done everything you can.

12.
THREE WISE, IF VERY ODD, MEN

*"When you can stop you don't want to,
and when you want to stop, you can't..."*
Luke Davies, *Candy*

Tarzana

AMONGST THE OTHER STRANGE and unlikely things I've done in this life are some cases involving rescue work and private investigations for the rich and famous in Hollywood. Some I can't talk about, for obvious reasons; others are a matter of record, and although my involvement may not be known about until now, I want to put some in here as yet a further example of the way life is full of surprises, as well as take a long, hard look at the seamier side of life in L.A.

Between 2002 and 2006, while I was following the other half of my life working on *King Arthur* for Jerry Bruckheimer and *The Prestige* for Christopher Nolen (*The Dark Knight, Inception, Interstellar*) and the odd TV "soap" appearance on *General Hospital* and The Young and the Restless, I took part in a number of cases involving the rich and famous. Some of these involved celebrities with addiction issues; others were stranger. One day a call came in from my contact at Chameleon, asking if I could help one of their clients with a problem. I went to meet the client, Danton Burroughs, who turned out to be the grandson of the famous writer Edgar

Rice Burroughs. He lived just outside of L.A. in a huge sprawling house called Tarzana. It was here that Burroughs had written the Tarzan books which, as well as selling millions of copies around the world, have been filmed more times than I can remember. It was a place of many legends—there was a screening room there, where all kinds of famous stars of the old Hollywood days had watched movies before settling down to some epic poker games. There were stories about people like David Niven and Errol Flynn having long drunken evenings at the house, which had given it a reputation.

I met Danton for lunch and he explained that some time earlier he had employed a man to look after the house. He was supposed to be a grounds-man, who lived in and helped maintain the house, but he was strictly an employee and had no lease. Despite this, the guy had decided he had a right to stay there and was refusing to move out. Really it was a form of blackmail because the family wanted to sell the house and develop the whole area. The caretaker knew this and was determined not to leave. Danton had tried to reason with him, but he just got more aggressive and refused to go unless he was paid a hefty sum. Danton had offered to pay his moving expenses, but wasn't prepared to pay him what amounted to a ransom. He said, "I've treated this guy very well—like a son in fact—and this is how he repays me. He's lived in this house for six years rent-free, and that's why he thinks he has a tenancy, but we have an agreement that states specifically that we are not paying him to maintain the property."

Danton's lawyers had already served the man with eviction papers, which he had ignored. Now he asked if I would go down and secure the house for him. He warned me to be careful because he believed the man had a firearm—someone else who had been sent down there had seen it and it had scared them away. Danton said he was also claiming there was toxic mold on the property and wanted money for that issue as well. Thus, forewarned, I took a camera with me and had a weapon in the car for self-defense if there was an issue. I also loaded up some chains and a padlock.

I drove to the house and parked at the bottom of the driveway. Because I was on private grounds I was entitled to carry a firearm with the permission of the owner (which of course I had from Danton), so I holstered my SIG and headed up to the house, noticing there was a vehicle parked there. I went up to the front door and put the key into the lock—

and the door literally exploded inwards. There was the guy screaming, "What are you doing, breaking into my house!"

I saw at once that he had one hand behind his back, but I couldn't see what he had in it. I said, quietly, "Well, first of all it's not your house. I have a key from the owner and you have been notified that you have to leave." But he was raving on about how it was his house and looked as if he might be on some kind of substance. I still couldn't see what he was holding behind his back, but he got more and more agitated as I kept saying that the house belonged to Danton Burrows and that he had been served papers to leave.

As we stood there, him shouting and me being as calm as I could be, it looked as if he was going to raise his arm. I already had my hand on my SIG P229, a powerful 40-caliber semi-auto—but as I went to draw it, luckily I saw at the last moment that what the guy had in his hand was a video camera. I saw the light glint off the lens and the eyepiece and that's when I realized what it was. I let go of my weapon immediately and pulled my jacket down so there was no chance of him recording me sticking a gun in his face.

He started filming anyway, and was saying into the camera's microphone, "Yeah, he's on my doorstep, right now," so he had everything I did and said on film. I kept my hands where they could be seen and told him again, "Look, sir, this is not your house, you are not the owner and you have been served with papers to leave. I'll do what I can to help you move, but you have to go because you are not a tenant."

Of course he ignored me and went back inside, slamming the door in my face and locking it. So I decided to wait him out. I parked at the bottom of the drive and sat there for three days, watching. I knew this would worry him, because he would think if he left the house, I would go in and change the locks. To make it clear I meant business I chained up the gates at the entrance to the drive, and locked us both in the compound—though there was in fact a gap next to the gate that you could easily just walk through.

While I was sitting in my car a couple of vehicles turned up and about half a dozen people got out and said they had come to visit their friend at the house. I said that I could not allow them onto the property, to which they responded that I could not stop them. One of the people was the guy's mother, and she said, "I want to visit my son and you are keeping him imprisoned." I responded that as far as I was concerned he could leave any time he liked. Then I said, "He's claiming there's toxic mold in the house—did he tell you that?" They all looked at each other and I said, "I can't allow you to go in there, because that would be a liability issue for the property owner, and you will be trespassing if you attempt to do so."

At this point the guy himself came out with his camera and said, "I'm locked in here, you're keeping me imprisoned against my will and you won't let my family in." I responded that he could leave any time he wished, but that his family and friends could not come in because that would be trespassing.

This went on for quite some time and he kept on saying I had better unlock the gate. He actually came out through the gap next to it to talk to the people, and then went back in again. As he walked past me he said, "When this is over, I'm going to come and find you."

What he didn't know was that I had my digital recorder going. I said, "Please do, but bring a friend." Then as he walked away from me I called out, "By the way, I just recorded you threatening me," and pulled out the recorder to show him. Then I added, "Oh, and when we go to court, which we will, this will come out. You just threatened me, and I am entitled to defend myself." He stood there for a minute, glaring, then went back into the house.

The next thing I knew, the police arrived, having been called by the guy himself. Some of his friends stayed and some left. The police asked what was going on and I showed them the paperwork and the eviction order and explained the situation regarding the toxic mold—and they said, "So this is purely a civil situation?" I told them it was and they explained to the remaining family what I had already told them, and then left. I knew the situation could drag on, so I called Rex so that I could take a break. Apparently, the guy had tried the same bluff—calling the cops—with him. It got him absolutely nowhere, because when the police showed up, Rex flashed his badge at them and they left.

Finally, after three or four days of this, the guy started moving his stuff. Danton himself came down at one point and asked how it was going. I told him the guy was packing and asked if Danton wanted me to confront him and check to make sure wasn't taking some of the family's stuff as well. Danton said he just wanted him out of the house so that he could conclude the sale, but unfortunately a lot of personal items—pictures and original editions of Edgar Rice Burroughs' books—disappeared from the house.

I said to Danton, "You're a good and gracious man—and I wouldn't swop places with you regarding all this money and the house and all this stuff you have to deal with—you have my sympathy having to deal with an idiot like this guy." Danton said, "It's one of those things, particularly in this town—people see an opportunity to squeeze a few bucks out of someone and they will."

At a later date, the thing went to court because the guy tried to sue everybody he could, including me, for false imprisonment. The lawyers told us he had a video that proved he was locked in the building. I said, "What it actually proves is that he was given plenty of opportunity to leave and that he was free to go at any time, and that I offered to help him move." To which the lawyer said, "Oh really?" I asked if they had seen the whole video. It turned out they had only seen parts of it, so I told him, "You should get a subpoena to see the whole thing, not just his edited highlights." That's what they did. When we got to court and the whole video was shown, the judge dismissed the case.

While I was waiting around outside the courthouse and the lawyers were still wrangling I got talking to one of them. He told me the guy was unlikely to get a penny and that in fact he was going to end up owing them. They were advising Danton to pay him a small amount just to get rid of him, but Danton didn't want to do that because it was a matter of principle. He told me that Danton had spent $100,000 defending this case, and that if he could settle it for $50,000 then it has only cost him $50,000. Originally the guy had been asking for $170,000, so for the lawyers to get their fees and settle so that everything went away, there comes a point where everyone had spent more money on a point of principle than it was actually worth. The lawyers had to work out the equation where their bills were not going to be bigger than any advantage Danton would get. I asked what Danton was going to do, and he said, "As a matter of principle, he's decided that whatever it costs him, he's going to go for it. He wants this over." I said, "Good for him," but I was thinking how crazy it all was.

Ultimately as I said, the charges against me were dismissed, and the claim against Danton settled. The claim against Chameleon was also dropped, and the judge ruled in Danton's favor, so the guy ended up owing them quite a chunk of change. It's what we call a satisfactory conclusion.

After this Danton used to invite me up to his house from time to time. He was a collector and hoarder and had original light bulbs from 1944 Hollywood street signs. He gave me two huge bulbs that came from streetlights left over from old Hollywood. Danton was a very giving man—he would walk around and show me stuff and say, "Here, take it if you want it." He gave me a first edition copy of *Tarzan and the French Legion* that had smoke damage from the night his drunken grandfather set fire to the house in Tarzana! It's one of my most treasured possessions.

THE MISSING PRINCESS

In March 2004 I got a call from a client requesting my help in tracking down a beautiful, young European Princess who had runaway to L.A. with her wannabe rock-star boyfriend. The boyfriend had a possible substance abuse issue and it was thought they were at the Chateau Marmont, a glamorous and well-loved Hollywood haunt of film and TV stars and hard partying rock-n-rollers alike. Although the princess was almost 18 the client had serious concerns for her wellbeing and wanted me to find her and confirm if she was there or not. If she were there I would have to keep a close eye on her. I had some pictures and information about the princess and as I liked the style of the Chateau Marmont and knew my way around the place, I booked a room for a couple of days, thoughtfully financed by the client!

I was trying to work the case in a very low-key manner by talking to waitresses and doormen and just hanging around the bar and restaurant so that I was seen and the staff didn't get nervous about me. I certainly didn't want them to think I was a paparazzi or a stalker, as this would only arouse the suspicions of the hotel security staff and hamper my efforts. So my usual cover of a visiting British actor was once again the best cover I could have and quite a natural fit for the clientele and staff of the famed Chateau.

The client believed the princess might be located in a room at the back of the main building where there were some private bungalows, in one of which John Belushi had died of an accidental overdose of a cocktail of drugs in 1982. It's a secluded area of the hotel, very exclusive with a private pool and you need a separate key to gain access. I had surveyed the area but couldn't tell if she was definitely there or not and there were no rooms available to book in the area to make the job easier.

I decided I needed a distraction to gain some reliable information before proceding any further. I called up my old mate Jason Connery and asked him to come and have dinner with me at the Chateau Marmont. I told him right away I wanted to throw his name about to see how people reacted if we said we are looking for a friend of a friend of ours who maybe was with this girl. If they heard the name Connery, they wouldn't think there was anything unusual about it. Jason agreed and we booked a table in his name. Once we were settled we talked to the waitresses about looking for this friend. Jason helped me by talking about royal connections in Europe to try to draw her out. But neither our waitress nor anyone else we spoke to had any useful info. I understood they all had to respect the confidentiality of the guests—but it meant there was no hard lead for me to follow. The waitress meanwhile decided to sell Jason on her next film project and there followed a hilarious conversation about the plot of her film script while she pitched us her acting career!

There we were, the son of *James Bond* legend, Sean Connery, who had played his creator Ian Fleming, and a retired intelligence operator and Californian PI, dining in a famous Hollywood hotel, surreptitiously looking for a runaway princess, and being pitched a film project by a delightful if slightly bonkers waitress! Once again the irony of the situation made me chuckle and shake my head.

Even with this inside track on the guests at the hotel our waitress was unable to confirm the presence of any royalty hiding in the hotel, so another ruse would have to be employed. I was just going to have to get into the private pool area round the back and watch and wait. So next morning I sat near the villa area entrance until one of the waiters came out and I was able to slip in and sit in the secluded area. I took a book and put a key on the table and went into the pool for a swim. I walked around the area as if I was staying in one of the villas and ordered a drink and a sandwich from the hotel staff, sitting in the sunshine waiting for people to come and go.

In the afternoon a petite blonde lady in her mid-thirties exited the room I had been given as a possible location for the princess, but this woman was definitely not my target. She returned a little while later and I casually watched her enter the room to see if there was anyone else in there, but the room appeared empty of company.

The same lady exited again later in the day and I casually wandered to where I could observe where she went. Then I knocked on the door of the room prepared to say that I was looking for a pal but had got the wrong room! My knock wasn't answered and I could hear no movement whatsoever from inside, so I concluded the princess (if she had ever been there at all) wasn't home. I went to my own room, dressed and spotted the lady who had exited the room in the bar area chatting with a small gathering of people that turned out to be a film crew of various nationalities. After opening jovial conversation with one or two of the crew about the state of the film business it became obvious that these folks were unconnected to my princess and the lady in the room was actually their unit's production manager!

There was no trace of the princess, and eventually I had to tell the client that I didn't think she was there. I think Jason rather liked being part of a surreal, if unsuccessful, surveillance operation though and we still joke about it and our wacky if harmless waitress to this day!

Arm and Hammer

Another job I did at this time was for Michael Hammer, grandson of the famous billionaire, philanthropist and art aficionado, Armand Hammer, one time owner of Occidental Petroleum. Hammer was suspected of spying by J. Edgar Hoover because of his many close Russian connections, but was reputedly a high level go between for several U.S. presidents and the Soviet Union during the Cold War. Michael owned a house in Pasadena that had been designed by famed architect Paul R. Williams. Michael is a warm, generous and gentle soul and he has followed in the family's grand tradition of abundant philanthropy in all it's forms and the preserving of a fine collection of world-class artwork.

One day I got a call from Muke Cohen, President of Chameleon Associates, a well-respected and highly vetted security and investigations company based in California for which I had already done several complex and curious assignments. Muke briefed me that Michael Hammers' house had burned down and they wanted me to go and secure what was left. The place was worth about $20 million—Michael had spent $5 million refurbishing it—and it looked as if the fire was a case of arson. The house had been used in several movies including *Rocky V* and *Topper* but was erroneously noted as having been used in the original *Batman* TV series, so there were lots of sightseers and the press was close behind. I had to stop people wondering around in the grounds, since apart from anything else, the building was not safe and there was a liability issue if the remains of the building collapsed on a sightseer.

When I got down there, it was absolute chaos. The press was there and all kinds of people were standing around taking photos and asking questions. I called Muke, and said, "There's something about this that seems a bit odd to me. I think I should hang around here for two or three days to see what I can find out." He gave me the go-ahead and I moved into the Coach House at the bottom of the drive.

Armie Hammer, Michael's son, who is now a star of film and TV and recently stared opposite Johnny Depp in Jerry Bruckheimer's remake of *The Lone Ranger*, was staying in the Coach House as well. I asked Peter Crabbe (my pal from the Eric Idle tour) to help me because I could not live there twenty-four hours a day, and he ended up sharing the security duty with me.

One night I heard noises at the back of the house, and thought that there could be someone creeping around. I couldn't see anyone, but I could hear sounds. It could have just been creaking timbers, but it sounded like somebody walking around. It's one of the profiling marks of an arsonist that they go back and revisit the site of the crime, so I was thinking that if this *was* arson—and after talking to several people from around the area, I was pretty sure it was—I was convinced that the culprit would come back for a look at his handy work.

I decided to wait. There was a hole in the fence that looked as if someone had come under it earlier—and I heard noises coming from that direction. I had tear gas and was armed because I was on private ground and thought the arsonist might put up a fight when confronted. Peter and I did a pincer movement towards the spot where we thought we heard rustling in the bushes. We were both ready to jump the guy—when out of the bushes trotted a coyote! We both went, "Oh my God!" at the same time and stood down. The coyote gave us both a look as if to say, "What are you doing on my patch?" and disappeared quietly into the darkness.

After talking quietly to neighbors and various workers on the site I began formulating the idea that if it was a deliberate arson attack it was not aimed against Michael at all, but was probably about anger towards somebody totally unconnected, and maybe even a case of misidentification.

There were a couple of people we put under surveillance, and one day I got a call from the Pasadena Fire Department's arson investigator, Jon Samardzich, who confirmed that it was arson. They wanted us to go and talk to them and I told them what I thought—that it was not about Michael at all and probably a serial arsonist who wanted to leave his mark on the famous house out of some demented and warped sense of notoriety.

As far as I know to this day the case has remained unsolved and what would have been a beautifully restored home was a ruined shell. I felt very sorry for Michael, as he's a wonderful and selfless man and didn't deserve this.

Stalkers in Paradise

A couple of jobs were concerned with stalkers—a common enough activity in Hollywood. The first was when I was asked to trace a subject who was stalking a female member of the cast of the TV show *Charmed*, and do a threat assessment to see if he was dangerous.

The only thing they knew about the guy was that he was possibly using a cybercafe in Hollywood—and there are quite a lot of those! They also knew what make of car he drove and his general MO. There is actually an L.A. Stalker Unit, but to qualify as a threat it has to be an explicit one of death or bodily harm. To say to somebody, "I'm coming to get you," does not count as a threat. You have to have evidence that someone has actually been threatened with harm before the LAPD will do anything.

This particular stalker didn't appear to be violent or threatening at first, although he did seem totally obsessed and unpredictable. The production was worried because of some of the things he had written, like a lot of stalkers do, in the belief that they should be spending the rest of their lives with the target of their unwanted attention. It was decided no chances should be taken and to make sure the subject did not have the means or ability to harm any of the cast.

We did a search and found what we thought was one of the places he might be using, and I drove around Hollywood until I found his car parked at a particular cybercafe. I knew roughly what he looked like, so for the next couple of days I went in and out, hoping to catch sight of him. His car didn't move, but I didn't see him in the place for the first couple of days. Then, a few days later, I went in again, and there he was.

In order to assess him I had to formulate an approach that he would not suspect. I had found out a bit of his background and knew that he was a Dungeons and Dragons player. From the fact that the car did not move I guessed that he didn't have or couldn't afford petrol so one night, while he was inside, I took a look inside the car. It was obvious that he was living in it.

So now I needed to set up a situation where I could approach and assess him and get him to start a conversation with me so he wouldn't suspect anything. I took a couple of books about swords, got rigged up with the monitoring equipment, and went into the cafe. He was sitting at a corner table, so I went and sat next to him and put my books down on the table and started reading. After a bit he initiated a conversation about swords. So I literally debriefed him for a couple of hours—talking about sword stuff, where I came from and life in general. I found out that he had come from the Mid-West to California and how his parents were sending money to support him. I could tell from the conversation that, although he was a certainly obsessed with *Charmed* and one of the actresses in particular, he hadn't broken any laws and wasn't, in my view, a threat. Nor did he have the means or ability to get close to her.

I made my report saying all that and it put her mind at rest. The subject appeared to be a harmless if annoying fantasist, and her present security precautions should be adequate to keep her safe.

Another stalker case I handled regarding *Charmed* was both poignant and tragic: I was asked to find the subject and check him out in case he was dangerous. We surmised he was homeless and living somewhere in Santa Monica. I had few other facts to go on, but not much. First of all, I found out what he was doing on Facebook. Then I befriended somebody's friend, who then "friended" someone else, until eventually I was able to write directly to him. I started by saying that I was getting a bunch of musicians together to create a musical project based on *The Greenwood*

Tarot concept—using a bit of truth to make the illusion work. I told him I had heard he was a good bass player and would like to meet and talk. He agreed and we met in a restaurant in Santa Monica. Amotz Brandes, from Chameleon Associates, came with me to assess the situation.

I actually felt sorry for the subject once we met him because he was clearly mentally ill and had emotional issues. We bought him lunch and talked to him about his life. He smelled pretty bad because he was obviously living rough; he didn't have a car and used to go into the library to get onto the Internet. It didn't take us long to work out that he was just another poor lost soul and no threat whatsoever to the client.

Afterwards I tracked down his family in Florida and wrote to them telling them I had met their son and what condition he was in and that he needed help. His father flew out and I spent a few days trying to relocate his son, but he did not want to go back. Then his mother came out and I spent some time with her, trying to reel him back in. But he didn't want to be found or helped, and sadly I don't think they ever heard from him again.

Watching over the Great and the Good

Other work at this period brought me into the dark and sorry world of drug abuse. Rex and I had both been working for a company called American Employee Defense and through them, Rex found himself involved someone who had a business helping celebs with substance issues. He ran a recovery facility on an estate in Malibu Canyon, as part of a charitable deal that these premises were used as a rehab center. It was very secluded, very private, and consisted of several separate houses. It was a perfect place to have a recovery sanctuary—although they had the usual problems with the press climbing over fences to get photos of their very famous clientele.

Rex called me up and told me all about the place. He was babysitting at the facility. He told me that there were several big celebs there and a lot of press interest. He needed somebody to be a perimeter watchdog and keep out anybody who shouldn't be there. Was I interested?

I agreed to do it and drove over. It was an amazing and beautiful property in a private valley. Rex showed me the sober living house. All the people living there were famous. They had gone through the program and were living a sober lifestyle with the help of support workers. Rex showed me other properties further down the valley where people were still on the program. He told me there were surveillance cameras everywhere but that if I saw anybody walking about they were probably press. My first job was to escort them off the property.

The first two or three days I slept during the day and was out patrolling during the night—which was perfect for me because it was a beautiful valley overlooking the sea. It was very quiet—occasionally the odd car came in and I checked who was in it—but that was about all. After a few days we went to the main house and I met with the counselors and some of the people staying there, mostly very rich and very famous. I learned that Mel Gibson was a big supporter of this set-up and was sponsoring several people there. Though I rarely met him there, I heard lots of good things about him. In no way am I defending what happened later on in his life, very publically, but he'd had problems himself in the past and was instrumental in sincerely trying to quietly help many others including Robert Downey Jr., who fought a long hard battle of recovery and finally made his way out of his personal darkness and went on to huge international success.

So I became, for a while, part of the strange world of addiction, which I found very interesting because I have never done any drugs—never even smoked a joint, though I have been in the presence of it and have been offered it. I had to be vetted by the organization of course—they couldn't just let anyone in —and they could not believe this. They questioned me insistently about drug use and I told them I had never done it. I told them that I liked a drink, and that according to the British Army that was not a problem, and that it was my understanding that the British Army runs on its consumption of alcohol. The whole thing was interesting for several reasons—not least because I wanted to learn about the whole process of addiction and recovery. That was what the work was all about—helping people conquer their addictions and find a way back into society.

For my own personal reasons I will for the most part honor the privacy of folks who we dealt with during this work unless their issues are already openly reported on and in the public domain.

One of those we helped was "Anna," the daughter of a very well known Hollywood figure who had become addicted to crack. Her boyfriend at the time was supplying both her and her best friend. Eventually, Rex and I had a friendly talk with him and persuaded him to leave Malibu for good. Later on, Anna got together happily with another recovering musician visiting the facility and they got married and now have a wonderful family!

I saw things then that made me believe that addiction is in the genes. Of course, opportunity plays its part as well. I spoke to Anna on many occasions and one day told her that she could do anything she wanted and that there were doors open to her that are not open to others. She looked at me a bit sadly and said, "When your father is this Hollywood institution and he's done everything you could ever want to do, what is there left for me to do? He's such a monumental figure—it's a lot to live up to."

One day we were driving back from an AA meeting—and she asked to borrow my phone to call her mum. As she was chatting she went bright red and hung up. I asked her if everything was okay and she said, "Yes—it was just bad timing." I asked her what she meant and she stumbled around for a few moments until I twigged. "Oh, you mean they were having a private moment?" She nodded. Then she said, "I know my mum, I'm sure something's going on over there." I said, "Listen, they're in their fifties, they have several grown children and they've been married for twenty some years. If they are still having a few 'moments', that's not a bad thing." It was a funny yet tender insight.

I was involved several times in rescuing Anna from her rampages when she fell off the wagon. I felt genuinely protective of her and thought she was bright and smart and would make it. I have said many times that misery loves company. One of the reasons we had to be around all the time was that recovering addicts could be triggered by seeing other addicts, as well as objects that reminded them of their addiction. We were always looking for tinfoil, which they were not allowed to use in the kitchen because just the look of it could set somebody off someone's craving for crack.

We also tried to help a really nice Irish kid with sparkly blue eyes, called Glenn Quinn, who had been working on a show called *Roseanne*. The part he had played was the boyfriend of Roseanne's daughter, but he came in because he had a problem with heroin and had been taken off the show because of it. I really liked the kid. He had a classic convertible

Mustang—red with a white roof. Sadly, he was a hopeless heroin addict. He had been in rehab a number of times, got cleaned up and then fallen off the wagon again. It was enjoyable talking to him and hearing his working class blue-collar Irish story—coming from the streets of Dublin, taking a gamble and coming to L.A. and doing well. He started working on the hit TV show *Angel*, in which he had a lead role, but the drug problem lost him the job again and he was written out of the series.

Glenn was desperately trying to get straight and get back into the acting game and I totally respected him for this. He had no money left at this point, but as usual the facility had offered him help for free to get him back into the program. We all chipped in time and effort as usual.

One night I was staying in a trailer we had set up, with a couple of rooms where we could get a night's sleep, when Rex called me. "You need to come down here. We've got an issue with one of the boys in the clean living house."

I went down to the house and there was Glenn with a large stretch limo and what appeared to be a pimp and two hookers in it. He had gone into the house to get some money—presumably to pay the pimp. After discussing it, Rex and I had to ask Glenn to leave to protect the other clients. He went quietly enough, but we were very concerned for him although there was nothing else we could do. He was now endangering the well being of everyone else at the facility.

About ten days later, on December 3rd 2002, Glenn was tragically found dead on a friends couch in North Hollywood after taking a massive overdose of heroin. He was 32. I felt very bad about it and wondered if there anything else I could have done to save him from this horrible fate. But after all, Glenn made a personal choice and it cost him his life. A big part of reaching the bottom is coming to an understanding of your personal responsibility for your own actions—accepting what you have done or will do and taking a different path. However, Glenn's passing did serve as a warning to others in recovery at the facility that when things go wrong with drugs they usually go very wrong indeed. Some folks learned that lesson from Glenn's tragic death. Others did not.

Another guy, whom both Rex and I had a regular interaction with, was "Rich," the son of a wealthy Army Colonel. He'd managed to waste virtually his entire inheritance—some $1.2 million—on his drug use, particularly crack. The reason we wrangled him was that his father was desperate to get him help and off the streets.

Rich was already HIV positive and we had a team out searching Sunset Boulevard because he was basically doing gay for play, or gay for dope. Rex and myself and an entire surveillance team all went to look for him over a period of a week. There was one particular Starbucks on Sunset where he might be, and we finally thought we had spotted him. I got out of my vehicle to make sure, went into Starbucks and walked up behind this figure. I remember calling Rex on the phone to say I thought it was Rich, but that there was one thing throwing me off—he was wearing a dress! Rex told me to stay there and keep an eye on him. Then he came in and took a look for himself. It was definitely our subject Rich—though I never did get to hear how he came to be wearing a long black dress.

We later tracked him back to a seedy motel on Sunset and the next day waited outside while a counselor went in and did the intervention. He used the ruse that Rich had been under surveillance for weeks and was about to get busted. The counselor said, "You either go with these guys (Rex and I) or you go to prison because there are some pictures of you over the last few days and they clearly show you using crack and whom you were buying from."

Basically we coerced him into rehab, but he was canny and had people attempting to drop off dope for him in the grounds of the facility. He was hopelessly addicted to crack and a real handful. How he got the messages out to people I don't know, but it was always a difficult situation with him because he was genuinely liked and could be totally charming.

He was funny, but also very aggressive—he wanted to fight everybody. This got him in trouble one day when he decided to pick a fight with another of the team helping at the rehab center, an ex-Riverside County police sergeant called Greg Preece. What Rich didn't know was that Greg was not only a big man, but also into MMA (Mixed Martial Arts) and had trained with the Grace brothers, who were two of the biggest MMA fighting trainers in America. When Rich picked a fight with him, Greg choked him out twice.

We used the same tactic with Rich again later. I asked Peter Crabbe to watch over his cabin, and told him, "Whatever you do, don't upset Peter." Now Peter looks like a six foot six giant—but he wouldn't hurt a fly. When

Rich asked why he should be careful not to upset him, I said, "Because he just came back from a warzone. I don't want him hurting you and that's all I'm saying." We got a week of peace from that.

On another occasion some Hollywood pals were sponsoring him to go to the Sundance Film Festival. Rex and I were too busy to go with him and the counselor got one of his mates, who had been in recovery for some twenty years, to go instead. On the day Rich was supposed to go his friend phoned up to say that he couldn't do it because Rich was loaded.

Finally they went off to the festival, but his friend said that Rich was going to get loaded and was going to want him to do the same. I said he had better talk to the counselor about it because there was no one else to go with him. Consequently, he was convinced to go along, and sure enough on the way there "Rich" decided he was going to get loaded, and his new friend got loaded with him.

For a while we used to say we thought nothing was going to kill Rich, then one day when he had been out of rehab for over a year and living cleanly in Santa Monica, I heard he was found dead on somebody's front lawn; another sad loss to addiction and another waste of human potential and talent.

A well of misery lies at the bottom of these addiction issues. Nowhere is this better exemplified than in the case of the singer Courtney Love. She came into the program all spunky and aggressive and everything you would expect from someone with her character. Rex and I were left to try and look after her. That was where we met Robert Tameny. He was very experienced and they brought him in as a counselor specifically to work with Courtney. Like many of these guys, he was an ex-felon but he had turned his life around while in prison and decided to do something positive. He was a very good counselor because he had been down all the addiction avenues tried all the drugs and understood exactly what situation these people were in.

Courtney had a reputation for being difficult, and always wanted to fight with everybody. One of my enduring memories of her time there was when her daughter Frances Bean, who was a lovely kid, visited her. There was a big legal battle going on at the time over who owned the rights to Kurt Cobain's fortune and she was in the middle of it. Her manager came to visit her but something about him set me on edge. Courtney actually asked me at one point what I thought of him, and I told her exactly that.

It was close to Christmas and there was nobody else available to keep an eye on things except for Rex, Robert and myself. For some reason we had none of the meds that were sometimes needed to help deal with the addiction habit and we didn't have a nurse on the premises, so there was nothing to help us if things went wrong. This worried me because I'm not a specialist in recovery therapy—I was just a baby-sitter stopping the addicts from escaping. Robert wasn't happy that there was no meds either; but it was Christmas and I wasn't going to abandon Courtney to her demons.

On Christmas Eve, she had got some money to buy presents, so I took her shopping in Santa Monica and I think she spent between $17,000 and $20,000 on absolute rubbish. We had lunch together, and although people knew who she was and were talking to her, it was a lonely, miserable Christmas Eve for her.

We went to the Grammy Awards a short time after that and Courtney managed to mislay about half a million dollars worth of diamonds at the Staples Center in between losing Francis-Bean and having me chase her all over the place trying to keep her clean! I later spent half the night on my hands and knees searching the floor of the auditorium looking for the missing bag of expensive jewelry. (Thankfully however, a friend had recovered them from under her seat and we retrieved them the next morning).

As we drove back to Courtney's home in the early hours with her fast asleep on Francis-Bean's lap our eyes met and I looked sympathetically at her with a sad, poignant smile, trying to give her support and encouragement. Frances Bean looked at me, weary and exasperated, and shrugged. Then stroked her unconscious mother's head with affection and with that genuine and stoical wisdom sometimes only the innocent can exhibit, she whispered, "What can I do? She's my mother." I nodded at her and got the feeling she was strong and bright and would probably make it.

I remember thinking that for all her fame and money, it was a sad and pathetic thing to watch. Courtney was a funny and smart girl and no fool—but when you look at what happened to her, you think: what a bloody waste.

Chasing The Dragon

One of the things I felt made me good at this job was the fact that I could stand outside it. I have personally never smoked anything because I watched my father die of lung cancer. I've never even partaken of a cigarette, which I think can be a gateway to more serious drug usage. I can be with a bunch of people who are smoking and nothing would make me want to smoke, and yet I know many ex-smokers and the worst thing for them is to be around other people who do!

For me—it just doesn't ring those psychological bells. This goes back to the point about addictive behavior. I think it's sometimes triggered by a collection of different things—social, psychological, emotional and genetic—a dangerous cocktail. One of the skills of counseling is to work out what the triggers are that push people—smart people—to become lifelong addicts and remain addicted to the point of endangering their own lives.

It seems that no one is immune to this sort of addiction. The rich and famous get addicted for all kinds of reasons—because they can afford it, because it helps them deal with the pressures of their lifestyle and because it's part of that lifestyle. Nor can all their wealth and success save them. They die just like the poor unknown and largely forgotten wretches who sleep under bridges and fall by the roadside every day.

The work took us to some interesting places and of course some equally strange situations. I remember working a charity event for the Musicians Union (MU) in which Kenny Wayne Shepard and Scott Weiland of The Stone Temple Pilots had volunteered to help. It was a concert at the famous House of Blues on Sunset Boulevard to raise money for the MU's own rehab program.

Rex and I were there to look after various people. We had been told that another client was coming in to MC the show and introduce the acts. He was going to be a target because the place was one of his old hangouts and there might be dealers around. At one point someone came over to Rex and I and said, "We have a problem. One of his old dealers is in the audience." So Rex and I asked the guy to step outside. Things got a bit heated because he had paid for his ticket, but of course what the dealers know is that their presence triggers cravings in an addict, and we knew that the client had struggled with this a lot. We didn't want him to go off the rails after all that hard work because this pusher was there. Ultmately, and after a bit of a standoff, we persuaded the dealer to leave, but it was not an easy evening for us.

Many good people have offered philanthropic support and help to others struggling with addictions, and soon after this event in Los Angeles Rickard Elmore and I were called to New York to meet with Trudi Styler, who is married to singer/songwriter Sting. A friend of theirs had been staying with them as a houseguest, and had fallen off the wagon and disappeared for two days. They guessed he was on a bender. So we met Trudi, who was very nice, very gracious and concerned for his safety. She was also footing the bill. They had some leads as to where he was and whom he was likely to be with, so Rickard and I went off looking for him. After three days we had still not found him, but then Trudi called to say she had finally heard from him and that he was on his way back to Los Angeles under his own steam.

Not long after this we were given us the job of helping to get another famous client back on track. There's a hotel in Long Beach that kindheartedly let us isolate clients who were having a tough time keeping clean in a location where we could keep their presence confidential and safe from prying eyes. Recovery is a process that requires support and counseling on a regular basis. I learned that it was a prolonged and daily battle for some. Rex was there with another one of our team and an Australian female masseuse who had forearms like Popeye. There were two guys watching the client all the time, and the masseuse was there to make him comfortable.

I had been chasing Anna all over Hollywood for three days at the time, and finally managed to get her back into the facility, so I wasn't able to go along on this particular job. The doctor who was there had given Anna something to help her sleep, but she had not been completely truthful about what she had taken, and there she had a bad reaction to some of the medication she was given; she nearly choked on her own vomit. Another female celebrity who was in at the same time had gone in to check on her and came to me and said, "I think there's a problem." Anna had fallen out of bed and was covered in vomit, so we had to clean her up and put her in the recovery position until she came round.

I was reflecting on the fact that you can never trust an addict to tell you the whole truth about what they have taken and the amount they have taken, when the phone rang and it was Rex asking how it was going. I told him what had happened with Anna, and Rex told me what had happened at the Long Beach hotel.

The management at the hotel was very hospitable—they gave a good discount because one of the bosses was a recovered addict himself—so we had the client in splendid isolation in a room with a balcony. There was no other way out, and Rex was sitting on a chair across the door. Then, somebody in reception called up and asked if he wanted to check to see if our client was actually in the room. Rex asked why, and they said they had just had a call from the guest in the room next to ours saying that somebody had got onto their balcony, walked through their room, said good evening and walked out of the hotel. The receptionist thought they had just seen our client walk out of the front door of the hotel!

Rex went into the room and found that the client was indeed missing. He called me from the balcony on the eleventh floor of the hotel, saying that he had either jumped the gap between his balcony and the next one, or had fallen eleven floors into the air-conditioning building below. He was about to find out which it was!

Rex found out later that the client had indeed made the jump, walked through the suite next to ours, got out, hailed a cab, and was probably back home before Rex had left the hotel to look for him eleven floors below. This particular client was a master of escape, and there is a scene in one of his films where he comes in through a window, walks through the room, says hello to the occupants and then disappears. It must have rung bells.

Sometime after I was asked to pick up the same guy from where he was staying in Santa Monica for a meeting. His apartment had a big wide balcony, and we were standing on it looking out over the ocean. I was saying what a great place he had there, and somehow the conversation came round to the hotel incident. I told him, "You are one talented and bloody lucky guy, not only with the breaks you've had, but also the fact that you're alive and people have stood by you. Don't throw that away mate. There are plenty of people out there who haven't made it and see you as a beacon of hope. When you've gone through all this and still come back and have a successful life and career you become an icon to those people. Don't throw that away—because if you do, I'll throw you off this bloody balcony myself."

Everything changed for him when he got married, recovered and got sorted out, but the balcony story has become something of an urban legend. The punch line to the story is that Rex said to me on the phone that night, "So let me try and get this clear—we almost killed Anna and her dad's best friend while we were looking after them—that's quite an achievement!" It was our usual sardonic and dark sense of humor, but when you think about the potential consequences of that night it's horrendous. It was one of the reasons I finally gave up this kind of work.

I can only express my total respect for people who work in this area. I will always remember the emotional and moral strength and dedication of most of the folks I worked with in the recovery world. It is a harrowing and challenging world, and the humanity required to stay engaged and positive almost seems superhuman. I honor their courage and their struggle.

Once, flying back to L.A. after chasing another client in New York, I was picked up and driven straight back to the rehab facility because they had new people coming in that night and needed all hands on deck.

A large, friendly African American who had been brought in to help with counseling, picked me up at LAX. As we were driving back to Malibu the guy looked at me and said, "You're a normie, aren't you?" We got chatting and I said to him, "Can I ask you a very personal question? I've heard a lot of talk about hitting the bottom. What was that for you—what made you stop and change your life?"

He told me he had been on the streets of South Central doing a bit of dealing and that he had quite a bit of money on him as well as some dope. He was with two life-long friends in his car and he got out to make a sale and then got back into the back seat. One of his friends was driving for him, and when he got in, they both turned round and shot him five times; then they dragged him out of the car, took his money and the rest of the drugs and left him in the gutter to bleed out, then drove away.

He showed me the bullet wounds to his arms, chest and hands. I said, "Wow, that's some kind of bottom." To which he replied, "That wasn't the bottom…"

LOOKING AFTER CHYNA

What finally ended my involvement with recovery work was my association with the wrestler Joanie Laurer, who fought under her WWE (World Wrestling Entertainment) name of "Chyna." I put almost two years of my life into trying to help her and rehabilitate her career—while working on other projects in between.

Robert, Rex and I—the three wise, very odd men—formed our own little rescue company called IGI, which became an elite company dealing with celebrities. Our first client was Chyna.

A lot of people get paranoid during their addiction recovery, but Chyna was a lot less mixed-up than some. There were some legal issues between her and the WWE regarding the use of the name "Chyna." She was also estranged from her family, and told me some pretty wild tales about her father. Our first job was to tie up the loose ends and put clear water between her and all those issues.

Some of the people she was involved with spent most of their time jacked up on steroids or worse, and there were some real concerns about the threats and violence that occur within the underbelly of wrestling. Several of her famous WWE contemporaries had died of heart attacks, overdoses or had committed suicide over the previous few years. There was also a famous sex tape that that had brought her a lot of notoriety but shattered her reputation. We ended up getting her isolated and secure on a friendly tribal reservation for a month, finding her a doctor and a therapist to put her onto the slow path to recovery.

I have to say I was very proud of this, and when she was in good shape, back in training and had a clear head she was a joy to work with. She was very intelligent, funny and she looked great and I thought she could have a career in comedy because she had great timing. We got her back to her *Playboy* cover form and things seemed to be going well. I actually found her an agent in Hollywood and some theatrical management, and I went with her to get her bank accounts sorted out because they were in a mess. We got her an accountant to get the IRS off her back and started down that road as well.

I traveled with her when she appeared on the *Howard Stern Radio Show* and it was clear that the radio "shock jock" genuinely liked and cared for Joanie. Stern was troubled by her last appearance on the show where she appeared to be heavily under the influence of drugs or alcohol and gave a rambling and incoherent interview. Now she was clean, sharp and in great shape, and Stern's production team seemed genuinely happy that she had turned her life around.

All this took place over two years and I ended up being like a minder to her when she went out and about. We all took it in turns, but I did most of it because she was up in North Hollywood, which is conveniently close to where I live. I drove her about and stayed close to her in the clubs and at the events she attended. I also found her an acting teacher, my old friend Michael Monks, and she got a part in a film called *Illegal Aliens* with actress and TV personality, Anna Nicole Smith, who I also met while in New York.

During the course of the filming the production company asked me to go up and visit because they were not very happy with the way things were going on the production. Chyna was doing very well, but there was a bit of friction between her and Anna Nicole Smith's manager, Howard Stern (not the radio personality). This guy, I have to say, I didn't like the look of from the start. John James (*Dynasty/The Colbys*) was acting as a producer on the project. He was a gentleman and a pro, and wanted the press to come and interview Chyna on the set; so I met with Anna and her son beforehand to make sure there was no tension. I thought Anna was charming but psychologically and emotionally fragile, and that she could break down at any time. I was very concerned because Stern was insistent that there would be no press on the set while Anna was there. I had been approached independently about Chyna doing an interview, which the producers were keen to do because any press at that point was good for the project. Stern was insistent that Anna would walk off if we had press on the set. I told him that she didn't need to be there at all, because the interview was about Chyna, not Anna Nicole. Of course, if she wanted to take part Anna was more than welcome, which would be good for the project; but the producers wanted the interview to go ahead, so it was going to happen whether he liked it or not.

I told Chyna I would not allow Stern to interfere, and that I'd deal with him in a professional but firm manner. After Stern realized that I was not going to be intimidated by him he begrudgingly relented and we did the interview on set. I remember also saying tragically and prophetically to Joanie that I thought Anna was not long for this world. Sadly, my words came true when she was later discovered dead from an overdose in her hotel room, five months after her son Daniel had also died from an accidental overdose of prescription drugs.

One of the toughest lessons I learned from all of this was that (a) you have to be careful who you wrap around you, and (b) you've just got to be aware that when you are dealing with people with addiction it can very quickly go wrong. I thought we had done a great job with Chyna; but as it turned out, I was mistaken.

After stints on the reality shows *The Surreal Life* and *Surreal Life – Fame Games,* filmed in Las Vegas, it became clear that Chyna was having issues again, with the possibility of a serious relapse. During the filming of *The Surreal Life* I was very concerned about the amount of booze freely available and the general atmosphere of emotional chaos that the show traded on. I visited the house and saw the actor and stunt performer Verne Troyer pretty much out of control.

I liked Verne and had met him previously in the rehab facility with his then-girlfriend Genevieve Gallen. Like a lot of addicts he was great when he was sober, and a bloody nightmare when he was not. We had talked about David Rappaport, who I had worked with on *Robin of Sherwood,* and his struggle with depression that eventually led to his suicide in the Hollywood Hills in May 1990. I had hoped that this would impress upon Verne how fortunate he was and encourage him to keep positive and focused on living a full and productive life.

I was later called by the producers to the house in Nevada to pick up Chyna's Chihuahuas, which were running amok and driving everyone crazy. The dogs ended up living with me for two weeks while she completed filming and they drove me bloody bonkers!

Soon after we were having a birthday gathering in The Robin Hood Pub, which might have been difficult except that some people can have a glass of wine once they have recovered and they will be fine. I didn't know how far it had gone with Chyna because, when she was with me, if I had a glass of wine, she would have a glass of wine, and if I had two glasses then she would have two glasses, and then we would stop. For this reason, I thought she was doing okay, and it wasn't until later that I found out she was drinking two or three bottles of champagne a night, and was not taking her meds. One of the issues with taking steroids for wrestling, particularly large amounts of testosterone, is that they burn out the thyroid's ability to manage emotions. The thyroid is very important in terms of balancing hormones and chemicals in the brain and reducing mood swings.

Apparently Chyna's thyroid wasn't working very well anymore so she was on daily medication to correct the imbalance. When she kept up the medication she was fine, but I couldn't be with her 24/7, and things were spiraling out of control behind my back.

The night we were in The Robin Hood Pub there was a girl there called "Maeve" who was apparently a financier who had come in to help put a film together. There was something about her that made me uneasy, and I went outside and called some contacts in New York to check out a building she said she owned; I discovered that it was in fact a rehab facility. It was possible that she had been an addict herself before she had travelled to Los Angeles.

By this time alarm bells were ringing in my head, but when I got back inside Chyna had already begun to strike up a friendship with "Maeve." That was the beginning of the end of my working with Chyna, because under "Maeve's" influence she decided that she didn't want to work with me anymore. She also fell out with her then boyfriend who I liked very much because he was stable, hardworking and a "normie."

Chyna had previously done a porno tape with her ex-WWE wrestler boyfriend Sean Waltman. She told me that she had been bullied into doing it and had not been paid. This turned out not to be true, and before we went our separate ways I confronted her about it. I told her that I knew she had received payment for the tapes and that she should give the money to charity or use it to rescue other people with substance issues. She said that was a good idea, and told me to use it for whatever recovery needs I might have and cover my own expenses.

I ended up getting back some of the money I had spent, because I wasn't being paid for all of the time I had put in, but was doing it out of a liking for Chyna as a human being. I paid back some of the debts that Rex, Robert and I had incurred working for her, and the rest went towards recovery work for other people. If someone came to us with a situation, or they had no money and their son was on a bender, I used that money to get them into safe hands.

Towards the end of the time I worked for her Chyna accused me of all kinds of deranged things, but I had moved on. About a year after this the production company on the film she had been making called me and asked if I would talk to her. The film was in trouble and she had contacted them and asked them to see if there was anything I could do to help. At the time I was just about to start the first *Transformers* film, but I did speak to her and we had a discussion about finances. I asked her if she still had "Maeve" around and she said yes, they were still friends, so I said, "I can't deal with her—I'm not going to get into a competition with the likes of 'Maeve' over this." I told her I cared about her and wished her well, and that I hoped her career would go well, but I wasn't going to give her any more time.

So that was the end of that.

Eventually, our own counselor, Robert, fell off the wagon for a period and ended up in jail. That was when I decided I was done with that work. I was battered emotionally by my experiences because I put so much into it. Also, show business work had picked up again for me and I was back in the film game. Rex carried on in the business for quite some time and has worked with a lot of people since, but by 2005 I had pretty much had enough. I don't think I will ever fully understand the addiction and recovery labyrinth.

One of the things that Rex and I used to joke about in the rehab house was that as soon as there was a break in the activities in the morning, or at lunch time, people would be outside smoking like chimneys, because that was the only addictive substance they were allowed. It might not have been drugs or alcohol, but they were still addicted to something. I think if people have that "addiction gene" they can become hooked on anything—even religion.

Substances are so readily available to high profile show business figures and celebrities in L.A., that it's the gateway to hell for susceptible people. It's not just the rich and famous, not just show business folk; it's also professional people from all walks of life—I also worked with surgeons, architects, lawyers, military and lawyers. Addicts will do anything to get a fix. That's why you can't always trust them—or in the long run feel sorry for them. You have to stay one step back and not get too involved emotionally or you lose perspective.

The people we helped recover, who got on with their lives, I am very proud of. I feel very sad for people that didn't and are either out there still with issues or didn't make it. But I came to realize we could never make decisions for people. You can make recommendations and show them new pathways, you can support them if they choose to do that—but they have to do it themselves. I have the greatest respect for those who managed to win the battle. I might have walked away in the end, but I can say I did the best I could.

HOLD FAST

215

18.

19.

20.

21.

22.

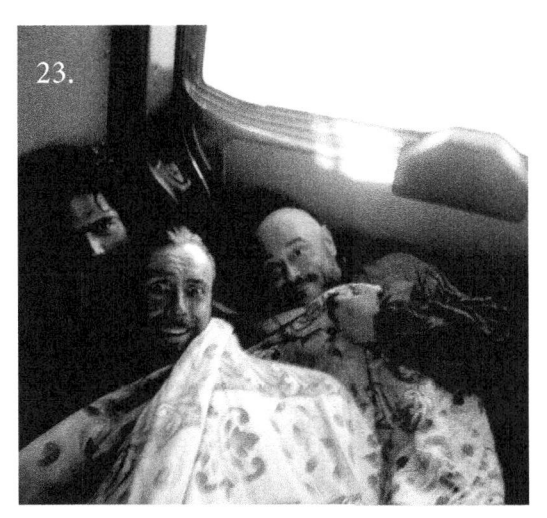

HOLD FAST

23.

24.

25.

26.

27.

217

Captions

12. Outside Carnegie Hall during the Monty Python tour with Eric Idle. Pic: MR

13. On exercise with HMS Fearless (L10) somewhere in the North Sea. Now scrapped this venerable and much loved old warhorse and Landing Platform Dock (LPD) was once used extensively by U.K. Special Forces. Pic: Anon

14. The legendary Harry Humphries and I during Transformers-Dark of the Moon at Launch Complex 39A, Kennedy Space Center, Florida with the Space Shuttle Endeavor ready for fueling for it's last trip into space.

15. The Excalibur from King Arthur. Quite an unwieldy weapon for Clive Owen to control during fights on the set. Pic: MR

16. My mate Optimus Prime. Pic: Abbie Bernstein

17. The Merry Men in one of my favorite haunts, The Robin Hood Pub in Sherman Oaks, Los Angeles. Pic: M.R.

18. Author in the butts wearing mixed shooting range 'battle rattle' and treasured 70s era smock and junglies. The early 'nice idea-poorly executed' SA80 assault rifle was later extensively modified by Heckler & Koch to improve reliability, durability and ballistics.

19. On the historic Launch Complex 39A at Kennedy Space Center, Cape Canaveral during filming of Transformers: Dark of the Moon. With sound crew members! Kevin Cerchiai and Scott Solan and the Space Shuttle Endeavor awaiting fueling for it's final mission commanded by one of my personal heroes, Scott Kelly. Pic: Pete Devlin (Sound Mixer)

20. Three Yorkshiremen. Backstage at the beautifully majestic Wang Theatre, Boston with Eric Idle and Peter Crabb on the last night of our eastern leg of the U.S. tour with Eric Idle Exploits Monty Python.

21. With the cast of Blood Type at the historic Prebendal, the home of Robin & Dwina Gibb during shooting of the sizzle-reel written by John Matthews and Wil Kinghan which I directed. Pic: Caitlin Matthews

22. An SBS LRIC (Long Range Insertion Craft) runs alongside HMS Fearless somewhere in the North Atlantic.

23. Pirates on parade! John Silver (Luke Arnold) James Flint (Toby Stephens) and Hal Gates (Mark Ryan) snuggle under a blanket after another long, cold, wet night of shooting Black Sails in Cape Town, South Africa.

24. 'I Am A Man'...With a little helpful support from wardrobe mistress Laura Baker while on tour with Eric Idle.

25. Keira Knightley gets her archery eye in during fight rehearsals for King Arthur. Good form I say! Pic: MR

26. Elizabeth Larner and I. Blondes & Bombshells - Quaglino's, London 1979. By Ronnie Cass, Robert Howe and Derek Braeger Pic: Stephen Hill

27. A Lockheed A12. The forerunner of the famed SR-71 Blackbird spyplane at San Diego Air Space Museum and the inspiration for the character "Jetfire" in Transformers: Revenge of the Fallen.

13.
BECOMING SEVERAL GIANT ALIEN ROBOTS

"You think you were born? You were built!"
— Lockdown: *Transformers IV: Age of Extinction*

Voicing Transformers

In SPRING 2006 my then-agent Brian McCabe called me and said that he had put me up for a job, and that the casting people wanted to see me. It was so hush-hush he couldn't even tell me what the name of the project was, or indeed anything about it. They were going to send me five or six pages of dialogue that they didn't want me to learn, but said that they did want me to do all five characters in one go, as if they were having a conversation between themselves with me using different voices for each one.

I went along to the meeting at the casting office and there was no one there but me. A very nice lady called Michelle Lewitt was looking at my CV and she said, "You just worked with Antoine Fuqua! What was that like?" I told her it was fine, that we got on really well, and that he trusted me with the sword and stunt guys. She asked me why I thought that was? I said, "Because he's the director and gets what he wants." To which she replied, "So you work well under pressure." I said, "Well, it's not really pressure if you're prepared. I like to be ready for any eventuality when we step onto the set in the morning." She said, "But isn't Antoine pretty intense and fires people off the set?" I said, "I have seen him do that, but usually the person deserves it, or they've not done what he asked them to do." She said, "You must have a thick skin." I jokingly responded, "Well, if you're walking around a set with a big sword over your shoulder, or an axe, people tend to treat you with a certain amount of respect. But we did genuinely get on."

Then I asked her, puzzled, "Is this an Antoine project?" "Oh no," she said, "It's Michael Bay." I did not have any preconceptions about Michael—I had heard about him from various people—Jason Connery had told me a story about Sean and Michael Bay working together on *The Rock*, but I hadn't heard anything that unusual about him. I think she was looking at me to see what my reaction was to what she had just told me, and said something like, "What do you think about that?" I said, "Well, I take people as I find them, and if they're professional and know what they're doing, it's my responsibility to make things work for them and help them get it in the can."

We left it at that and I recorded the scene in Michelle's office that was eventually filmed at Griffith Park Observatory. I did all the voices, including the character of Jazz with a Sean Connery voice. Michelle filmed it and about a week later I got a call that told me I was going to be working on the set of *Transformers*!

All I knew about the job at this point was that it was going to involve voicing some of the characters. Although some people class this as voice-over, it's not just that. It's voice-over multiplied by ten. I knew a bit about the franchise because the animated stories were being aired in the U.K. while we were shooting *Robin*, so I started reading as much as I could to familiarize myself with the characters.

When I showed up for that first *Transformers* outing, back in 2006, it actually didn't take me long to work out what I had to do. I got it from the moment Michael showed me the first primitive "animatics," which are simple "wire framework" drawings animated very simply to show what's going to happen with the robots in the scene.

The first scene we shot was the one where we are at the Witwicky household, and the robots are in the back garden, trying to be inconspicuous. I said, "That's funny, you've got giant robots trying to hide around the house as if they can't be seen." Michael said, "So you get it?" I said,

"Yup! I get it." He just said, "Okay then! Let's go."

That was it. The most important technique I learned, right from the word go, was being able to follow cues from a position near the monitor. I was used to that because when you're doing fights you have to be watching the monitor most of the time. I would stand there with a headset watching the actors so that Michael could give me the cues when he wanted me to say the lines, or when he wanted the electrics to be sparked. I knew what he was trying to achieve technically, but it was sheer blind luck that the experiences I've had in my career behind the camera had equipped me for this. I could not have planned it if I'd tried!

I was also very fortunate to have sound guru Peter Devlin on the set. He had also worked on *King Arthur*, and is an internationally respected ex-BBC sound-mixer whose team have worked with Michael for over a decade. Having them in my corner was a huge technical advantage.

One of the critical decisions in my career that really equipped me for this role in the *Transformers* franchise was not an acting job at all. It was working with Bob Anderson on *First Knight*. The decision to work behind the camera, to learn what happens on a big set, was a huge education. Everything I learned on that set was directly applicable to the work I was doing on *Transformers*. For instance, in some shots the actual sword blades had not been in the weapons at all. When they did the final big fight between Richard Gere and Ben Cross, they just used the hilt sets and painted the blades in using CGI later so that they seemed to move faster. Bob Anderson had two sets of swords made without blades—just hilt sets—so they could do the sword moves and then the visual effects guys could put the blades in later. So in the last fight, when Richard finally goes bonkers and is moving really fast until he finally slashes Ben across the throat, there were no actual blades in the swords.

Knowing about that kind of CGI technique prepared me for Transformers. Obviously the technology is much more advanced and we were painting giant alien robots into the film rather than swords. But I remember thinking at the time that if the technology took off, there would be nothing that couldn't be done.

So the concept was not new to me when I started on *Transformers 1*. What *was* new to everybody was how it was going to be applied. I had seen *Jurassic Park*, where dinosaurs interact with human beings, and I knew that the technology was going to change everything. What you are trying to do is get the actors to interact with things that often aren't there, and still deliver off-camera dialogue. It would be too difficult for one person to do five different voices in a live-action film and keep them all unique and different; you would need five different actors, one for each character. On *Transformers* in the post-production phase I would go into the studio and do all the dialogue, because the thing that takes time is the rendering of the actual robots, and they wanted to edit the scene into some kind of a near-final cut, then paint the robots into the action. Today the Industrial Light and Magic (ILM) team, headed by Scott Farrar, have it down to a fine art, but back then it took time to add the details for the transformation of the robots. I would go in and do the dialogue with initial line drawings so that they could time-out the scene and work out the editing. Once they have a something close to a final cut of a scene they can start rendering the final version of the film. I voiced scenes several times for the scratch-track until Michael was happy with them and he could decide how the scenes would flow from an editing standpoint. Michael could then choose the bits of dialogue that he wanted to keep in the film.

In *Transformers* I had done various lines early on, including bits of alien language and off-screen military lines, but I wasn't sure how they were going to fit in. At that point Bumblebee didn't speak, and therefore had no lines. Then one day Michael just said to me, "Try these lines." It was the dialogue about wanting to stay with the boy, Sam Witwicky. We just wild-tracked it in Michael's editing suite at Bay Films, but I had no idea how, or if, it would be used.

I had done many scratch-track lines this way and it was my voice that the other actors would hear when they went in to re-voice the original robots. They have a guide track of vocals to follow—and I believe Michael told them to say the lines exactly as I had spoken them on the track. That's why a lot of people have commented that the voices sound a bit like me—same intonation, pacing and so on—when, in fact, it was other actors actually speaking the lines.

Brian called me some time after and said that the production wanted to use my Bumblebee lines; Michael had decided to keep them in the film. I told Brian that I didn't recall doing any Bumblebee dialogue, as he didn't speak in the version of the scenes I had seen! We went back and forth for a while, but eventually the sound mixers on the production called me and played the lines for me and asked, "This is you, right?" "Yup! That's me alright," I said. I had forgotten all about them!

I have been able to work with some wonderful and talented actors on all four of the *Transformers* movies. Shia LaBeouf was great from the beginning—very open and approachable, very relaxed for such a young actor—professional and confident. We often ran lines together. He got on well with the crew, absorbed direction and delivered lines with ease and spontaneity. John Turturro ad-libbed a lot, as did Shia.

To Michael Bay's credit, he allows the actors to do this. He always says, "Go ahead! Try it." He knows there's nothing to lose. If it stays in the film, it stays in; if it doesn't, it doesn't. There were several of moments where Shia did this. He was naturally funny, and his delivery was magical.

Julie White was also a brilliant improviser, and together with Kevin Dunn almost entirely improvised the whole masturbation scene with Shia, which was hilarious!

At the beginning of the first film we were all trying to work out the best way to deliver the robot lines. This was the first time it had been done in the way we were doing it on a special effects film of this scale, and it was then that I realized I needed to be next to the monitor so that I could take cues from Michael *and* Shia at the same time. That style of working was developed, as far as I'm aware, for the first time on *Transformers*. It was groundbreaking in every aspect, and it's still the way we do it, although we've refined the technique quite a bit over the last four films.

When *Transformers* was released it generated a reasonably positive response from the critics and a massive cheer from the fans. It generated $700+ million at the worldwide box office, and spawned a whole new Transformers toy revival and interest in IMAX cinemas. It pushed the boundaries of what CGI could do in film and amplified Michael Bay's clout as one of the most bankable directors in Hollywood. The film was a massive worldwide commercial success on many levels. People went to see it in droves, which is what this business is about—because if they don't play well you won't get to make another one for a very long time!

People can get very critical about a popular film like this—a real crowd-pleaser. But what needs to be remembered is that it's a roller coaster ride—you go, you pay your money, you sit on the ride, and for two and a half hours it takes your mind off the troubles of the world, and you believe that cars can transform into alien robots. It's entertainment, not Shakespeare. There's usually a little moral story in there as well—it does have its moments of morality and human reflection as well as iconic and universally archetypal themes.

There are those who knock the *Transformers* franchise because the movies are based on the original toy line featuring giant alien robots that disguise themselves as vehicles. I've had many conversations about inanimate objects not having souls, and it's a very interesting aspect of the whole thing. What would happen if there were a type of sentient alien entity in the universe made out of some form of living metal? Imagine if an alien race like that really existed somewhere out there. Would it be so different from ours? We simply don't know what might or might not exist out there in the universe. During the convention tours I've been doing around the world to promote the films, the whole idea of living machines has become a kind of urban myth. I've had kids come up to me and ask, "Is my dad's car a Transformer? My dad says his car turns into an alien robot at night while I'm asleep." I always say, "I'm sure your dad knows the truth—but it's a secret he's not supposed to tell."

I think everyone was taken aback by the commercial success of the first film—and I was certainly surprised when I heard those last lines come out—the ones Bumblebee says when he finally gets his voice back. I am very grateful for that; I am now, for the rest of my life and career, associated with Bumblebee—one of the most popular and easily recognizable film franchise icons anywhere in the world. You can buy an actual Bumblebee Camaro from Chevy with the *Transformers* logos on the side and on the steering wheel; it's yellow with black stripes. A lot of people buy the parts separately and add them to their cars. I have been to Japan twice, Hong Kong, New Zealand and Australia, all over America and back to the U.K. just to talk about the *Transformers* franchise and about being Bumblebee, Jetfire, and now Lockdown.

REVENGE OF THE FALLEN

With all I had learned from *Transformers* I was very happy to be called back for the second of the series, *Transformers: Revenge of the Fallen*. In that movie, as well as doing voices for some of the other characters in the early stages of shooting, I got to develop a new character for the film franchise: Jetfire.

For me, this film is one of the most memorable of the four because of the scenes shot at a top-secret facility in California called Edwards Air Force Base. There's a hanger there that looks as if it's lined with blue foam pyramids. It's actually a giant testing complex the size of three football fields laid side by side, with no internal support structure. There's also a big gantry in the middle of it that looks as if it could hold something very large and heavy indeed. On the film it looks like a CGI shot because it's so vast, but it's actually a real stealth-testing hanger.

We filmed the scene there where Optimus Prime first reveals himself to the then Secretary of State and some of the servicemen had been allowed in to watch. I asked them, "What do you do in here?" One guy said, "I can't really tell you what goes on in here except to say that this is where we test the stealth aircraft. We bombard them with all kinds of waves—microwaves, radio waves, radar and all kinds of stuff, to see what sort of signature they reflect. The foam pyramids are there to absorb all these waves so they don't leak out, very much the same as in a recording studio," he said, "You should have seen what we had in here last week."—And he was laughing as he said it—"We've never seen anything like it before. It was hanging up there and we were all wondering just what it was?" Which just goes to show that there are things in development that even the guys who fly them have to ask: "What is that?" It was all very interesting.

We were constantly developing the way the robots were filmed. In some of the scenes in *Transformers: Revenge of the Fallen* I actually stood on a stepladder with a loud speaker near the head of the robot whose dialogue I was speaking. By then we had refined the process: I wore earphones so that I could hear both the other actor and what Michael was saying. They gave me a radio mic and put a speaker on the set so that I could be near the monitor. In this way, everyone on set can hear everything I'm saying without me having to shout down a loud hailer—I can use my normal speaking voice. The process was evolving into a fine art.

We did a lot of shooting in various locations both in downtown Los Angeles and at the Air Force Base, particularly for Jetfire. I had already recorded some of the dialogue for the character early on, but still didn't know what he was going to look like. Then in the post-production phase it became apparent that some of the back-story of the film wasn't clear. At that point, Jetfire became a much more important figure. He explained a lot of the plot and history of the robots, and Michael brought me in to try a chunk of dialogue to explain what was going on.

We went over the material several times as I developed the voice for Jetfire. The first time I saw the ILM renditions for what he would look like on screen I said, "That's a SR-71—a Blackbird Spy Plane!" I told Michael about the one in San Diego outside the Aerospace Museum, which I had driven past on my way home from the theatre when working on *Neville's Island*, and often used to pull over and look at. I remember saying that the most interesting thing about it was that when you walk around it there are some angles from which you can't tell it's an aircraft at all because it's so flat and sleek. It's not surprising it was so often mistaken for a UFO.

Michael wanted the voice of this character to sound noble, but old and cranky, so that was how I did the voice. I actually started with an impersonation of Ray Winstone, and it worked so well Michael kept it in. When the film came out, Ray rang me up. "Marky, you cheeky bugger, I've just seen that film—you nicked my voice. I've been *Beowulf*, a gangster, and now a giant alien robot—you owe me a beer!" I remember Michael asking me curiously, "Who is that—who are you doing?" I told him it was Ray, and said he was a mate of mine and wouldn't mind. Michael said, "Carry on."

That's how Jetfire got his voice.

Michael really liked what I did. He got the scriptwriters to put in extra lines to flesh out the history of the Autobots and Decepticons. At one point I was trying a line and he said, "Just say it the way you would normally. It's so much better when you do it naturally." So we changed some of the lines to the way I would say it and filmed my face in the studio as I was reading them so that they could match the movements of my mouth to Jetfire's face.

It was during this that I had a bit of fun. There's a scene where Jetfire, who had not shown he was alive for years, stands up in the Smithsonian and staggers about feeling stiff and creaky. I was asked what I would say under the circumstances. Would I curse? What English curse word would I use? So I went through a few: wanker, tosspot, etc., and Mike "Hoppy" Hopkins, the ADR and Supervising Sound Editor said no. Then I said "bollocks"—and they asked what that meant. I said, "There's a weapon they used in the 17th century called a Bollocks dagger, which is used as left hand thrusting weapon for sword and rapier." Bay looked at me a bit suspiciously and went off into the control room for a few minutes. Then I heard, "Right, it is a 17th century dagger." So the word bollocks was adopted into the *Transformers* lexicon.

The tag to the story is that when the film was about to go out on American network TV they had to remove all the swear words, so I was called back in to replace the word. I went into the studio and Mike Hopkins said, "You cheeky bugger, we've got to get rid of bollocks, so you'd better come up with something similar with the same intonation." We ran through the same things we had done before—none of which they liked and then I then said: "What about cobblers?" They asked, "Cobblers—what are cobblers?" I said, "Well, it is sort of like bollocks, except that my mum would say it." So they replaced the word bollocks with the word cobblers for the network version of the film. And they paid me to do it!

Dark of the Moon

Revenge of the Fallen was critically slaughtered but was a massive financial success. Again, the proof of the pudding is in the eating—it was bums on seats. When we came to number three, *Dark of the Moon*, I was very intrigued by the story, because throughout my life and career I had heard various stories about the astronauts and what they had seen on their way to the moon, what they had witnessed, what they had actually found and in particular what the governments of the world were not telling us about alien contact. So I was very interested to see how the filmmakers were going to deal with this, especially since they open the film with the discovery of a crashed alien craft on the dark side of the moon.

It gave me great pleasure to run around again to various locations for the film, but the most memorable one was Cape Canaveral, Florida where I was lucky enough to be able to stand on the historic Launch Pad 39A with Michael, Director of Photography Amir Mokri and Shia, right underneath the Space Shuttle *Endeavor*. I could have reached out and touched it. For me that was a marvelous experience. They had the "Crawler," the huge five million pound machine that carried the Apollo missions and space shuttles along that crawlway, running up and down as we filmed a comedic scene. The crawler consumes around one hundred and twenty five gallons of fuel to move just one mile. It travels forty-two feet per gallon because it moves at only two miles per hour.

You need a security clearance just to stand on 39A, and there are NASA employees that have worked there for twenty years and never been able to stand where we were going to be filming. Michael's clearance had taken a while to arrive and I was late and hadn't been cleared. So when I got there I went straight into the permits office. I was waiting a while, and then one of the guys that came out and said, "You've got previous?" He was referring to my old security clearance. He added, "It came up at once, so you're clear to go." So I was able to go out right away and stand on that historic and sacred ground.

Once again the cast and crew were truly inspiring to work with. On *Dark of the Moon* I got to work with the incomparable Frances McDormand. One day I was sitting in a chair off to one side of the set, and she came over and grabbed me and dragged me off into a corner and said, "You're the robot guy—right?" I said, "Yes. How can I help you?" She said, "I have no idea what I'm doing here. I need you to stand with me, come with me wherever I am so that you and I can work together." So I literally ran around the set giving her cues or running the dialogue. It was great to be working with her like that—I felt honored.

At one point I sat down with Peter Cullen, who has been voicing Optimus Prime since the original cartoon. He had come to record some lines that we were going to use later. He said, "I couldn't do this. I don't know how you do it. You're running all over the place all the time. How do you know what to do?" I said, "Because I've done a lot of this behind the camera work and I know what Michael is trying to get."

I also got to know Josh Duhamel, who plays Lennox, over the course of the three films. He's such a nice guy—very down to earth. I remember doing a scene with Josh when we were up against the clock and the atmosphere around set became very tense because the company needed to wrap the location by a certain hour. The scene ended up being cut. Josh was great about it and I remember saying to him, "I hope that was alright for you in there. I'm just trying to get what Michael wants." He said, "Don't worry about it. I'm just so glad you're here, because I know you're doing what needs to be done."

Josh's character is a Special Forces officer, and to help him get this element right they brought in the living legend that is Harry Humphries. I believe Harry got a Bronze Star, a Navy Commendation Medal and a Purple Heart after two tours in Vietnam and over two hundred combat missions. He was an original member of Seal Team 2 and is mentioned many times in Richard Marcinko's book *Rogue Warrior*. We had met in Ireland on *King Arthur* and got on very well. Right from the beginning Harry was massively supportive. Very early on he took me over to Michael and said, "Michael, this is Mark. He's a friend of mine." Michael said, "Yeah, yeah, he's doing the voices." But Harry laughed and said, "No, Michael, Mark is a *friend* of mine—play nice please?" He said it in a very simple jokey way and Michael just smiled at him, shook his head and said, "Okay Harry!"

Harry did all the coordination between the military and the production company, whether it was sourcing an aircraft carrier, F-18 jets or Black Hawk helicopters. During filming of *Dark of the Moon* we were working in a NEST (Non-Biological Extra Terrestrial Species Treaty) base film set, built in the historic Spruce Goose hanger in Playa Vista. This expansive soundstage was originally the birthplace of Howard Hughes's legendary, massive wooden aircraft, which flew only once in 1947. In the script NEST was the organization that succeeded Sector-7 as the joint allied defense force against Decepticons, and it could deploy a large amount of hi-tech weaponry, vehicles and personnel around the globe. We were in the base and deployed two or three Predator Drones, several Black Hawk Helicopters and an Apache Longbow Helicopter, as well as several armored Humvees and ATVs. I actually totted it all up and said, "Harry, I think we have probably got about $130 million worth of military kit here." He said, "Oh, it's more than that." Then he told me, "We've got a flight of Chinooks—C47 twin-rotor Helicopters—coming later as well. So it's more like $200 million." Harry is the man who procured all the hardware so we could make the film. He's a great guy and has worked on all the *Transformers* films, and everyone has the greatest respect for him. He takes the actors who are playing soldiers out to do some training and running about, giving them pointers and basically outperforming the lot of them.

Alien Life Forms

One of the greatest thrills for me when working on *Transformers: Dark of the Moon* was getting to meet astronaut Buzz Aldrin. Buzz came onto the set and I got to meet him and shake hands with him. I knew he could throw a good right hand because once when he was challenged about whether he actually went to the moon, he punched the rude and intrusive interviewer on the jaw! I would certainly have liked to engage him in conversation, because four or five of the Apollo astronauts have come out and said, "There's stuff up there we can't talk about!" They know a lot more about what is up there than most people believe. I think a lot will be revealed before too long. I know there's a movement to disclose more information and that it's widely believed that what was released was a deliberate disinformation campaign, as with the stories of ritual magic being used against the Germans in World War II. I think talk of UFOs has been used to hide some of the things that are really flying about up there. I'm sure we have much more advanced aircraft flying than people would imagine. After all, they were testing nuclear powered aircraft in the 50s—that's a fact. So if they were testing them then, who knows what they actually have flying right now.

Ben Rich, the director from 1975 to 1991 of Lockheed's Skunk Works, the secret development facility where they designed the F-177 Stealth Fighter, and where the B2 Bomber and the SR-71 spy plane were designed and tested, was reputedly quoted before he passed away in 1998, "We already have the means to travel among the stars, but these technologies are locked up in black projects, and it would take an act of God to ever get them out to benefit humanity... Anything you can imagine, we already know how to do."

There is something flying now that looks like a triangular wedge. Its popular online name is Aurora. We also know that a hyper-speed vehicle nicknamed "The Lozenge" exists. Launched from Vandenberg Air force Base, a DARPA research vehicle known as the HTV-2 (Hypersonic Technology Vehicle) reached speeds of up to Mac 20 before its "controlled splashdown" in the Pacific Ocean. Also known as Falcon (Force Application Launched from Continental U.S.), it's been tested and has come apart in flight, but they know it can fly. In England there's a company working on an aircraft called the Skylon, and when I was young they were already talking about a reaction-engine—an engine that would push an aircraft almost into sub-orbit and come down again at hyper velocity. This HOTOL (Horizontal Take-Off and Landing) engine would mean that we could fly from London to Australia in about three and a half hours. The concept was rumored to have been snapped up immediately by the military and has been used, I believe, to create the much-discussed Aurora spy plane. It was also associated with phrases like "pulse detonation engine" and "wave-rider" and "scramjet." There are traces of aircraft leaving Area 51 and other places in America—you can see them on Google Earth—and of something flying at hyper velocity that literally tracks right across the surface of the earth. Something is probably flying very high and very fast and its shockwave is setting off earthquake sensors in California as it re-enters the atmosphere and breaks the sound barrier.

I remember that one of the astronauts said that when they got to the moon they found that they were being observed and tracked by other craft that had been waiting for them. Personally I think it's possible that there are other things on the moon. I think there are things on Mars that are not going to be revealed yet because no one wants to admit there could have been life there once, or that it could have been an advanced civilization, part of which could have migrated to earth before the dawn of humanity as we know it today.

Whether these entities became Atlanteans or the *Book of Enoch's* Fallen Angels, it's possible there was already some kind of life here; the planet is old enough for entire civilizations to have risen and fallen over the last seven million years. It's also possible that life developed on Mars, especially if there was water on Mars in the ancient past, as is now widely believed.

Very credible people have said that the pictures you see of the Moon and Mars have had stuff painted out—stuff NASA doesn't want to be seen. I think it's possible they found something on the moon that they decided needed to keep secret until they had a greater understanding of what it is. It's entirely possible that they did find something, or at the very least that something they found opened the door to the possibility of a civilization being there before. I believe they were in two minds about it, and that's why they've sent an unmanned rover craft to explore further.

My opinion is that the powers that be in the governments of the world—maybe just the big five—are fully aware that alien civilizations have been visiting Earth on a regular basis for a long time, but that their technology and science is so far advanced that we can't fully determine how it works yet. So when the critics sneer at the idea of the possibility of giant alien robots existing in the universe they are failing to recognise that such things are a possibility—however strange that might seem.

I don't know about Roswell, or Area 51, but I do know about the RAF Bentwaters case. I would say this is one of the best UFO cases ever looked into in the U.K. I've spoken with people from Bentwaters. There were even questions asked in the House of Commons about the case. It happened at an F-111 Nuclear Strike Base, where the security people are all supposed to be highly trained and disciplined. The Assistant Commander of the Base, Colonel Halt, saw what can only be described as an alien craft as, apparently, did several others. Was the entire base hallucinating, and if they were, why are they in charge of a U.S. nuclear strike base? And why is this nobody's responsibility?

The Americans said that as it happened outside the Base it was the responsibility of the U.K. Ministry of Defence, and the Ministry of Defence said that they saw no defense issue, so therefore it did not happen. But we know something did—there are multiple witnesses and even radar sightings—the MOD stopped people from investigating further because it was totally unexplained. Maybe it was a test craft they were using to see if they could sneak up on a secret base in the U.K.? Who knows? It's never been explained. Both the guards and Col. Halt believe that what they saw was alien technology.

I have seen documents that show current and/or future designs for airframes that are actually being tested, and one clearly shows a flying disc, a flying triangle, various wedge-type crafts and various B-2 type boomerang shaped craft—which we now know are already flying. The other designs were either in development or are already out there.

Even though these are obviously of earthly origin, I am firmly convinced that we have encountered things like this that are not. I have always remained open to the idea that there are alien intelligences, and that we have probably bumped into them. I imagine they are watching us with some kind of disbelief and wondering what the hell is going on down here. We might well be a case study for civilizations around the cosmos!

Any alien intelligence must be thinking: these human beings believe in some entity out there—a god—and three of the major belief systems all subscribe in the origins of the same god, but they are willing to kill each other over the fact that each system has a different prophet and are willing to cause havoc, death and destruction to their fellow entities because their prophet must be the only one that is genuine!

I ask you, does that make any sense? You can see why an alien race could be watching us and thinking, we really don't want this "infection" creeping out into the galaxy. It might come back to infect us!

TRANSFORMERS: AGE OF EXTINCTION

In 2013, I was engaged on *Transformers: Age of Extinction* and found that working with Michael was as exciting, challenging and exhilarating as ever. I also really enjoyed working with Mark Wahlberg and Stanley Tucci. Michael called me over one day because Stanley had asked about me and Michael had told him I was in the new TV show, *Black Sails*. Michael wanted me to tell Stanley all about the show, on which he is executive producer. So we talked about the history of the show and about Toby Stephens, who plays Captain Flint in the show. Stanley said, "I know Toby, he's Maggie Smith's son. Is he good?" I said, "Yes, he's fantastic, he has the genes—after all he is Sir Robert Stephens' son as well. Theatre is in his blood." Michael said, "Tell Stanley about the tattoo thing on the back of your head." I told him all about the history of the privateers and the possible involvement of the Knights Templar and other Secret Societies as well as the history of the All-Seeing-Eye I had inscribed on the back of my head for each episode.

Working with Stanley Tucci was fascinating. I was watching the monitor with Amir and what we saw was one of the shots where Stanley is talking to Optimus—an angry bitter exchange. This scene was quite a turning point in the film, and they were doing this big push-in camera move. As we were doing the dialogue, I was trying to time my lines with enough emotional force so that Stanley could deliver *his* final lines, which were something like, "We don't need you anymore," with real emotional heft. I had to respond to the other Autobots with, "Autobots, we are done here." He then had to react to the fact that I have acknowledged that we were done. It's a very simple thing, but you have to time it. Stanley has to walk into frame, they push in, and he says the line. I then have to give a beat where he is watching to see what my reaction is, the camera dolly settles, and then I do the other line so the close up is on him and he can react to the line. It's all about timing, watching the monitor, listening to the actor, knowing where the cameras are moving to and from; there are 3D cameras and close up cameras—it's quite a technical zoo.

In the early days they used everybody to try this on-set voice technique. The script supervisor read the lines, the first AD read the lines, and they brought in other actors. Reading the lines is one thing, but watching the other actor and the camera moves while delivering the lines so you don't get in their way is another thing entirely. If you don't know the camera moves and have to stand by the monitor and take direction from Michael, you're lost.

A quantum leap happened for me in *Transformers: Age of Extinction*. For the first time I had three actors, including Mark Wahlberg, dialoguing with three or four robots, all voiced by myself. On these particular two days I was Optimus Prime because Michael wanted to try a more aggressive tone to create more tension in the scene and provoke a stronger reaction from Stanley by bringing a different confrontational edge to this crucial exchange.

Another time we were doing a scene with Mark Wahlberg, Nicola Peltz and Jack Reynor. I was standing next to Michael and he was giving me directions while I did the dialogue. As I stood there, he looked at the monitor and said, "Hold it. Here's what we're going to do. They will come into frame, we're going to rack focus on the robot called Hound (voiced by John Goodman), say the line, and then rack out and let them get on with the scene."

Technically you have to understand what is being done here—they are actually pulling focus—not even on one of the robot heads on a pole — literally on thin air. So they rack focus, which means they zoom in, get the line and then pull out again—all in time with the other actors. There isn't really a name for any of this. Sometimes it's called performance capture— but that's when you are wearing a special suit covered in camera focus dots. It's not really that—it's called on-set robot voice because they don't know what else to call it! Technically it's a lot more complex than that.

As Michael stated in an interview, the character of Lockdown, whom

I play in the movie, is a very interesting, mysterious and complex being. He roams the galaxy freely and is focused and dispassionate about his missions. He doesn't really want to take sides at all. To him it's all just business. He has absolutely no interest in the future fate of humanity. Lockdown's ship has epic history too, and there's a lot of backstory about that ship and it's origins in the Transformer's mythos that might be revealed in future films.

On this occasion I was sitting in the trailer waiting to go down to the Nicholson Terminal on the massive River Rouge docks where we were shooting, and I was going over the dialogue in my head and trying to imagine the character and the scene, which was pretty dark and violent. There were several sections of dialogue that needed to be covered, and this was where we were going to reveal a new Transformer.

We often use placeholder names for the characters in the script for security reasons but I had a good idea who "NP" was from researching the *Transformers* mythology for the past productions. As I ran over the lines in my head I wondered what I could bring to this character voice-wise that had not been heard yet in the three previous films. I thought about the best villains in recent movies and how an advert for the latest Jaguar F-Type stated that all the best bad guys in films had British accents! I began hearing Anthony Hopkins in my head doing the lines and remembered my conversation with him in London's Soho district in the 80s.

Stillness is the key. A calm and cold proficiency focuses the presence. I ran the dialogue again in my head and decided to go for a more Hannibal Lecter/Anton Chigurh tone for Lockdown—very controlled, amoral and sociopathic to match the dialogue in the scene, yet contrasting the massive scene of mayhem and merciless carnage going on all around. This was a bit of a gamble because usually my V/O technique is to simply deliver the lines so the other actors could hear them clearly and react. In this scene the other actor was myself and the scene only involved two Transformers. Time to bring the "A" game, change it up a bit and deliver something new and different to the *Transformers* universe!

As we worked on the scene I decided to watch the action on the monitors in the Porsche Cayenne camera car, so I ran alongside the vehicle as it drove across the set. This made it easier for me to time the dialogue to the camera-tracking move and see what they were seeing.

I used an old hand-held mic singing technique of getting very close to the head of the mic and almost whispering the dialogue. My pal Peter Devlin must have realized what I was doing and quickly pumped up the volume so the effect was loud, sinister and yet very intimate in a scary way because my voice echoed sonorously across the dark and ominous dock complex.

At one point I was so focused on the monitor in the Cayenne that I got very close to the car and Michael shouted at me to mind the crane as it rotated above my head. In fact I was running so close to it Michael was worried about me getting my feet run over by the vehicle!

But I knew this was my chance to throw in a wild card and try something new and previously unheard. Michael would sometimes ask for something more aggressive or something with a specific sound or accent if he has a particular character aspect in mind. This process is a lot of fun, and we play around with a lot of vocal tones in post-production. In the process a voice from the set will sometimes stick in Michael's head. This time I'm very happy to say it was Lockdown.

Working with Michael Bay on all the Transformers movies has been a huge pleasure—and continues to be so. He may have a reputation for being demanding to work for, but really he's just pushing the boundaries of film and inviting people to come along for the ride. He expects the best from people, and demands that you bring your "A" game. There's been a lot of discussion about Michael Bay's effect on the film industry, and that alone is enough to make you think about the huge effect he has had on making movies.

As of this writing *Age of Extinction* has grossed over $1 billion worldwide and is the highest grossing film ever in China, making it the tenth highest earning movie of all time. I'd call that a success by any measure.

Michael's shooting technique, the way he keeps the camera moving, has spawned a style of its own that comes uniquely from the way he works. The term "Bayhem" was coined to describe the insanity of what goes on, on set, and has come to define a unique movie style that encompasses editing, camera movement, composition and the layered background and staging that defines a complex visual experience. It is studied and copied by aspiring film students and highly accomplished professionals alike. Michael's cinematic style is almost a character in his movies, and yet he also delivers definitive character traits and studies that help the actors flesh out their roles in his films. An example includes the use of lighting and rotating close-up photography to bring the viewer right into the very heart of the drama and the minds of the characters being portrayed.

Technically, Michael is the most proficient and efficient director that I have ever worked with. He lives and breathes and exists for that film set; he knows every aspect of it. It's not just a job to him—that's what people misunderstand about the way he approaches it—it's his life. If you work with him you have to have the right attitude. For example, during the filming of one of the scenes in *Transformers 4* he wanted to speed up the whole process, so he snatched the script out of my hand and started cutting lines. I was doing the lines that were in the script for the other actors and he just started crossing them out. We were able to cut quickly from one speech to the next and he got what he wanted—it was efficient.

There is one more thing I will say about Michael Bay, which is something you can't say about many people in Hollywood. He's loyal. If you show that you can hang with him technically and keep up with the speed at which he works—he will be loyal to you. *Transformers: Age of Extinction* is my fourth film and my fifth project with him, and I know that he will always go to bat for me if I need it.

Recently I was coaching Christian Bale for his part in *Exodus*—working on his archery skills. He had worked with another fine director, Michael Mann, on *Public Enemies,* and I asked him what it was like. Christian said, "He's got a reputation for sure. It would be easy to say he's difficult, except that he's the hardest working man on the set." When they were shooting *Public Enemies* he shot for virtually twenty hours a day, night shoots and day shoots, and he would usually only get about four hours sleep. Christian said, "It's easy to knock people if you don't understand they are literally carrying this massive creative edifice on their back." I knew exactly what he meant. It's the same with Michael. It's a 24/7 process with him, because we are talking about a $200 million project and a multi-billion dollar franchise with thousands of jobs and careers at stake.

In some recent articles in the press Michael has been called an "auteur." In its purest sense it's a title he well deserves and of which he should be rightfully proud.

14.

TRIBAL STATES—THE RESERVATIONS

*After taking their land and converting everything that was holy
and good into money, the white man became aged and foolish
and then gambled all that money away at Native American casinos.*
— Carl-John X. Veraja

Bullets, Baccarat and Bougainvillea

IN AND AROUND THE TIME I was working on *Transformers 1* and *2*, I also found myself engaged in other work, which not only brought its own rewards, but also introduced me to some extraordinary people—members of the Native American nation.

As many of you will know, certain tribes have become the owners of a number of extremely lucrative casinos in recent years. These can have a turnover of one million dollars per night in the higher limits rooms, which is no small amount of revenue. However, this has brought its own problems—the kinds that come with being part of the gambling world. My involvement with this again came through Merrit Rex, who had been co-operating with a tribal member working for one of the Gaming Commissions.

The gaming commissioner was a retired Police Chief. He had done one of Chameleon's Human Intelligence Courses, which I had attended and subsequently taught. This teaches the human intelligence questioning techniques used by El Al and Israeli Intelligence to gather insightful and actionable information. It's called "predictive profiling:" a technique of tactical questioning that helps ascertain the motivations people have for doing certain things. By profiling here I don't mean profiling the person, but their actions. It's a simple tool used to define intention and motivation, but it works very well. It has been taught to security personnel from many major American corporations in the transport and avionics industries, and is a very effective and financially frugal method.

The commissioner had obviously learned from the course and remembered us. He had an issue where the son of a tribal member who was buried on the reservation wanted to visit his father's grave. Although this kid was a member of the family he wasn't a full member of the tribe, which you have to be to automatically get onto the reservation. He didn't live there either and had become a police officer in Arizona. He had not been adopted into the tribe and didn't have full benefits, including visiting rights and an income from tribal revenues.

Some tribes share a stipend from the casinos or the other businesses they control, and every member gets a monthly payment. Some of these payments can run upward of $20,000. Some tribes don't do it that way. One that I worked with in Washington paid all the money into a big fund, with a dividend at the end of the year—but only after they have paid out for schools, education and medical bills. It's a really democratic system that provides jobs and pays out a Christmas bonus to all their members.

One of the problems with having this monthly payment system is that some of the people involved don't have an education that can help them manage this kind of financial flow. Many don't have a job either or suffer from drug or alcohol addiction. The kids in particular have no drive to do anything. Some of the older members have been forced to leave because of patterns of this kind and live off the reservation.

To add to this, most tribal people are understandably suspicious of government agencies because they are officially an independent state within the U.S. Federal system, with a legal tribal government. So the only agencies that have actual legal rights to interact with the tribal councils are agencies like the FBI, DEA, DOJ and ATF (Bureau of Alcohol, Tobacco and Firearms).

That was the environment we were working around and, of course, anything that generates the kind of money that a casino can accumulate also attracts every kind of organized criminal operation that you can think of.

The issue with the kid who wasn't allowed to go onto the reservation to visit his father's grave was a thorny one. He had rebel-roused a bunch of disenfranchised tribal families who had been excommunicated from the tribe, and there was going to be a big meeting followed by a march on the casino. The kid had also threatened to blow-up the casino and other acts that were considered to be Terror-Soft situations.

Chameleon asked if I would manage the incident. I told them I would need a pretty big team—at least 12—so that I could put operators into the crowd. I also wanted to put people on the kid himself and serve him with papers in Arizona so that he would know he was under surveillance. I came up with a whole plan, which was then put into effect.

The tribal rangers then felt that their noses were out of joint because strangers had been brought in to do the job they thought they could do alone. But all of the rangers were well known to the families who felt aggrieved, so we were given the go-ahead. In conjunction with the tribal police, we put a team together to monitor what was going on in the crowd, and we knew during the course of the day that it was going to fizzle out. We let the ringleader in Arizona know that we were aware of the threats he had made, and that the casino had a legal responsibility to act upon it. He also knew that he was under surveillance. This kind of approach usually defuses this type of situation, and sure enough the kid went back to work and never left Arizona. Once people knew this they lost interest and the day ended peacefully.

The casino was very pleased with how it turned out, because those who wanted a confrontation didn't get it. Commission members came to us and said that it was the best way to handle the situation—to defuse it—and that the tribe was impressed with how we had taken care of a potentially explosive issue.

ON THE GAMING FLOOR

Almost two years later they brought another problem to us. Originally it was seen as an internal problem, which then blew up into something else. This time Walter McKinney and I were involved independently of Chameleon. Walter had been a police chief at Hawaiian Gardens, which was infamous for lots of things including casinos and bingo halls that were started by various mafia families in a huge money laundering operation. The Israeli Prime Minister Benjamin Netanyahu had been seen there, and there were a lot of interesting business connections as well.

The Indian casinos have a strange relationship with the local people because they are pouring millions into the local economy and employing local people, but in its wake is what casinos always bring: gambling addictions, money laundering, loan-sharking, intimidation and card cheating scams being just some examples. Other issues, such as public drunkenness, petty crime, DUIs and drug dealing are not unique to casinos, but can sometimes complicate law enforcement efforts.

Thus, there was an interesting dynamic between the reservations and the local policing agencies, and although the tribes are very proud and independent, they sometimes need help. Because they knew Walter and me, we were invited to go and look at a problem they had with one of their own managers. He'd been suspended from the Table Games Department (the casino was built like a corporate business with different divisions) and they'd had multiple problems with him.

This particular guy had a colorful background with a history of work in various casinos around the country, but he also had been reputedly associated with various scams and skims; he was certainly in a position to be able to cause some considerable financial damage if that was on his agenda. Because the tribe knew Walter and I were open-minded and didn't know the people involved personally we were given the full backing of the Tribal Council.

This particular tribe had three levels of government: a Tribal Council, a business development corporation and a gaming institution with it's own policing and investigations department. Although Nevada has a State Gaming Board that licenses everybody, California does not. Instead, each tribe has a casino with its own Gaming Commission. They are often very competitive and don't co-operate with each other, so intelligence about what is going on generally tends to be scarce and patchy. Also, they tend to not be as familiar with outside law enforcement or intelligence work. So when a sophisticated and complex bunch like the Vietnamese crime syndicate known as the Tran Gang moved in, the tribe didn't know until it was almost too late.

We were there to look at the gaming floor that was run by a particular individual. It became obvious very early on that they had a serious problem with infiltration by Tran gang members. We were given a letter of indemnity to go and interview people and gather information. However, that was far from easy because surveillance, which is the most confidential thing in a casino, was not exactly open to us. We knew that anyone who could penetrate it had carte blanche to steal at will, and it looked very much as if the Tran gambling teams had done that.

We set about interviewing the people we thought were going to be helpful—tribal members and people who had worked there for years and whom the tribe trusted. Then, we cross-referenced that information with the HR Department, to which we had full access, and started getting an idea of who belonged to which group.

We ran it like a straightforward human intelligence operation, and ended up with dozens of possible targets and a whole matrix of information regarding who was doing what on the floor.

Another case blew up soon after in San Diego. At least thirteen Tran members, including a big boss, were arrested by the FBI and were accused of stealing from fifteen tribal casinos across America and Canada. Tran associates would travel around planting dealers in their pay in the casinos, and then skim off the profits. I was shown the FBI files later, and in the course of eight to ten days they had taken something like $700,000 using a false shuffle, which fixes it so that the card counter/shuffle machines don't mix the cards properly. In Las Vegas, any good stage magician will tell you they could memorize the order of three decks of cards. There have been others who could memorize five decks. They train to do it, and can remember all the cards in the order they come out. The Tran had a system set up where they had teams on the tables that knew exactly which cards would be coming up. They would bet against each other, and took a lot of money that way.

Around this time I had been looking into similar old cases and got my hands on a just released and previously secret indictment, of the kind that is kept sealed until the police or the FBI want to move in and make some arrests. Shortly after this we went into a meeting with the tribal representatives. As we were talking over what we had discovered about the table games I said, "There's another issue that I want to bring to your attention. The authorities in San Diego have just unsealed this indictment. It mentions every casino in Southern California that could have been infiltrated—all along the western coast from Canada down. The strange thing is that this casino isn't listed."

Of course, they said that their defenses were just too good, but I responded that I did not want to insult them, but that if this was happening in San Diego, just a few hours drive away, and they were not mentioned, something was very wrong. If they believed their defenses were that good, why were we looking at the table games? It was a red flag.

They said they thought the FBI had spoken to the Gaming Commission chairman, but that nothing had come of it. I said that I thought they had a different kind of problem and that we should look into it. They told us to go and talk to the Commission and see what they could tell us.

I had met the chairman before and got on well with him. He was famous for sitting at his desk with a .45 in front of him, so that the weapon was pointing right at whomever he was talking to! Most people were cautious and respectful to him and he was straight with them.

He told us that the FBI had come with an affidavit to do a co-operative deal with the tribes, but that they were sent away from this casino. I asked him who was responsible for that, and he admitted that it was an unresolved question. The main reason that no one had tried to resolve it was because they didn't think they had a problem. I said, "Mr. Chairman, thirteen or fourteen people have just been arrested in San Diego, and I can guarantee at least another 30 will go. If your casinos are not mentioned in this document, it means that they're taking money from you and you don't know it."

This was clearly difficult for him to swallow, but he admitted that they'd had some previous issues with a guy called Ricky—a common Vietnamese name. This guy, in the middle of a game, would hand over a block of cards to somebody playing at the table. That was one of a number of red flags that should have been noticed. There had been instances where dealers had volunteered information, both to the individual we were investigating over the issue of the table games department and to the Gaming Commission. They said that one individual even gave them a Tran business card and told them that they could make a lot of money working with him.

With the authority of the Tribal Council and the Gaming Commission, we started digging. The more we looked the more we found. We had help from lots of brave people who came forward, despite threats of blackmail and worse. We learned quickly that one of the dealers had already been murdered. Walter and I went to look at what is called the "Murder Book," and found that the case was still unsolved. The woman and her boyfriend had both been executed in a horrible fashion. He had been found shot to death, and she had been cut into pieces still wearing her casino uniform. Her face in particular had been brutally slashed and mutilated.

I asked some people from a different cultural group—who were opposed ideologically to the way the Tran operated—what the cutting of a woman's face meant. They said that in their belief system if you are scarred in this life, you would be known as a traitor in the next life because of the scars on your face; the scars go with you, and there is no escape in the otherworld.

By this time we knew there was intimidation going on, so we stepped into a different gear, which meant being armed most of the time. I carried a .223 Ruger Mini-14 rifle in the trunk of my car and sometimes had my .32 Seecamp semi-automatic pistol strapped to my ankle while working on the reservation. We took precautions like that because we knew that some of the people involved were utterly ruthless. Walter and I led the way on this job. I worked very well with him. He is a smart and solid man who knew what he was doing. He also had the contacts with the Feds and the other agencies that we needed to liaise with.

I started by recruiting crucial C.I.s (confidential informants) to penetrate the organization, since as a white Yorkshireman I stood out in an Asian cultural environment. In fact, we managed to penetrate several operations, both Asian and Italian. One of the Italian gangs was running a sports ring in Nevada, where sports betting is legal. We discovered that one guy was actually running a sports book on the casino floor, right under the nose of the guy who was supposed to be protecting it! He was recruiting supervisors and dealers to bet with him. This gave the organization leverage because when you've got people, let's say a supervisor, who is in debt to a sports book they can be pressured into turning a blind eye to what else is going on at the tables.

This kind of thing is quite common. They were having poker parties at people's houses where some of the supervisors' fleeced money from the new dealers by making them pay to play in their own homes. Of course, that was against the HR rules and regulations regarding non-fraternization, but these situations completely broke security and fractured the chain of command.

We discovered that all these things were going on quite openly. Loan-sharking was also prevalent and people were buying jobs and borrowing money to do it. We discovered that one family in particular was behind a lot of this, and had to find out which members were involved.

It took nearly two years in all, and was one of the most complex operations I've ever been involved in. It needed a lot of careful thought, planning and work because there was real fear on the reservation and threats and intimidation were common.

Another nearby casino had utterly rejected any kind of involvement from the Feds. They had actually opened fire on an LAPD helicopter that pursued a speeding vehicle onto the reservation. Three or four guys started shooting at the helicopter with rifles, but one of the police was a SWAT sniper and killed all three on the ground.

There was almost open warfare between law enforcement on the outside and the gangs running the illegal operations on the casino floor. You have to understand that these were multi-million dollar businesses. The casinos are huge, luxury gaming floors with water features and elaborate decorations, as big as anything in Las Vegas. They take as much money daily as any of the Las Vegas casinos. There was a whole range of groups moving their pieces around the board. We set about trying to interdict and dismantle some of that.

Once we started unfolding it, the aim was to pull some of the people out of the middle. It got to the point where even the schedulers who organized the work force were identified as playing a key part in it all. A lot of people volunteered information in private. When one woman in particular, who was actually in charge of running the scheduling office, contacted us, Walter and I met her off casino property. She told us how it was fixed so that certain dealers would be on certain tables when high rollers were in town.

By this time, a new guy had been brought in to run the casino while another, among those we were investigating, was suspended. We asked her why she had not gone to him about this. She said that she was fairly certain he knew all about it but did not want to get involved. I told her we needed to know who was paying off whom. Despite the fact that people with a criminal record were not supposed to be licensed, some people were coming from Las Vegas who had association with organized crime, and were working as dealers on the gaming floor.

The woman started to tell us how the scheduling was being fixed and I said, "I don't know how we're going to handle this, because if we go to the tribe the guy running it now is going to know, and they're going to ask him what's going on in the scheduling office." I told her to be careful, because the whole thing could easily backfire on her.

Very soon after that I got a call from the tribe telling me I should come in and see the Gaming Commission because a very serious accusation had been made against us. When I asked what it was, they told me that Walter and I had apparently kidnapped one of the employees from the scheduling office, taken this person off the reservation and threatened them to get information! Of course we asked where this had come from, because we knew at once that it was in response to the woman from the scheduling office coming forward. We found that it went all the way to the top, to the boss of the whole casino complex and his underling.

I went to see the Chairman and told him it was not true, and that I wanted him to call the woman we had met with so that he could hear what was going on from her. I also suggested that he should talk to the person who made the complaint. The Chairman did just that. He got the girl up to his office and told her what we had been accused of. She confirmed that both she and her husband had been present when we spoke to her, that they had collaborated willingly, and that we had identified ourselves to them both. Then she told the story just as we had reported it.

Everyone sat there looking stunned. They were finally starting to get the picture.

Consequently, the CEO was first suspended and then fired. His underling was kept on because he told them that he had just done what the CEO told him to. They should have fired him as well, in my view, but they chose not to.

Some members of the families issued threats against Walter and me throughout all this. One guy, who I won't name for obvious reasons, threatened me personally several times—until the police finally kicked his front door down in the middle of the night and handed him over to the Department of Justice. By that time we were liaising with both them and the FBI, who sent an agent with whom we cooperated regularly. We gathered a lot of intelligence for them, and they did the same for us. During this time we discovered that one of the people working as a floor supervisor at the casino was actually wanted by the FBI, and when they caught up with him, it led to the arrest of several others with whom he was connected. Ultimately, the cooperation between the Feds and us resulted in sixty-five arrests, and we began to have a very practical and effective working relationship with them.

On another occasion the FBI needed some help identifying a member of a highly lucrative identity theft operation being run out of various eastern block countries. It was stealing hundreds of thousands of dollars a month from U.S. banks via ATMs. We cooperated in cleaning up this fraud scam and helped break up the operation. It was actually quite simple and practical, and involved using stolen ATM information to get cash from ATM machine, launder the money on the tables and then cash out the chips, totally obscuring it's origin in one simple cycle.

Of course, we had to take precautions when we were working on this because millions of dollars and a variety of organized criminal gangs were involved. I had my hand on my firearm several times during this whole operation, but when Walter and I went to meet a CI in a restaurant in the middle of the desert we were both on edge. We both thought it was a set-up. We parked our cars in darkened corner of the parking lot so that we could watch what was going on. Three motorbikes came roaring out of the distance and parked. We guessed that the guy we had come to see was with them. We got out of our cars and went over to talk to them. As we got closer it looked like there would be trouble, and both of us had our hands on our weapons. But it turned out that the guy had brought his sons with him because he didn't know whether he could trust *us*!

We ended up going into a Cantina, where he sang Mexican karaoke. He was known there, so our meeting didn't look out of place. Sadly, afterwards he was persecuted and ended up getting fired. Indeed, to show how serious this all was, more than one of the people we worked with and who acted as an informant passed away. A couple died under very mysterious circumstances, and I believe to this day that at least one of them was murdered. We had visited him in prison and he gave us great intelligence related to millions of dollars of fraud and graft. We managed to get him out to cooperate with law enforcement, but he was dead only ten days later. It was assessed to be a heart attack but it seemed rather too convenient.

The long-term effects of what we achieved are a matter of record. The result in terms of the Tran investigation was extremely successful. Most of that particular gang were arrested and jailed. As I have explained, part of the job was to recruit CIs who would give us information about what was happening on the casino floor. We were very successful with that and had a lot of streams of information coming in. We had to piece all of this together and make a coherent picture of what was going on. We call this "intelligence fusion" in military terms, and "link analysis" in criminal investigations and police work. We had everything from compromised dealers, who were in debt to loan sharks or had just been intimidated and threatened, to floor men and bookmakers trading favorable treatment or influence peddling.

In one case, one of the floor men at another casino was a main player. A CI gave us his name, and I called my contact at the FBI and told them about him. It turned out that they already had a warrant out for his arrest and had been looking for him. They asked us to let him stay working there for a month so that they could keep him under surveillance. When he was eventually fired and left the reservation they arrested him. In all, about 45 people were arrested as part of an international, organized criminal conspiracy. There was every form of corruption going on—people buying jobs, sex for jobs, loan sharking and various kinds of cheating on the floor—sometimes involving Native American families. We are talking large amounts of money here—as much as $30—$35,000 a hand of *Pai gow* poker.

I enjoyed working with the Tribes; I came to respect them and their attitude. I don't know why they trusted us so much—maybe it was because I'm not American, even though I am white. They are a very trusting and, in a way, naive people: loyal and stoical. They really do want to keep corruption out of their environment, but they only have a short history of running casinos, and not so long ago they were very poor; so money management is something they have a problem with. I asked the Chairman once why all this corruption was happening when some of the tribal members were being given as much as $20,000 a month. He said, "A hundred years ago we were raiding each other's villages and stealing cows and horses. Now it's about who has the biggest pick-up truck and who's married to the more powerful or influential person." The rivalry between them is still there and hasn't yet refined itself, but they are trying to do good social things for the whole tribe.

They have built schools and have a health insurance system for their own tribal members, but there are still a few people who will turn a blind eye to whatever is happening because a lot of the people who opened up the tribal lands to gaming were already involved in organized crime. The tribes bought their first machines from those organizations. All of that is part of the dynamic they are trying to grow away from, and they have made significant changes to the way they do business. Walter and I stood in front of the tribal leaders several times, explaining what we had done, how we had done it and who had been involved. Some of it was difficult for them to hear—how this business they thought of as a benign money making machine was riddled with corruption and all kinds of criminal activities.

We were also very grateful to the people in the Asian community who helped us unravel the very sophisticated Tran operation. Sometimes the bad guys parked vehicles outside the casino and were in radio contact with gang members inside. They were tracking the gaming using computer software that had algorithms that could work out what the next cards would be: a very high-tech operation. There was a big insurance scam going on as well, and of course they were involved in the brutal intimidation of dealers. Interestingly, one of the CIs that came forward with information told us that, in his culture, cheating is not seen as a bad thing as long as you don't get caught. It simply means the person being cheated is not smart enough to understand they are being robbed, and if they don't understand that and can't do anything about it, that's no shame on the person who is cheating, but rather shame on the person who is being cheated. The same goes for intimidation: it was seen as the casino's fault for not having enough security.

They didn't do any of this in Las Vegas because if they had been found in Nevada working the same operation it would have had a very different outcome; they would have been buried in the desert. They did it on Indian territory because, and I say this with great respect for the tribal people, they knew that because of the system, where there was no unified gaming organization covering the whole thing and each tribe had their own Gaming Board, their chances of getting away with it were much higher. So they hit and ran. They bounced from Indian casino to Indian casino up and down the west coast, including Canada. They saw them as easy pickings, largely because of their stoical resistance to outside help. The FBI had gone to them, and if the tribe had cooperated sooner they might have stopped the problem long before we were brought in.

The whole operation was often extremely harrowing. People who thought it was funny and believed they were invincible often shone "red dot lasers" on us at the casino. They would say, "got to watch out for those red dots!" I saw this as the usual infantile tactic of the bully and simply replied, "We don't use those anymore. I could be in your back garden by your two orange trees and bougainvillea by the hot tub, and you wouldn't see or hear a thing. In fact, I'm still good for about 200 meters in twilight. Think about that next time you let your dogs out for a crap or point that thing at me." Bullies usually don't like pushback.

Somehow, I was still keeping up the other half of my life while all this was going on, so that at one time I was going from being a giant alien robot in *Transformers* to working on the reservation. Two alien worlds indeed.

Old Magic

You might ask what it is that makes me do this kind of work—what I find satisfying about it. Apart from the fact that I'm helping people, as much as anything it's the challenge. Looking at all the bits of information you gather and putting it together to solve the puzzle. You look at something and ask: *What does this mean? Why would someone do this? How does it work?* I do this work because I can, and I don't mean to sound blasé but it does take a certain kind of mind-set and creative process. It takes vision and experience to look at it and see what's happening. It's very like intelligence work—putting together unproven and unverified information and looking for a pattern that you might recognize from another type of fraud or crime.

The work is a mixture of the challenge and the satisfaction of being able to put the whole picture together. Of course, being able to do that doesn't always mean that you get a good result or resolution on your own, because you don't have the tools to do that. Sometimes you need outside help from the DOJ or the FBI for example, because we have no powers of arrest. It's like what you see in the recent movie *American Hustle*. I watched that movie the other night and was chuckling because everything you see in that film I learned from listening to Bob Dick. I was laughing because I knew where the story was going.

You might think that this work would make me as dark and cynical as the issues I'm dealing with, but it doesn't. For the most part I still believe in the general goodness of mankind, but I also believe that we often act very stupidly. Mankind has to be one of the daftest creatures every created. If things get too much, I can take all the worst things that humans do to each other—murder, theft, manipulation, extortion—and channel it into the earth. Sometimes, on a very practical and visceral level, "the wolf must guard the sheep." I'm very comfortable in that role, and quietly proud of having been effective and of service to those who needed help in the shadow labyrinth.

I've written about this in connection with the tarot and contact with the natural world and the power within it. This helps clear my mind and gives me a place to take it and discharge it—not physically of course, but spiritually. The earth is very deep and very forgiving.

With this approach I found that that working with the Native Americans was wonderful, because of course they have a strong tradition regarding their links with the earth. That is all still very strong in them, as is their respect for elder wisdom. They have a political and familial structure called the Silver Feathers—the Tribal Elder level of wisdom—to which they turn in search of knowledge and insight. I felt a real kinship with that, and with the good husbandry of the land they were given. Their relationship to the environment—keeping it renewable and not interfering with the eco-system so that it benefits everybody—is something I really respect them for, and making it a working reality in the modern world is quite an achievement.

I had an opportunity to sit down and talk with Elders on the Council, and we talked about the similarity between the European Wheel of the Year and the Native American Medicine Wheel. Although it varies from tribe to tribe, the similarities are quite striking. We share the idea of totem animals as well—spiritual beings in animal form who act as guides and protectors in our interaction with the universe—and the characters of these animals are often the same.

Everything about this belief system spoke to me at a very deep level. I was very comfortable with the tribal people, and it made working with them amongst the most satisfying things I have done in my PI career.

I still carried my faithful Walther PPK/S, while working on the reservation, but felt I was in touch with my own roots again, despite being so far away from home.

The magic was still there.

15.
HOLD FAST: SAILING UNDER NEW COLORS

*"Now and then we had a hope, that if we lived and were good,
God would permit us to be pirates."*
~ Mark Twain - *Life on the Mississippi.*

BEING PIRATICAL

I FIRST HEARD ABOUT *Black Sails* in July or August 2012, when my manager Sandy Oroumieh called to tell me that Michael Bay was working on a new project. It would be his first for TV production, and was collaboration between the U.S. cable network Starz and his own film and TV development arm, Platinum Dunes. It was a prequel to the famous book *Treasure Island*, by Robert Louis Stephenson, and would feature younger versions of some of its famous characters. Sandy thought there was a part in it that I would be just right for.

I called Ian Bryce, the producer of the *Transformers* franchise and one of the best hands-on producers I have ever met in the business. Unflappable and icy cool under pressure, Ian is the steady hand and ever-practical presence behind the massive, kinetic and sometimes hungry beast that is the *Transformers* filmmaking machine. Ian explained that he wasn't involved in the *Black Sails* directly but Andrew Form was, and he was in the next office. He'd ask Andrew to speak to me and he'd call me back in fifteen minutes. True to his word, as Ian always is, he called me back and told me that Andrew was waiting for my call. Andrew was very complementary and said that Michael spoke highly of me. He thought I was absolutely right for the part. He also said he'd set it up and I would definitely get a call from Starz

I did indeed get a call, as did Sandy. Starz casting left a message on my voicemail and said they would like to see me. They sent me some pages and when I read them, I knew in my bones that I really understood who this character was and that I really wanted to play him. I went into the audition and knew I had done a good job and that the casting director was happy. But about a week later when Sandy called the casting office, they said, "We're not going any further with Mark. This is going to be cast in South Africa, where the series will be shot."

We thought that was the end of it. I filed it away in its little box and got on with my life.

At that time John Matthews and I had undertaken a book tour with *The Wildwood Tarot*, which we had worked on together the previous year and which had sold really well. We started out in Atlanta and headed on to Seattle. While we were there I got a call from Platinum Dunes asking where I was and when I would be back in Los Angeles.

They wanted me to go back in to re-audition for the show, and that as soon as I got back I was to meet with the producers.

Second, and most importantly, I knew that Michael Bay must have gone out of his way to open this door, and that he was a loyal and honorable man. He had always been relaxed and fun to work with, and we had certainly had a very good relationship during the three previous *Transformers* movies we had filmed at that time. I was going to repay the favor and go with the flow out of loyalty and respect for him.

Soon after I went to meet Jon Steinberg, one of the co-writers and originators of the show. After we'd talked for a while he asked me if I had any questions about the part. I asked if he could give me some of the framework of the story so I could get it into my head. He gave me a rundown of the show, which is set in the so-called Golden Age of piracy, which most see as stretching from the early 1700s to the middle of the 18th century.

Jon asked me what I thought about the character of Gates, the quartermaster, who I would be playing. I replied that I really understood him because I had lived through events not unlike those that dictated his life.

Jon asked what I meant. My answer was simple, "I served in the British Army as a non-commissioned officer, and we have a saying: it's the officers who give the orders, but the sergeants that carry them out. Gates is the pivotal point between the crew, the men, and the officer class. It's the Sergeant's job to make it happen and he is the Sergeant. To do that he has to have a range of skills to deal with a range of people, in order to do whatever needs to be done." Jon was enthusiastic and told me that what I had said was absolutely spot-on. So we read the lines a couple of ways and he seemed happy.

A week or so after that Sandy got a call from Brad Fuller at Platinum Dunes to congratulate me on getting the part and wishing me well in Cape Town! I left on New Year's Day, and that was the beginning of a new journey.

The flight to Cape Town from Los Angeles was a test of mental and physical endurance—probably the longest I've ever done. I was flying Virgin Business Class, which is luxurious and comfortable but even so, it's twelve hours from L.A. to London, then some waiting time before you go on for another twelve hours. It's a full day in the air but you lose two nights sleep, so that by the time I got there I was already exhausted and very jet-lagged. Still, I had a very nice first evening with Neil Marshall, who is an easy going and affable chap as well as a renowned director of films and TV. Neil confessed to being a huge *Robin of Sherwood* fan and I knew then that this was going to be a wonderful and challenging experience!

THE RHYTHM OF THE HEAT

I was curious to see how things had changed in Africa because of my experiences there when I was younger. I'd heard all the stories, good and bad, and was interested to see for myself.

The first place they put us up was the Mount Nelson Hotel, which is one of the old Colonial hotels in Cape Town. It's is an amazing place and famous for its afternoon tea, and I had a room there that looked out over the mountains. The first thing you see when you drive into Cape Town is Table Mountain. It's the most extraordinary, magical lump of rock I have ever encountered, and it came to dominate, in many ways, my emotional response to Cape Town and South Africa. Later on, I went up it in a cable car. It has a very strange but definite energy about it—awesome and magical at the same time. I used to sit in a restaurant on the waterfront many a night, watching the sun go down and the clouds roll over the top of that mountain—it was an extraordinary sight and different every evening.

Cape Town itself has a wonderfully cosmopolitan atmosphere. People said that the harbor with all the boats, where we were staying, was not the real Cape Town, and that we had to go into the townships to really experience it.

At one point I bumped into Max Beasley, an old friend of mine who was also there shooting a TV show called *Mad Dogs*, and he told me that you still had to be careful about carrying too much money on you when you went out because, as with any big city, there are good areas and bad areas and you need to have your wits about you.

We all had apartments in a gated complex. Mine looked out over the Marina Complex at the front, and onto Table Mountain at the back. It was idyllic. A lot of the photos I posted on Facebook at the time were just day-to-day pictures as the light changed.

Mid-series I had a couple of really big scenes coming up that were critical to the storyline. I had a long weekend ahead, and wanted to get away, clear my head and absorb the scenes. I randomly asked one of the assistants if she could recommend a place to go and she suggested a seaside town on the West Coast called Paternoster. So I hired a car and drove up the coast and stayed at a place called *The Oystercatchers Haven*. I booked an upstairs room with a small terrace with a table so I could relax and watch the sun go down while I read the script and did a few emails.

On my way in I had seen a plaque on the wall that looked like it related to Nelson Mandela, but I hadn't read what it said. While I was having breakfast next morning, I asked about it. They told me with great pride that it commemorated the fact that Nelson Mandela had stayed there, in fact in the room I was in. He had written part of his book, *A Long Walk to Freedom*, there.

I was amazed, thinking that I had been sitting in the same chair and looking out at the same view he must have seen. Of course I had to ask them what he was like. The New Zealander who ran the hotel, said, "I'm not given to saying stuff like this, but he's the only human being I have met in my life who had an aura—I could actually see it. I'd never seen anything like it before, and I have never seen anything like it since."

During the last few days I was in Cape Town I managed to book myself a tour to Robben Island, where Mandela had been imprisoned. They have ex-prisoners doing the tour of the place. I was in a small group of about five or six people, and while we were walking around somebody asked him how he got involved with the ANC. He told us that he was recruited in South Africa, and then went to Swaziland, Tanzania, Mozambique, and Congo and then to Angola, where he was recruited by the East Germans and flown to East Berlin. There, he was trained by the Russians and finally flown back to Africa—Rwanda I think—where he passed on what he had learnt. I think he then went to Zambia but was expelled because the Zambian government didn't want anything to do with what was happening across the border in the then-named Rhodesia. He was eventually arrested and ended up in Robben Island, where he met Nelson Mandela. This brought back the things I had experienced years before when I was in Lusaka at the Intercontinental Hotel and it was teeming with spooks—KGB, CIA and SIS.

It's funny how things go round in big circles. I was so focused on the show that I didn't really get into discussing politics, but there is a strong political rivalry to this day between Mandela's tribal associations and Jacob Zuma, who is currently President of South Africa. I talked to the drivers about it because they had all been supporters of the ANC, but a lot of them said that they don't support it any more because all the money and aid they had been sent was squandered through corruption. They said that ten years after the ANC took over, the new houses and services that they were promised still haven't happened. For them, nothing has changed and corruption is still rife. They are torn between their loyalty to what was once the ANC, and all they achieved, and what they see now as a betrayal of the Mandela legacy.

BEING MR. GATES

The part of Gates was a job I had waited 17 years to get. After smaller parts on shows like *Frasier*, *JAG* and *Alias*, here at last was something I could really get my teeth into. Gates is the Quartermaster of Flint's ship, *The Walrus*. He's well aware that he's playing a younger man's game, but he has no ambitions to be captain. He's happy with the crew and has a good relationship with them; and they trust him because he's even-handed. Some of them feel he is "Flint's man," and will do whatever Flint says, but most of them respect him.

At this point, Flint (played by Toby Stephens) is the most successful pirate captain around—though he is going through a bad patch, which is causing trouble amongst the crew. There are various characters that want to throw him aside and bring in a new captain. What Gates knows, though the rest of the crew don't, is that Flint is looking for a Spanish treasure ship that has so much gold on it they will all be rich. But first he needs a document showing the detailed course the ship will be taking so that he can ambush it. They need two ships to do this because *The Walrus* is not powerful enough to take on a treasure galleon, which is basically a floating castle with 100 canons. Gates knows this, but while he is letting Flint run this game, he also knows that Flint is running a game on *him*, and he actually says that to him. One of the lines I really enjoyed saying was, "This is one of those occasions where we both pretend that I don't know you are lying."

That's the basis of their relationship.

Gates knows that Flint has this other game up his sleeve, but is willing to support him because when all is said and done, he thinks it best for the crew, and for himself. He uses whatever leverage he has with the crew to get them to go along with Flint's plan and, because they are of so many different cultures and belief systems, he has to blend in with them like a chameleon.

In one scene Gates gets involved in a negotiation with the character called Mossiah (Ernest Ndhlovu) in an effort to save his old friend Flint, and enters a hut where African and Jamaican members of the crew practice the Obeah magical belief system. Gates has to draw blood and swear before an Obeah Shrine that he'll pay Mossiah what he owes him. Mossiah is convinced to support Gates because he says, "I know your word is good."

The relationship he has with the crew is sound. With Billy Bones (played by Tom Hopper) it's almost a father-son dynamic. He knows that Billy is honest and clear-headed and a little naïve, but that he's respected. Gates guides and advises him as well as protecting him, preparing for the time when he can eventually take over the job of Quartermaster.

Then there's Jack Rackham (Toby Schmitz), one of the characters who is based on an actual historical pirate. Jack is the Quartermaster of *The Ranger*, the ship belonging to the black-hearted Charles Vane (Zach McGowan). Gates has an interesting relationship with him, which sadly we never really got to play out. We did one scene where Rackham pulls Gates apart psychologically in a single long monologue, and during the course of this I had to sink further and further into depression as I realize that what he was telling me is the truth—that I am too old, and that nobody would trust me as a Captain. He basically gets into Gates head. It was a great scene, and at the end Brad Fuller and the rest of the cast and crew actually stood up and applauded.

I wish that we could have done more scenes like that, because both Rackham and Gates are Quartermasters and both have the same set of problems dealing with their crews. They understood each other. Rackham has his own captain, Charles Vane, to deal with—a real sociopath. Gates knows he's a good Captain and good in battle, but that he can't be trusted. Gates of course has Flint, who is as cunning as a wagon-load of monkeys.

Then there's my relationship with Eleanor Guthrie, played by Hannah New, who is the power broker in the township of Nassau, where *The Walrus* is berthed. She basically runs the port like a mafia boss. Gates knows that she has a deep friendship with Flint, and respects him because he's the most successful pirate captain in Nassau. At one point I have to negotiate with her for a loan to keep Flint in power.

All of these relationships are complex, political and cunning.

I knew from the start that I wanted to bring something a bit different to the look of the character. For a start he's supposed to be in his sixties, so I decided I would go with the flow. They aged up my eyes to give me more wrinkles, and decided that a diet of pasta and oysters and game would probably help me look slightly more aged than I actually am. I decided that was the way to go with the character, heavier and stouter than I actually am, so that's why he looks the way he does physically.

Getting the right overall look for Gates was an interesting process. One problem I had was with my costume, because the main costume lady was not there when I arrived, so they just threw some stuff together. It didn't fit me very well. It was a bit baggy and haphazard. Later they changed the costume to the one you see in most of the shots—the longer coat and darker shirt that fitted and worked better.

I got on particularly well with the make-up girls. They were really keen to help give me a distinctive appearance. We tried a bearded look, which didn't work at first, until they hit on the idea of giving me mutton-chop whiskers. One thing we discussed at length was the tattoos. It was their idea to put the words "Hold" and "Fast" on each of my hands, but my idea to have a tattoo on my head.

We tried various things: symbols to do with the sea and the equator and birds, but I told them I wanted an esoteric symbol. That's how we ended up with the All-Seeing Eye, a symbol associated with the Freemasons.

This was all part of a desire I had to bring a bit of metaphysical background to the character. I knew this resonated with a certain part of the audience from my experiences with *Robin of Sherwood* and its wonderful and eclectic fan base. Because of my history of writing books about tarot cards and esoteric history, I wanted to get it into *Black Sails* as well. John Matthews, who knows just about everything there is to know about pirates, had often discussed possible links between the Knights Templar and pirates with me. One of the things I've always speculated about is what happened to the Templar fleets that disappeared after Pope Clement V shut down the Order in 1307. The Templars were masters of sea trade and seamanship in general, and traded ideas with the Assassins and various other Middle Eastern groups; so it seemed unlikely that they just vanished without trace.

The theory is that they simply changed their names and flew a different flag from their masts. It's been suggested that this was when the skull and crossbones became the flag under which pirates traditionally sailed. Nobody knows if this is true, but wherever you find Templar graves throughout the world, you also find the skull and crossbones.

When Queen Elizabeth I later wanted to establish fleets of privateers to help her relieve the Spanish of some of the gold they were exporting from South America, she authorized a number of sea captains with letters of marque that gave them permission to raid any ship they liked. Her advisor, the Elizabethan magus and alchemist John Dee, would have known about the existence of secret societies that were descended from the Templars and others. There has long been speculation that there were links between these societies and the privateers, who morphed into pirates as soon as peace was declared between the French, the Dutch and the English. That's why the privateers rebelled against the British Crown. They felt they had been betrayed. One minute they were working for the Establishment, attacking any ship they fancied, and the next it was illegal, and the British Navy was sent to round them up or blow them out of the water.

I wanted to have a little reference point to this lineage, whether or not it was true, so I had the All-Seeing Eye, an old esoteric symbol that you will find in Freemasonry and on the American dollar bill tattooed onto the back of my head. A lot of people believe the Templars also knew this symbol. The producers liked it so much they often shot me in such a way that you could see the symbol clearly. It was just a little nod to the lineage between pirates, Knights Templar and Masons.

I remember saying it would keep people talking for years.

I tried to suggest subtle historic notes like this wherever possible,

There's a scene where I hand over the role of Quartermaster to Billy Bones because I am about to become the Captain of another ship, *The Ranger*. I become Captain, but don't really want to be; I'm bullied into it by Flint because he needs someone he can trust. So I recommend Billy Bones to take over as Quartermaster for *The Walrus*. I happened to have a Bosun's whistle of the period and, during the course of the scene, I wanted to pull this whistle out and throw it to Billy Bones as a gesture that I was giving the power of the Quartermaster to him. I asked the director Sam Miller if it was all right to do this and see what it would look like and he told me to go ahead.

Happily the scene made it to the final cut.

Flint's Man

I got on really well with Toby Stephens (Flint) right from the start. We had almost met years earlier when I visited Bob Anderson on the set of the James Bond film *Die Another Day*, which co-starred Toby. We were probably in the same lunch tent at the time, but I was busy chatting away with Bob, so we never met. But we have a lot of friends in common in the business, and all I'd heard were lovely things about him, so I was very excited that we were working together. He's a wonderful actor, and one of the most charismatic people I've ever worked with.

We went out for dinner early on and started talking about our backgrounds and histories; we were brutally honest. Toby talked about his father and mother, Dame Maggie Smith and Sir Robert Stephens, two of the greatest actors of their generation. I talked about my close friendship with Jason Connery, from whom I had learned a lot about having famous acting parents. If any child of an acting dynasty wants to go into the profession as well, it's a double-edged sword because you are always going to be judged by your parents' achievements.

We laughed a lot both on and off the set. While we were sitting in makeup, being aged up and tattooed, we discovered that the best way to deal with the tedium of that was to take the rise out of each other. Of course it was all in good fun, but not everyone understood that. There was such a constant stream of mockery and abuse between us that people were asking, "Do they mean it?" We played with a very eccentric British humor, which carried us through a lot of long nights and otherwise grueling days of filming.

We actually had permission to laugh. One night we were on set at three o'clock in the morning. It was raining, so we couldn't shoot this particularly intense, emotional scene, and we were waiting to come on. We went off into a hut and I can't even remember what we were talking about, but we were laughing our heads off. Finally, Brad Fuller, the executive producer, came over. I gave Toby a look that said, "Uh-oh, we're in trouble," because I thought we were making too much noise. But Brad said, "I've been watching you two for an hour. You've done nothing but giggle like idiots. What the hell are you laughing at?" I just said, "I'm not sure you'd understand. It's British 'Carry On Film' humor; schoolboy humor if you like." Brad looked at me and said, "It's three o'clock in the morning, it's raining, we can't shoot and we're in the middle of this depressing scene. We need some humor, so you have permission to laugh." We took that as permission to fool around and crack jokes from then on. So we did, for five months.

The bond we established made a lot of difference to the way we worked together. Gates' most essential dynamic is with Flint. Flint is the captain of the ship, and his oldest ally and friend. Gates respects Flint for his seamanship and vision, and thinks he's one of the best sea captains he's worked with. Flint in turn sees in Gates something that is of value to him as a quartermaster. That's one of the pivotal relationships within the show. A lot of things revolve around that relationship, in terms of keeping Flint in a position of power as the captain. Because of Gates' relationship with the crew, he has to negotiate with different groups, different cultures and basically cajole them into honoring him. "If I'm following Flint, you've got to follow me." Those machinations are very important in the show.

Of course there are a lot of great action sequences on the show. Those sea battles are among the scariest and most exciting I've ever been involved in, and they really make you wonder how anyone survived in one piece in the real thing. There were enough, arms, legs and heads flying about the deck of *The Walrus* to make you really think about that.

A stunt team did most of the swordfights. I longed to get into all of that, but I've spent thirty years of my life, either on the stage or in film and television, throwing myself around sets with swords, guns or whatever, and I understand there's a time to step aside and let the younger guys take care of that. When you get to my age, you become an elder statesman. You get to stand back and watch other people do it, until finally they throw you a bone and say, "Okay, do this." They obviously thought I was perfectly capable of throwing a couple of punches, waving a sword about or pulling out a pistol, so I had no stunt double on the show!

Memories of Other Times

I have to say that working on *Black Sails* was an amazing experience, even after a lifetime in this business. I had never seen anything like the size of the production. Most TV shows work with a much smaller budget than feature films, which means that the production values are less extravagant and detailed. Not so with this production. Possibly because of Michael Bay's input I could see it was going to be huge right from the start. Not only had they built the entire township of Nassau on the lot at Cape Studios, but also two full sized ships, mounted on gimbals.

A lot of the time my head was back in the time of *Robin of Sherwood*. Thirty years ago my very good friend Jay Larkin, who has since passed away, was working on the public relations side of the American distributor for *Robin*. Jay said to me that one day cable television would be the source of the best-produced quality drama, not only in America, but also around the world. This was because, at some point, they would have the budget and technical know-how, and the audiences, to be able to do what networks then were struggling to do, which was to find audiences for niche shows.

Robin of Sherwood was a cult, groundbreaking show in its day. There were controversial issues even then, about the level of violence, for instance. There were guidelines that you couldn't cross on network TV. We had a pagan god of the forest being a good guy and the representatives of the Church being bad guys. We had organized criminals—the outlaws—who were good guys. You couldn't do that on television until then, until a company called Goldcrest, the British TV network HTV and the U.S. network Showtime came together to make *Robin*, to make it viable for the audience it captured. It was a landmark. So, I believe, is *Black Sails*. It's an extraordinary show with a deep historical and cultural basis and a powerful set of characters. Those are what made *Robin of Sherwood* work so well.

Neil Marshall, who directed several episodes of *Game of Thrones* as well as the pilot for *Black Sails*, turned out to be a huge *Robin of Sherwood* fan. Lucas Ettlin, who was our director of photography on the show, came up to me at one point and said, "You're Nasir!" When we were shooting later on, he brought his brother around to come and say hello and he said, "We used to run around in our back garden with rulers stuffed down the back of our shirts, to simulate Nasir's two swords, carried in a sheath on his back, having swordfights in the garden." So the show still has a resonance.

For me personally, a lot of understanding about where you place a part, where you fit into the group, the ensemble, and how you compliment each other, feed off each other and feed other people came from my work on the older show. I had experienced and enjoyed those things on *Robin*, and I was able to apply them to *Black Sails*.

I think the show will change a lot of things about what we see on network TV. I think it's also going to be a ground breaking show for Starz in the sense that pirates are so iconic and so international, and that this is a new way of seeing them. I think what series creators Jon Steinberg and Robert Levine did by taking a hugely familiar story like *Treasure Island*, and taking iconic figures like Flint, Billy Bones and John Silver, and planting them in an historical reality where you have characters that really existed gives you the best of both worlds. It's very similar to the way *Robin of Sherwood* had an iconic character like Robin Hood next to Richard the Lionheart. This opens a door for the audience to step through because it's familiar. Then you can expand the relationships, the dialogue, the interplay and the politics—the dynamics of those characters. I think it was a very, very smart thing to do.

The other thing they did that was very wise was to bring Michael Bay in at the beginning in terms of production values. Michael is a creative genius. I've been privileged to stand at the side of the monitor on the set of *Transformers* when he's giving direction and interacting with actors like Stanley Tucci, Kelsey Grammer and Mark Wahlberg. Michael's production values are high and visually stunning. Bringing his eye into the mix from the start made *Black Sails* epic.

Ten years ago, maybe even seven, this show would have been impossible to make the way we did it. What makes it possible now is the technical advances. Both the ships were on gimbals, and could be moved around for battle sequences where they came up alongside each other. The gimbals rocked as well, so it looked as if the ships were rocking in the water.

Quite a mechanical feat!

Most days we were looking out from the tank at the African bush, stretching for miles, with an airport down the road and a freeway about a mile in the distance. But with the help of CGI and green screens, you'll believe these boats are at sea. The first time I saw some of the stuff at a *ComiCon* event in San Diego I could hardly believe it myself. It really did look like the ocean, which is one of the most difficult things, CGI-wise, to do, because everything is moving. I knew then that we were at a place where anything you can imagine can be filmed.

I recall I told Jon Steinberg early on that until you've been out on a ship in a big sea, you really don't understand the power of the ocean. I have nothing but total respect for the people three hundred years ago who were sailing across the Atlantic and Pacific in what was essentially a wooden boat with no sanitation, and with only rudimentary navigation devices.

I'd worked on big RN warships like *HMS Fearless*, which was a helicopter platform or LPD (Landing Platform Dock) and amphibious warfare vessel. Fearless was also an aging veteran of the Falkland Islands campaign (Operation Corporate) and had been the HQ of Brigadier Julian Thompson, CO of 3 Commando Brigade during the conflict.

Once I volunteered for intelligence duties during an exercise with the SBS out in the North Sea and the weather turned very nasty indeed. There was an eight or nine force gale and even the big warships were literally being tossed like toys into the air by the roiling sea. I remember having to go past the bridge in the middle of the night, and they were having a big pow-wow about the fact that the storm was breaking up the entire fleet. There were Type 22 frigates and even bigger ships like Type 42 destroyers retiring from the exercise with big cracks in their hulls because the ocean was picking them up and shaking them and slamming them down again so hard.

I had to go down a ladder on the super-structure to avoid the bridge and onto the deck below. While I was climbing down, the entire ship was rolling almost at forty-five degrees. I was hanging onto the ladder, and as I looked down, there was the ocean and massive waves, and I remember looking out into the darkness and thinking: *You'd better not let go boy because if you do, they won't even know you've gone.* I would have been out there in the freezing water and that would have been the end of me. But as I looked out at that ocean I was thinking how extraordinary the power of nature is. Until you've been on an ocean in a powerful storm and seen what it can do to even a big warship, you have no idea how deadly it is. Those early seaman have my sincere respect for what they did during the period in which *Black Sails* is set.

The ocean itself is such an emotional place. Water is sometimes assessed to be a Jungian archetypal representation of our emotions, which is maybe why there's a real relationship between human beings and the sea. It's all to do with the depths and the unknown. Some people have a different relationship with the ocean than others. I was given a wonderful speech in the show, where Flint and Gates discuss their lives and their relationship to the men, the boat and the ocean. It's a beautifully written statement about the pirate's relationship to the sea, and the starkness and brutality of that; the simple nature of this very powerful element that we make our living from, that we have a relationship with, but that eventually will swallow us up. There will be no marker, no headstone and no legacy. We leave behind nothing: we're just swallowed, taken by the sea. It's an amazing speech, and for me it embodied the relationship between seagoing men of that period and the ocean they spent so much of their lives on.

Out of Africa

There are many different ways of looking at what led people to become pirates. For some, it was just about profit, whereas for others it's a dream of autonomy and freedom. I think you have to look at it in the context of what was happening around the world at that time, when new nations were being forged and old orders toppled. *Black Sails* is set not long before the American Revolution of 1776, and unrest was already fermenting in the Colonies. People were flexing their muscle against what they saw as traditional power and control politically, and new alliances were forming, new ways of viewing the world. The acceptance of different religions and different spiritual concepts were beginning to be considered. There was still a lot of the world yet to be discovered and exploited. The concept of a nation of free men who fought and struggled against the powerful ruling classes of the time and found their own way of living in a democratic society—all of that was in the general consciousness of the period, and it has some really in-depth exploration in the show.

There is very little similarity between the pirates portrayed in the show and the modern world of piracy. What we're seeing now are people who are ordered by warlords to go out and raid. They don't live on their boats and sail around the world; it's physically impossible to do that any more. Maybe if you had a nuclear-powered submarine you could stay under the surface and travel the world, but a modern-day ocean-going pirate vessel would be hunted down by satellites and aircraft and blown out of the water. Modern pirates run out in their little boats, raid along the coastline looking for wealthy yachts. They take prisoners for ransom along with whatever is in the boat and haul it back to their masters. That's not the same as rebelling against the British Navy or the Dutch East India Company, or anyone that was seen as the powers-that-be in the 17th and 18th centuries. I don't see much modern equivalent to that, except in the level of violence, but there's no doubt that piracy was a very dangerous and brutal business, then as now.

These were not nice people, and it was made clear from the start that this show was never going to be *Pirates of the Caribbean*. No peg-legs, no

"Arrr, matey!" I love the way one of the critics reviewing the show said that Captain Jack Sparrow, memorably played by Johnny Depp, would have not survived five minutes with the *Black Sails* pirates. This is a historical look at the way these people functioned, the spirit of the age if you like, how that spirit of rebellion echoed through that period and how these people lived and what they would do to live that life.

This kind of understanding fuelled a lot of the scenes Toby and I did. Some were very emotional, and in one of them I was talking about friendship and said to him that he was the last friend, the only friend that I had left in the world.

Some really good stuff between Toby and I went on the editing floor, but we did do some remarkable scenes. We had one that was almost nine minutes long and is, I think, the best thing I have ever done. The more we showed what we could do, the more they gave us, and the more dialogue they gave to Gates.

All of this was pointing the way towards the most difficult aspect of the part. I had known almost from the start that Gates was going to be killed off at the end of the first season. I'm still not sure why. The talented and highly professional director T.J. Scott of *Spartacus* fame helmed the final episode and he was under great pressure dealing with the many different issues in the final script. T.J. did a wonderful job and kept the show moving, tense and alive.

Consequently, Toby was very upset by it and it was all very harrowing. We had grown close and developed a close and humorous camaraderie during the filming. We both came from the same place in terms of taking everyone along for the ride crew and cast-wise and genuinely respected and trusted one another.

We had previously discussed the various ways the death had been written and Gates would meet his end but none of them seemed practical or realistic. There was one version where Flint stabs Gates in the back and another where the character is burned and disfigured in a battle. I believe it was Chris Albrecht, CEO of Starz, who actually came up with the idea of strangling, then snapping Gate's neck.

A very personal, intimate and vicious demise and from one that there would be no going back. It still seemed rather unbelievable and shoddy, and Flint's response to having just killed his only ally and closest friend seems truly amoral and sociopathic.

I guess that's what Chris Albrecht wanted from the character and Toby is such a good actor he pulled it off beautifully.

During the final scene Toby became very emotional and was holding me so tightly around the neck that he almost choked me. I had to "tap out" and stop filming as I was actually loosing consciousness. We had little chance to rehearse the move during the morning of that day and we were basically improvising the whole thing. He also was crying and physically shaking with adrenalin as I lay there and tried to keep my eyes open as if I was dead. I was soaked with his tears and he was trembling with emotion. It was one hell of a way to go!

On the last night before we all went our separate ways I bought dinner for the cast. I wanted to say thank you to everybody I'd worked with, because they all threw themselves into the show.

Once we were all sitting there I found I couldn't think of anything much to say—not something that happens to me very often! When they all started calling for a speech, I thought back to my days on *Robin of Sherwood*, which I knew that several of them had loved from their childhood, and said, "It's been a tremendous pleasure and honor working with everyone, and I wish you all one thing from this show. I know you've all heard me talk about *Robin of Sherwood*, but I have friendships that have lasted thirty years from that show, and what I wish for all of you is that you take away that depth of friendship and respect for each other, and that you still have that in thirty years time, as well as the success and acclaim this show will generate for you all." It was a sentiment I meant, and I think they were all quite moved. I know I was.

It's in the Cards

I bumped into Toby Stephens back in L.A. a few months later, and he joked about this book and asked if I was writing an adventure story—"Bravo 2 Ryan?" I told him he was going to be in it but, although we laughed, the conversation made me think, once again, about all the amazing things I've experienced over the years. I began to consider how I would end this book—not that it's really the end because I intend to continue doing whatever the universe throws at me for a while yet. I tried to think how I might sum up everything I had written about here.

As ever, the universe reached out to help me.

As part of the razzmatazz surrounding the premiere of *Black Sails*, I attended a reception where there were all kinds of people doing interesting things. I'm not sure why she was there, but I noticed a lady off to one side reading tarot cards. Now I've had quite a lot to do with Tarot over the years, creating *The Greenwood Tarot* with Chesca Potter in 1996 and *The Wildwood Tarot* with John Matthews and Will Worthington in 2011.

So of course I wandered over and sat down for a chat. At first she thought I wanted a reading, but I told her I was interested to see which deck she was using. Imagine my amazement when she unwrapped her cards and there was.... *The Wildwood Tarot*! When I told her who I was she nearly fell off her chair. "The Wildwood is my favorite deck. I love it and think it's the most beautiful deck ever produced." High praise indeed! I then found out that she was Lisa Greenfield, one of the most famous Hollywood psychics, who has done readings for countless A-list stars—many, I assume, with the deck I had created!

We had a wonderful conversation, ranging over many things, and I told her a bit about my own philosophy of life, especially in terms of making things happen and creating your own reality. She was fascinated and asked me to explain some more. I responded with what I have said here several times—that I believe that when you use a creative impetus to move forward down your unique path, somehow the universe responds.

I have never allowed myself to be inert, to wait around for something to happen. There are times to be patient and times to be still, but I have always felt that if you push on the universe opens a pathway for you to make something happen. That's why asking questions is so important. The questions you ask open a vacuum into which the universe brings possibilities and potentiality. This is equivalent of the Grail Question, because in the myth it's asking the universe, "Whom does *this* Grail serve?" that sets off a new and magical chain reaction.

I believe that the more you question, the more the universe reacts. This might seem a long-winded way of saying that the journey of self-discovery, shaping what you do through life, is each individual's gift to bring into the mix. A lot of people stumble into that through fear or insecurity. But that's the beginning of magic. The real magic is taking that intangible creative impulse and saying: I am going to make this happen.

To draw from the imagination, the consciousness, and turn that into a reality—whatever it may be—to create it and manifest it into reality: that is real magic.

What I want to say here, to leave for all of you who read this, is really very simple. It's this: *attitude and intention define outcome.* How you define what it is you are trying to achieve and how you approach that defines how the outcome will unfold. In your conscious thought processes, if you see things as negative and destructive, you will create and attract that; but if you see creative and positive ways forward and work with that impetus, you will attract the creative and positive. It seems to be the nature of the universe. It doesn't mean of course that we all don't end up, at some point in our lives, knee deep in trouble. But to find your way out of that you have to return to what was true in the first place. That process of going back, of identifying what makes you happy, what you want to achieve, and committing to that journey in a positive and creative way is the key to ultimate personal success.

The magic is in everyone's hands.

Acknowledgements

A number of people helped us in the writing of this book, in particular: Sandra Edwards, who bravely typed up the transcripts of our long rambling conversations. Lutine de Boer and Dayna Linton for correcting and reformatting the original U.K. text. Brian Hamilton and Merrit Rex just because. Ray Winstone and Clive Mantle for their friendship and love over the past three decades and Jason Connery and Alison Cross for being our first "test" readers and for always being there. A special thank you to Michael Bay without who's support, good humor and friendship over the past eight years various chapters and stories in this book could not have been included.

And finally for those many brave souls still out there in the shadows protecting innocent souls and shedding light in very dark corners.

Further Reading

Some background reading for things discussed in this book.

COLLINS, Andrew, *The Seventh Sword,* Arrow Books, 1992

DAVENPORT, Elaine, Paul Eddy, and Peter Gilman, *The Plumbat Affair,* J.P. Lippincott, 1978

DICK, Robert, *The Bagman,* Kensal Press, 1985

DORON, Meir and Joseph Gelman, *Confidential: The Life of Secret Agent Turned Hollywood Tycoon. Arnon Milchan,* Geffen Books, 2011

FOLLETT, James, *The Tiptoe Boys,* Mandarin, 1994

FORMAN, F & John Lisners, *Respect: the Autobiography of Freddie Forman: Managing Director of Crime,* Arrow, 1997

FORTUNE, Dion, *Sea Priestess,* Red Wheel/Weiser, 2003

MANDELA, Nelson, *A Long Walk to Freedom,* Abacus, 1995

MARCINKO, Richard, *Rogue Warrior,* Pocket Books, 2004

MARKSTEIN, George, *The Cooler,* BCA, 1974

McNAB, Andy, *Immediate Action,* Corgi, 2005

MEER, Fatima, *Higher Than Hope: A Biography of Nelson Mandela,* Penguin, 1990

MOORCOCK, Michael, *Elric of Melniboné,* Grafton, 1989

PETROCELLI, Daniel and Peter Knobler, *Triumph of Justice - The Final Judgment on the Simpson Saga,* Crown Publications, 1998)

PREECE, Greg, *Justice for None,* Palisade Press, 2003.

RYAN, MARK (with Mike Grell), *The Pilgrim,* ComicMix 2009

RYAN, MARK (with Chesca Potter), *The Greenwood Tarot,* Thorsons, 1996

RYAN, MARK (with John Matthews & Will Worthington), *The Wildwood Tarot,* Connections Publishing, 2011

SHELDRAKE, Rupert, *Morphic Resonance: The Nature of Formative Causation,* Park Street Press, 2009

THOREAU, Henry David, *Walden,* Dover Publications, 1995

WATSON Peter, *War on the mind: The Military Uses and Abuses of Psychology,* Hutchinson, 1988

Filmography of Mark Ryan

2014
Granite Flats (TV Series) - Benjy Fitzhugh
Street - Uri
Transformers Universe (Game) - Mixmaster / Lockdown (voice)
Transformers: Age of Extinction - Lockdown (voice)
Black Sails (TV Series) - Gates
- VIII. (2014) - Gates
- VII. (2014) - Gates
- VI. (2014) - Gates
- V. (2014) - Gates
- IV. (2014) - Gates

2013
Community (TV Series) - Constable Edmund
Conventions of Space and Time
Transformers: The Ride - 3D - Bumblebee (voice)

2011
Transformers: Dark of the Moon - Military Drone Operator

2009
Transformers: Revenge of the Fallen (Game) - Bumblebee (voice)
Transformers: Revenge of the Fallen - Jetfire (voice)
Siblings - Boris

2008
The Thirst: Blood War - Reeve

2007
Transformers: Beginnings (Video short) - Bumblebee (voice)
Transformers: The Game (Game) - Ironhide / Hoist (voice)
Transformers - Bumblebee (voice)

2006
The Prestige - Captain
Special Ops: Delta Force - Lt. Colonel Anderson Savage
My Elaborate Toaster (TV Short) - Mark Gossamer

2005
Alias (TV Series) - Cooney
- Authorized Personnel Only: Part 2 (2005) - Cooney

2004
Return to Sender - Mark Schlesser
Perfect Opposites - Nigel

2002
Eric Idle: Exploits Monty Python - Various

2001
JAG (TV Series)
- The Iron Coffin (2001)

2000
Charlie's Angels - Fencing Opponent
Nuremberg (TV Mini-Series) - Maj. Airey Neave
- Episode #1.1 (2000) - Maj. Airey Neave

1998
Conan (TV Series) - Barkeep
- Red Sonja (1998) - Barkeep

Frasier (TV Series) Winston
- Where Every Bloke Knows Your Name (1998) - Winston

1993-1997
The Bill (TV Series) - Franks / Micky Dale / John Randall
- Warnings (1997) - Franks
- Somebody's Home (1996) - Micky Dale
- A Duty of Care (1993) - John Randall

1996
Evita - Waiter in Junín Bar
Casualty (TV Series) - Dave Newman
- Flesh and Blood (1996) - Dave Newman

1995
First Knight - Challenger
Harry (TV Series) - DI Small
- Episode #2.5 (1995) - DI Small

Peak Practice (TV Series) - Chris Palmer
- Light at the End of the Tunnel (1995) - Chris Palmer

1994
Doomsday Gun (TV Movie) - SAS Man

1989
The Phantom of the Opera - Mott
William Tell (TV Series) - Barbarian
- The Lost City (1989) - Barbarian

1986
Dempsey and Makepeace (TV Series) - Jimmy
- Extreme Prejudice (1986) - Jimmy

1984-1986
Robin Hood (TV Series) - Nasir

1985
Corsican Brothers (TV Movie) - Bernardo de Guidice

1982
The Final Option - Mac

Printed in Great Britain
by Amazon